Working a
"Perfect Game"

Cactus League umpires about to take the field, March 8, 2019, Tempe Diablo Stadium. As lined up: Mike Winters, Gerry Davis, Lance Barrett, and Jim Reynolds.

Working a "Perfect Game"

Conversations With Umpires

By Bill Nowlin

Summer Game Books

Copyright © 2020 by Bill Nowlin
Summer Game Books Edition Published May 2020
All rights reserved.

Several interviews and partial interviews in this book originally appeared in *The SABR Book of Umpires and Umpiring*, published in 2017.

No part of this publication may be reproduced, stored in a retrieval system, or transmitted in any form by any process – electronic, mechanical, photocopying, recording, or otherwise – without prior written permission from the copyright owner and the publisher. The scanning, uploading, and distribution of this book via the internet or any other means without the permission of the publisher is illegal.

ISBN: 978-1-938545-60-3 (print)
ISBN: 978-1-938545-61-0 (ebook)

For information about permission, bulk purchases, or additional distribution, write to

Summer Game Books
P. O. Box 818
South Orange, NJ 07079

or contact the publisher at www.summergamebooks.com

Unless credited otherwise, all photos in this book were taken by the author.

Other Books by Bill Nowlin

BOSTON RED SOX IN 5's and 10s (The History Press, 2020)

THE BOSTON RED SOX KILLER B's: BASEBALL'S BEST OUTFIELD, by Jim Prime and Bill Nowlin (Sports Publishing 2019)

RED SOX vs. YANKEES by Bill Nowlin and David Fischer (Sports Publishing, 2019)

BOSTON RED SOX IQ: HALL OF FAME EDITION (Black Mesa Books, 2018)

TED WILLIAMS – FIRST LATINO IN THE BASEBALL HALL OF FAME (Rounder Books, 2018)

TOM YAWKEY: PATRIARCH OF THE BOSTON RED SOX by Bill Nowlin (University of Nebraska Press, 2018)

SO YOU THINK YOU'RE A RED SOX FAN? by Bill Nowlin (Skyhorse, 2017)

THE BOSOX CLUB: 50 YEARS by Bill Nowlin (Rounder Books, 2017)

FROM THE BABE TO THE BEARDS by Bill Nowlin and Jim Prime (Skyhorse Publishing, 2014)

DON'T LET US WIN TONIGHT: AN ORAL HISTORY OF THE 2004 BOSTON RED SOX'S IMPOSSIBLE PAYOFF RUN by Allan Wood and Bill Nowlin (Triumph Books, 2014)

521: THE STORY OF TED WILLIAMS' HOME RUNS (Rounder Books, 2013)

FENWAY PARK DAY BY DAY: THE FIRST HUNDRED YEARS (Rounder Books, 2012)

FENWAY PARK AT 100: BASEBALL'S HOMETOWN by Bill Nowlin and Jim Prime (Skyhorse Publishing, 2012)

AMAZING TALES FROM THE RED SOX DUGOUT by Jim Prime and Bill Nowlin (Skyhorse Publishing, editions in 2012, 2017, and 2020)

FENWAY PARK TRIVIA (Rounder Books, 2012)

CURSE IN THE REARVIEW MIRROR (Black Mesa, 2011)

THE GREAT RED SOX SPRING TRAINING TOUR OF 1911: SIXTY-THREE GAMES, COAST TO COAST (McFarland & Co., 2010)

PUMPSIE & PROGRESS (Rounder Books, 2010)

RED SOX BY THE NUMBERS by Bill Nowlin and Matt Silverman (Skyhorse, 2010)

BOSTON RED SOX IQ: THE ULTIMATE TEST OF TRUE FANDOM (Black Mesa Books, 2009)

THE ULTIMATE RED SOX HOME RUN GUIDE by Bill Nowlin and David Vincent (Rounder Books, 2009)

RED SOX THREADS: ODDS AND ENDS FROM RED SOX HISTORY by Bill Nowlin (Rounder Books, 2008)

THE RED SOX WORLD SERIES ENCYCLOPEDIA (No Longer the World's Shortest Book) with Jim Prime (Rounder Books, 2008)

WHEN BASEBALL WENT TO WAR edited by Todd Anton and Bill Nowlin (Triumph Books, 2008)

TED WILLIAMS AT WAR by Bill Nowlin (Rounder Books, 2007)

LOVE THAT DIRTY WATER: The Standells and the Improbable Anthem of the Boston Red Sox by Chuck Burgess and Bill Nowlin (Rounder Books, 2007)

DAY BY DAY WITH THE BOSTON RED SOX by Bill Nowlin (Rounder Books, 2006)

THE 50 GREATEST RED SOX GAMES by Cecilia Tan and Bill Nowlin (John Wiley, 2006)

BLOOD FEUD: THE RED SOX, THE YANKEES, AND THE STRUGGLE OF GOOD VERSUS EVIL by Bill Nowlin and Jim Prime (Rounder Books, 2005)

THE KID: TED WILLIAMS IN SAN DIEGO edited by Bill Nowlin (Rounder Books, 2005)

MR. RED SOX: THE JOHNNY PESKY STORY by Bill Nowlin (Rounder Books, 2004)

FENWAY LIVES by Bill Nowlin (Rounder Books, 2004)

THE FENWAY PROJECT, edited by Bill Nowlin & Cecilia Tan (Rounder Books, 2004)

TED WILLIAMS: THE PURSUIT OF PERFECTION by Jim Prime and Bill Nowlin (Sports Publishing, 2002)

MORE TALES FROM THE RED SOX DUGOUT: YARNS FROM THE SOX by Jim Prime and Bill Nowlin (Sports Publishing, 2002)

TED WILLIAMS: A SPLENDID LIFE by Bill Nowlin and Jim Prime (Triumph Books, 2002)

TALES FROM THE RED SOX DUGOUT by Jim Prime with Bill Nowlin (Sports Publishing, Inc., 2000)

FENWAY SAVED with Mike Ross and Jim Prime (Sports Publishing, 1999)

TED WILLIAMS: A TRIBUTE by Jim Prime and Bill Nowlin (Masters Press, 1997)

THE EARLY DAYS OF BLUEGRASS (Rounder Books, 2019)

THE ROUNDER BOOK OF BLUEGRASS MUSIC TRIVIA (Rounder Books, 2016)

ALEXANDER BERKMAN, ANARCHIST – LIFE, WORK, IDEAS (Christie Books, 2014)

WOODY GUTHRIE, AMERICAN RADICAL PATRIOT (Rounder Books, 2013)

WHEN FOOTBALL WENT TO WAR by Todd Anton and Bill Nowlin (Triumph Books, 2013)

Bill is editor or co-editor of an additional 50 or so books.

Contents

Foreword by Larry Gerlach		ix
Introduction		xi
Author's Note		xiii
Part I: The Interviews		1
1.	Phil Cuzzi – True Perseverance	3
2.	Ed Hickox	29
3.	How This Book Came To Be	37
4.	Ted Barrett	39
5.	Laz Diaz, Chris Guccione, Cory Blaser, and Clint Fagan – group conversation	45
6.	Ted Barrett, Angel Hernandez, Chris Conroy, and Pat Hoberg – group conversation	69
7.	Jim Joyce, Greg Gibson, Chad Fairchild, Carlos Torres – group conversation	85
8.	Tim Timmons	97
9.	Tim Welke	114
10.	John Hirschbeck, Bill Welke, James Hoye, and John Tumpane – group conversation	123
11.	Jeff Kellogg	136
12.	Brian O'Nora	146
13.	Mike Winters, Mike Muchlinski, Mark Wegner, and Marty Foster – group conversation	149
14.	Dale Scott, Dan Iassogna, C. B. Bucknor, and Lance Barrett – group conversation	155
15.	Fieldin Culbreth, Jim Reynolds, and Paul Schrieber – group conversation	165
Part II: Being an Umpire		175
1.	The Varied Backgrounds of Some of Today's Big-League Umpires	177
2.	Relatives in the Game	188
3.	What Else Might Some Umpires Have Done if They Hadn't Made it to the Majors?	196
4.	Umpire School	200

5.	The Long and Difficult Road to the Majors	207
6.	Getting "The Call"	216
7.	"Nobody Notices You Until They Notice You"	225
8.	Instant Replay	238
9.	Favorite Games to Work and Favorite Positions	244
10.	Spring Training	255
11.	Ejections	258
12.	Injuries	264
13.	Evaluation and Selection for Postseason Play	269
14.	Keeping a Clear Mind to Work That Perfect Game	275
15.	After Umpiring	282
Appendix		287
End Notes		291

Foreword by Larry Gerlach

Major League Baseball Rule 8:01 stipulates: "The umpires shall be responsible for the conduct of the game in accordance with these official rules and for maintaining discipline and order on the playing field during the game." While umpires are an essential participant in baseball—no umpire, no fair or orderly game—they work, except for controversies, in anonymity. And fans, even the most avid, are unaware of the administrative structure and daily realities of major-league umpiring.

Questions abound. What motivates someone to become an umpire? How does one become a professional umpire? Why do so many umpires for so many years endure the rigors and low pay in the minor leagues knowing the odds of reaching the major leagues are great? What it is like traveling from city to city during a season that stretches for seven months from February through September—and beyond in some cases? How does an "on-the-road" job impact their personal and family lives? What are the reactions of witnessing first-hand great players and performances and participating in World Series and All-Star games?

To answer these questions and many more, Bill Nowlin, prolific baseball historian, conducted interviews mostly prior to games with umpire crews in their dressing room in Boston's Fenway Park over the course of four years, 2015-2019. The informality of group interviews produced unusually spontaneous, candid comments, unlike the guarded and planned responses in more formal situations. The interviewees, 87 in all, range from veterans like Ted Barrett, to minor-league umpires who serving as short-term vacation replacements during the season. There is, alas, an unavoidable omission: the experiences of female umpires. To date only males have reached the major leagues, but that will eventually change given the growing number of women going to umpire schools and working in the minor leagues.

The interviews, effectively broken down into extended individual responses and collective comments about a variety of issues, are both entertaining and educational, providing insights not only into the personalities of umpires, but also a detailed understanding of their duties, working conditions and lives off the field. And they remind us that umpires are unique individuals-- sons, brothers, husbands, fathers, members of communities—who have lives away from the diamond. For all the varied personalities and experiences there is a common theme: these are remarkably skilled individuals who love baseball and are dedicated to ensuring the integrity of the game. The title—*Working a "Perfect" Game*—is doubly apropos as baseball, truly America's National Pastime, is the perfect team game and every umpire wants to call the game unerringly.

Nearly 40 years ago I wrote *The Men In Blue: Conversations With Umpires* (1980), a collection of autobiographies of major-league umpires at a time when they did not attend an umpire school, were divided into National and American leagues with different umpiring techniques, had to buy their own uniform and equipment, had no union so received meager pay and no benefits, and made decisions without the scrutiny of television and instant replays. Given the great organizational and technological changes in baseball and umpiring since then, this unique and timely book about the lives and experiences of present-day arbiters is destined to become a classic of baseball literature. It will forever change how readers view baseball games and umpires.

—Larry Gerlach
November, 2019

Introduction

Working as a major-league umpire is a tough job. You're on the road almost constantly, hardly ever home. You're in the spotlight almost constantly, berated or challenged if a call is questioned, but almost unnoticed, overlooked, and forgotten if all your calls are correct. You're working to enforce the rules of a game in which the minimum wage for players is greater than any amount you can hope to achieve. When the game is over, the players and coaches have a group of 30 or more teammates to choose from to socialize with. They are in their home park half the year. Their homestands typically last a full week and sometimes 10 or 11 days. You've got three fellow umpires, maybe a friend in town, but twice a week you've got a plane to catch to get on to the next city.

There are benefits, though. There is a real camaraderie within the umpiring community, one that includes fellow umpires but also families and friends. You've made it to the top of your profession. You're part of The Game, a game you've come to care deeply about. You get pretty good pay by most standards, and a job that is pretty secure once you make it. Your career can last longer than the typical ballplayer. There are inner rewards, too, satisfaction after a game in knowing that you had positioned yourself properly and made the right calls. For the right person, it's a good job, even something of a calling.

Becoming a major-league umpire, though, is far from an easy road. It takes years and years of dedicated effort. You've got to excel at umpire school and then serve what usually amounts to about an 8-to-10-year apprenticeship, working your way up through the minor leagues, working under more basic conditions, for very little money, with no job security, and being constantly evaluated and graded at every level as you rise in the ranks. Most wash out – even very, very good umpires. Ron Kulpa told me that on his first day of umpire school one of the instructors said, "Look around the classroom. Usually only one person per class makes it to the big leagues." There were 182 people in the room.

It is probably worth mentioning right off the bat that a minor-league umpire typically earns between $2,000 and $3,900 per month, and for a shorter season than major-league umpires have. Major-league umpires, however, are much better paid – earning a range, largely depending on seniority, from $120,000 to $450,000. Benefits such as per diems and vacation are described in the book. In 2019, the minimum major-league salary for a player was $555,000. Salaries for both groups are set through collective bargaining, and will likely change over time.[1]

Becoming an umpire takes perseverance. It takes grit. Some have been fortunate, and through the timing of retirements and the like, have made it to the majors earlier than others.

Others have had obstacle after obstacle thrown in their way. And some had bad luck with timing.

The goal of it all, veteran major-league umpire Tony Randazzo once told a writer for the *Chicago Tribune*, is to have a perfect game. He didn't mean what everyone else thinks of as a perfect game. "I love umpiring because it's never the same. Every day is different. I couldn't have a job and sit behind a desk for eight hours. That's just not for me. Every three days I'm in a different city. I've traveled all over the United States and met some great people. Plus, I like the challenge. I want to have a perfect game."[2]

Clearly that could be taken more than one way. Asked to explain, he said, "We all strive to get everything right. We want to get everything right. As far as balls and strikes, safes and outs, all that stuff. We don't want to miss anything. That's what I meant by a perfect game."[3]

—Bill Nowlin
Cambridge, Mass
February 2020

Author's Note

In Part One of this book, we will hear from a couple of dozen of today's 76 major-league umpires, talking in conversation about their backgrounds, their work, and their lives. Several of the conversations are in a group setting, with two or three or four of them sitting around a table in the umpires' room before a ballgame. In some instances, I had longer conversations with individual umpires. Over four years, I talked with 72 major-league umpires and a number of Triple-A umpires hoping to make the grade.

Note: At the end of the book is a complete list of umpires interviewed and the dates on which we conversed.

Chapter 3 explains how this book came to be.

In Part Two, we look at a number of themes and subjects related to contemporary big-league umpiring.

Let's start by hearing the detailed story of two umpires – Phil Cuzzi and Ed Hickox – telling about how they got started umpiring, the challenges they faced along the way, and sharing some of their thoughts about the game and their work.

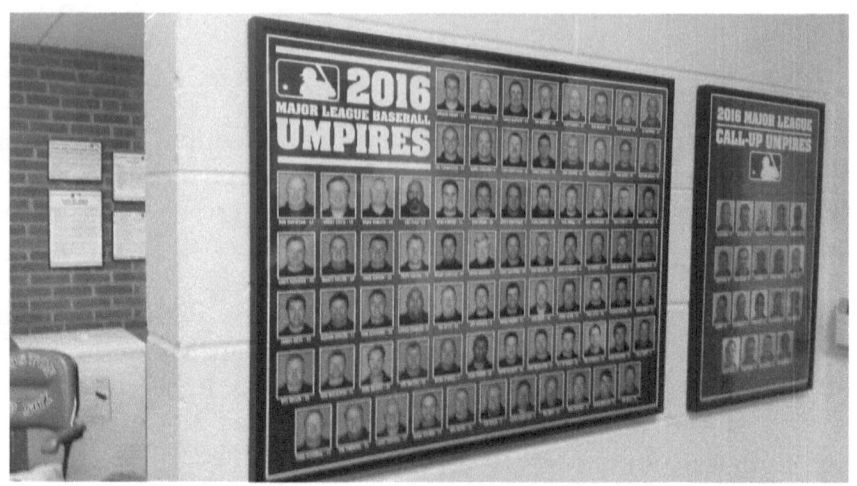

Framed posters depicting 75 major-league umpires and 19 call-up umpires, 2016. Fenway Park umpires room, Boston.

PART I

The Interviews

Phil Cuzzi leaving the field after working the plate at Fenway Park on June 23, 2019.

1

Phil Cuzzi

Phil Cuzzi's story is one of true perseverance. We met up at Fenway Park on August 4, 2018. He had some friends coming to visit so we talked for a bit then and then followed up phone a week later, on the 11th.

Interview with Phil Cuzzi at Fenway Park on August 4, 2018, and on the telephone on August 11, 2018

Bill Nowlin: Yesterday was a fast game.

Phil Cuzzi: That was certainly the quickest Yankees/Red Sox series that I've ever been a part of, or even seen.

BN: It was 2:15. They're usually closer to four hours.

PC: That's what we were expecting, yeah.

BN: Porcello only gave up one hit all game and threw something like 80% strikes.

PC: It was a well-pitched game on both sides. Porcello threw a great game.

BN: The game before [on August 3], I thought it was all over in the first inning. Gregorius gets up and hits a three-run homer and there's still nobody out for the Yankees. And then the Red Sox turned the tables the other way around in the fourth inning, scoring six runs before there was anybody out in the fourth inning. You never know!

PC: That's baseball. That's why it's a great game. You never know what's going to happen day to day, and inning to inning.

BN: Other than a game that's a quick game and that's well-played, and doesn't have controversy, do you have a favorite kind of game in a way? An 8-0 game?

PC: Really, just the opposite. I like to be out there for a 2-1 game, a well-pitched game, a well-played game, and a game that's played at a decent pace. It's much easier to keep your concentration during that time. I would think for the players it's the same thing.

BN: I think especially the fielders. I don't think they like to stand around while the batter or pitcher keep stepping out.

PC: Absolutely, yeah.

BN: Those of us who go to a lot of games, it's nice to save 15 or 20 minutes when you can, but I think it tends to produce a better quality game. I understand the mental game between the pitcher and that batter, and that's good. But still…

PC: When it moves along, I think it's better – even for the fans. I think it's more enjoyable for the fans as well.

BN: So how'd you get into umpiring?

PC: My first job out of college, I was a schoolteacher. I taught for about four years.

BN: At what level?

PC: I taught at a middle school – junior high school. I taught ninth graders.

BN: That's about the roughest age group.

PC: Well, normally you would think yes, but because the school was 7, 8, 9, the 9's were the kingpins of the school and they acted a little more maturely than they would have if it was a 9 through 12 setting. I loved it.

BN: I remember what I was like in seventh and eighth. What did you teach?

PC: I taught graphic arts. I really enjoyed it, but I just thought there was something missing. I was young at the time. I was just out of college. I had the dream of having a family, and I just didn't want to feel that I always had to have a summer job, a second job. So someone suggested, "Well, you have a pretty good personality. You like to talk to people. Why don't you try sales?" So I went into sales and I sold – actually, the company was out of Worcester, Mass. – it was called Wright Line. I worked for them selling computer accessories. This was back when computers used tape. I sold tape and disk storage cabinets, etc. My goal was to make more money. I did. But there was still something that was missing. I said, "There has to be more to life than closing an order."

One day I was at Yankee Stadium with my buddies, and for whatever reason I just started focusing on the umpires on the field, watching them rotate around the field, and I said, "What a great job that would be." What kid in America doesn't want to grow up and play major league baseball? What a great job that would be. You're kind of in charge of the game.

One of the friends I was with said, "You know, I see in the back of *The Sporting News*, there's an umpire school. I'll give you the paper and you could write away." So I did. I wrote to both schools, which at that time was Harry Wendelstedt and Joe Brinkman. Harry wrote me back a handwritten note and so I said, "Okay, that's where I'm going to go."

So I went off to umpire school. I told my father that I was going to do that. For my father, who only had an eighth-grade education, me graduating college was a big thing. Me becoming a schoolteacher, I had made it. He couldn't understand how I was going to chase this wild dream – leave teaching and then a sales job, but my family was always supportive... But that's really how it began.

BN: You weren't married at the time?

PC: I was not married at the time, which in a way was a fortunate thing. I was single, going to umpire school, and not making any money in the minor leagues. It helped that I didn't have those kind of responsibilities.

BN: You were born in Newark. Is that where you grew up also?

PC: I grew up in Belleville. Went to Belleville High. It was a great town in which to grow up – same town as Frankie Valli, Connie Francis...

BN: You could have had another career, singing,

PC: Well, no, not if you heard me...I only sing in the shower and my wife doesn't like me to even do that.

BN: You played baseball and football?

PC: I played baseball and football.

BN: What position did you play in baseball?

PC: I was a catcher, and I think that helped me as an umpire.

BN: I was talking to Chad Whitson the other day. He was a catcher, too. You put in that time behind the plate. You know where the strike zone is.

PC: Seeing the ball coming at you, seeing the batter swing in front of you. You know, one of the biggest things at umpire school is that the guys who have never done it before, when a bat was swung in front of them, they all flinched. I didn't have that because I was used to seeing the ball coming at me. I think it definitely helped me.

BN: It's a good thing you didn't have to umpire in the 1860s when they didn't have masks. What kind of work did your parents do?

PC: My father was a sheet-metal worker. Union guy. And my mother was a homemaker. I had two sisters and a brother. It was a great way to grow up. Dinner was on the table every night at 5 o'clock and every night we ate as a family.

It wasn't like today. Even though we were involved in our own activities, we didn't travel. For us, travel was playing at a field on the other side of town. Today kids are on traveling teams and go out of state for soccer and baseball tournaments. It's really much different.

BN: I went to the Wendelstedt School just for three days last year, to see what it was like. I have been so impressed talking to you guys over the last three years, the care that goes into it, how one of you can get a call right but still realize you weren't in as good a position as you could have been to get a better angle – and then lose sleep over that.

PB: A lot of people don't realize that. They think we're just out there...and sometimes even players, they think that we're just out there and we don't care as much as we do if we miss a call. The ones that really understand it may be mad if we miss a call, but they know they're not more mad than we are.

Of course, replay has changed a lot of that, but even still no one wants to be overturned. You're still missing a call. Even though they make it right, and the ramifications may not be the same if you miss a call and it changes the outcome of the game. We don't really have that any more – which is a good thing – but in our minds and in our hearts, we're still missing a play. It's still very disappointing when we pull on the headset and they say we have to overturn the call.

BN: I stayed home yesterday and watched the game on TV and they did a thing where they showed a picture of you – because you're the crew chief – and they said they wanted to take a poll of all the viewers as to whether they should mike the umpire – the home-plate umpire or the crew chief – and also to be able to hear what was said if there was a challenge. The poll was predictable. People did want to hear.

PC: They do want to hear that.

BN: You might not want them to hear! It was like 80 percent.

PC: I'm sure. That doesn't surprise me. Last night, Adam [Hamari] was miked behind home plate.

BN: Oh, was he?

PC: Yeah. Every national game, the home umpire is usually wearing a mike, unless it's a Triple-A umpire. They can't play the replay conversations, or confrontations – anything that might embarrass a player, an umpire, or the Commissioner's Office. They'll sometimes show "Sounds of the Game" and it's usually something very light. Of course, fans want to hear the juicy stuff, perhaps, but…

BN: You don't have the sort of stuff you used to have, with Earl Weaver coming out…

PC: That's true. Very true.

BN: Of course, I never heard what was said. I've just read Ron Luciano writing about it.

PC: Mm hmmm.

BN: You were a National League umpire when you came up.

PC: Yes, I came up a National League umpire. The thing I'm most proud of is that Al Barlick was the umpire – he was working for the National League at the time – and he's the one who saw me working at Louisville and he's the one who gave me my shot.

BN: You were only there for a couple of years and then you were released. What happened? They just told you there was no room? It seemed kind of quick – 1991 to 1993.

PC: My road was never an easy road and that started from umpire school. There are some guys who go to umpire school one year and go out into the minor leagues. A lot of guys go a second year. I had to go four times.

BN: Four times! Wow. That's dedication.

PC: Some called it dedication. Some called it stupidity.

BN: Well, here you are!

PC: I became obsessed with it.

BN: You had to pay each time.

PC: I had to pay each time and the hardest thing about that was that I borrowed the money to go to umpire school the second and third time. If you went to umpire school and you didn't make it, and if you had in your mind you were going to go back, you had to wait another year. What do you do in the meantime?

When I really got serious about it – not that I wasn't serious the first time, but when I really became obsessed with it, after my third time people thought I was crazy even to consider going back a fourth time. I had been to Harry's school and then I went to Joe Brinkman's school, and then I went back to Harry's school. In between the last times, I was fortunate enough...I said, I have to umpire at the highest level I possibly can over the summer and just get as much experience as I can, as many games as I can. I was fortunate enough to be selected to go to the Alaska League. I'm sure you're familiar – living here – with the Cape Cod League. It's similar.

BN: I went up to a game two years ago – the Midnight Sun Game.

PC: Yes, in Fairbanks.

BN: Fairbanks, yeah.

PC: Fairbanks, absolutely. It was a great experience. Not only a great experience to be in Alaska and to see all that, but it was a great experience professionally. After that I went back a fourth time. I either got better or they said, "He's going to keep coming back until we send him out to the minor leagues." That's what they did. So in 1985 I got to the New York-Penn League.

BN: That's really something. I never would have guessed. Didn't they try to discourage you after a certain point? Maybe that's why you went to the Brinkman School after the first two years. I'd heard they often welcome people back a second time and might help set someone up for a collegiate position or something like that.

PC: Yeah, it was just to get a change of venue or whatever. Sometimes... I'm reluctant to say it, but it almost feels like when I went to Harry's school twice and then I go to Joe's school, they almost looked at me like I'm damaged goods. Why should we take him when Harry didn't take him for two years?

BN: I can understand that.

PC: So then I went back to Harry's the fourth year and then…[phone call interrupts from friend arriving at the park.]

[Second portion of the interview was conducted by telephone on August 11, 2018. Phil was working games in Kansas City.]

PC: I had lunch with Steve Palermo's wife. It was nice to see her.

BN: Great. I really miss Steve. As a supervisor he'd come through Fenway Park maybe three times a year and I always enjoyed sitting with him.

PC: We miss him. He was a great mentor. He's missed. That's for sure.

BN: Yeah, I knew he lived there. I guess when you're an umpire it helps to live kind of centrally, if you can.

PC: Yeah, we always joked about it. We'd say if you lived in Chicago, you could probably get home every off-day. You're that central. I think the key is to be near a good airport. Me being outside of Newark – of course, I don't fly home across the country to be home for an off-day, but I can get anywhere from Newark, that's for sure. This is a tough airport – Kansas City – to get in and out of. A lot of times you have to connect, to get in or out.

BN: When you started as a National League umpire, do you remember feeling a sense of rivalry at all with the American League umpires?

PC: No, I don't remember feeling a sense of rivalry. Perhaps a joking type of camaraderie. I just remember the tremendous sense of pride that I felt. In part, I'm sure, that was due to the fact that it was Al Barlick who gave me my chance.

BN: The American League umpires had those big balloon protectors.

PC: The American League, yeah. I don't remember who it was – if it was Palermo or it was maybe Richie Garcia. They said they felt as though the National League guys were at an advantage working the plate because they were able to get closer and felt as though they [AL umpires] couldn't see the low pitch as good with the balloon. I could kind of see that, but since I never wore the balloon, it's tough for me to say firsthand.

BN: You would think it would kind of get in the way.

PC: You would see how it could, but the other side of it was it certainly offered much more protection than the inside protector. Of course, it wasn't an option for us when we came in.

BN: Kind of a side question – when you taught graphic arts, was that like cartooning or drawing?

PC: Basically, we did printing – offset printing. We did silkscreen printing. We did linoleum block cutting.

BN: Do you draw, yourself?

PC: Not really. My father was able to draw, but I didn't really have… I could look at something and kind of come close to duplicating it, but I really can't say that I'm an artist.

BN: I just kind of wondered if you'd ever drawn or sketched umpires at work.

PC: No, no, I don't have that ability, no.

BN: Speaking of your father, is he still living now?

PC: No. I lost both my mother and my father.

BN: Did they see you make the major leagues?

PC: Yes. Not as a full-time…under contract. They did see me work as an up-and-down umpire at Triple A.

BN: So they knew you were on your way and probably making it, well along on the path.

PC: Yeah, and that was a very difficult time for me – not because I didn't have the support of my family, because I did, but my father wasn't really a sports fan. He lost his father when he was, I think, in the sixth grade. He was born in 1915 so we're talking about in the Twenties. He just had to go to work. He was supportive but after it looked like I was getting a very slow start – I told you, I went to umpire school four times – he was trying to be the voice of reason, as any parent would. He said, "Listen, I give you credit for trying but you tried it and it didn't work out" and basically, "What are you going to do now?"

BN: Yeah, I was the first person in my family to graduate from college.

PC: As a schoolteacher, my father thought that I had made it. I was the first of his children to go to and graduate from college. I remember as a schoolteacher working at the company he worked for and the guys that he worked with said, "Oh, you're the teacher. Your father's always talking about the teacher." So when I said I was leaving teaching, he couldn't wrap his arms around that at all. But he was still supportive.

BN: Well, he…probably knew you were a good kid. You don't have to comment on that. (laughs). The first couple of times you went to the Wendelstedt School, what did they tell you? There weren't any jobs for you? Did they give you any sense of what they perceived as your shortcomings? You've got to work more on this, or work on that?

PC: After the first year…I'll be the first to admit that after my first year, I didn't think that I should have made it out. I went down to the umpire school thinking I already know about baseball. I've played baseball my entire life. Umpiring is baseball. But then when I got there, I realized that it had nothing to do with the fact that I played baseball. It was a completely different animal. Learning all the rules. I kind of stumbled through it. I agreed that I shouldn't have gone out after my first year. I was told, "You have some ability, but you just have inexperience." Harry Wendelstedt said, "Sometimes we prefer when people don't have experience because then we don't have to break their bad habits." He said, "My suggestion is take this next year and just get as much experience that you can, at the highest level that you can. And then if you decide that you want to come back, you come back." And that's what I did.

BN: Did you work at schools mostly?

PC: Yeah, I worked at summer leagues. The [umpire] school ends in February, and what do you do in New Jersey until the summer time. I umpired some JV high school baseball in my town. When the summer came, I umpired the highest level of summer ball that I could. Just trying to get experience. That was the hard part. If you didn't make it, you had to wait a whole 'nother year.

That was a long four years. In between time, I had to just pick up work. So I was substitute teaching in my town. I was painting. I was bartending.

A friend of mine owned an office furniture business so I was unloading trucks. Just whatever I could do, while waiting for umpire school to start again the following January.

BN: What year was it that you essentially…graduated?

PC: '85. So my first year in the game was '85, New York-Penn League.

BN: So I guess you worked your way up over six years until you got your first big-league work.

PC: '91, yeah, that was my first. At that point [1985], I was 30 years old. Fortunately for me, they had little choice but to either move me up or move me out. You can't make a career of being in the minor leagues, that's for sure. Before I got into it, guys became career minor leaguers. Fortunately, the system changed a little bit and they realized it wasn't fair for anybody. The leagues were happy if they had an…older guy, if you want to call it…a career minor leaguer, because he kinda knew the lay of the land but it just wasn't fair to keep a guy holding on if he had no chance at all to have one league or the other – American or National League – interested in him. So they put in a retention policy, which was good. I think it was something like if you weren't going to be promoted in, two or three years, then you were released, if there was no major league that was interested in you.

BN: You worked a bit in '91, more in '92, and then did you get released?

PC: Yes, I did get released. You know, all during that time everything was building up to expansion – the Rockies and the Marlins – so we knew that that was going to create four jobs. Then there was two retirements. I don't remember who. That was going to be like an unprecedented six jobs that were going to open up in…

BN: '93 was the first year for the Rockies.

PC: '93, yeah. Those years building up to it…the first year, '91, I was called up for – I think it was six games, but it was a great start. The '92 season, I was called up as a fill-in Triple-A umpire. Based upon the amount of time I was being used, I felt I was certainly within the top six. [Cuzzi worked 10 games in 1991 and 42 games in 1992.]

BN: They were using you in games, yeah.

PC: And then in '93, we all went to spring training. Ed Vargo was the guy in charge of the National League umpires at that time. He had everybody in the same place, by West Palm Beach, for spring training. We jokingly called it Camp Vargo. I guess there was probably 15 or 20 guys that were working spring training, all in the same boat, looking for six jobs. I thought that I had an excellent chance to be one of those six. That didn't happen. We had this meeting at the end of spring training and he announced the names and of course there were six guys that were extremely happy and 15 guys that were extremely disappointed. I think that at that point they were looking for me to just go away. I said, "You know what? I'm not going to go away." That was the toughest season, that '93 season, because I wasn't being used at all. [Cuzzi was called up for 19 games in 1993.]

I remember being in a Triple-A city and an umpire got hurt in a city close to the city I was in, and them flying in a guy from across the country. I thought, "Well, the handwriting is on the wall." But I said I'm not going to quit.

BN: Back then, when you were getting called up – like in '92 – were you getting the same kind of daily pay that a major league umpire was getting – like the way it works now?

PC: Yes, we would get the same per diem and we would get the same first-year salary prorated for however many days we worked.

BN: That's obviously a great deal for guys who have been working through the minor leagues.

PC: Oh, without question.

BN: Guys now coming up who work with you on different crews and stuff, all of a sudden they're making whatever it is as a callup – 10 times as much money per game as they were making in Triple A.

PC: Yeah, we jokingly used to say, "Well, it's all back pay." For all the years we worked and didn't make any money. It's different today, because if we have doubleheaders, they always send in a Triple-A guy to help us work that doubleheader. He'll work two games on the bases and whoever works the plate will only work one game. When I was coming up and down, we didn't do that. They didn't have that.

BN: You just worked other jobs then.

PC: Oh, definitely. Once the season was over, even going up and down, you couldn't rest on the laurels of… The most fortunate thing for me was that I was single, I had no expenses, I was still living at home. There were guys who had families, so they really had to work when the season ended. So did I, but I just didn't have the pressure. I always worked, in just a variety of jobs as I mentioned.

BN: So there was quite a stretch there when you didn't umpire and I had read that you just happened to meet Len Coleman at some point.

PC: Yeah, well, the first thing that happened was I got a phone call from my Triple-A league president, who was Branch Rickey III. He called me the day before Thanksgiving. When I got the call, I said, "Branch, I don't want you to even tell me because I know why you're calling." He said, "I'm sorry. This is just…the National League no longer has interest in you and I wish you the best of luck," and this and that. He was very nice about it, but they gave him a dirty job to do and he did it.

It was just devastating, of course. I'd sensed it was coming. At that time, going up and down, I had had the opportunity to work a lot of games with Jerry Crawford, who at that time was the president of the umpires union. He said, "I've seen your work and I don't think that it was fair." He said, "We're going to fight for you, and let's see what happens." I was flattered by it because being a Triple-A umpire, I wasn't a member of the union, so to think that they were going to fight for me as a non-member, I felt good. Most importantly, it gave me hope, because I wasn't really ready to turn the page.

A lot of things had happened over those three years before I actually did go back to work, and one was that Bill White, the National League president, was going to retire. He was kind of a lame duck. Len Coleman came in, so for that year Bill White didn't really want to have anything to do with it when they approached him – even though sometime over that first winter after the '93 season, I got a phone call from the attorney of the union. He said, "Hey, we're fighting for you and I just want you to be prepared to go back to spring training." I said, "OK." There was hope.

Then spring training came and went. And then, if you remember, there was a players' strike [mid-August 1994 until the following spring]. There was an umpires' strike [just before the 1995 season began]. And there was the change in the National League president. As good as it was that the union was trying to fight for me, I went from the back burner to off the stove completely.

The very ironic thing is that when the umpires went on strike, I got a phone call to cross the picket line and go back to work. It was from some guy in Florida. I won't tell you what I told him before I hung up the phone, but certainly I had no intention of doing that.

BN: As you mentioned, your father had been a union man himself.

PC: Yes, he absolutely was. I remember long before I began trying to come back into baseball, when I was substitute teaching, I saw an ad in the *Newark Star-Ledger* and the Newark teachers were on strike. They had an ad for substitute teachers to make like $100 a day or $150 – some exorbitant amount of money compared to what substitutes were making and I said, "Hey, Pop, look at this, what the Newark schools are paying!" He gave me a quick schooling about unions and crossing a picket line.

Fast forward. It was three years later and in that time the umpires were back to work, the players were back to work, and Len Coleman was now the National League president. After three years it was difficult to just keep sitting around, just knocking around at different jobs. I decided that as well-intended as the union is, I have to just take matters into my own hands because it's my future.

I tried to call Len Coleman on the phone for probably six months. He had no reason to take my call – and, in fact, didn't. But I got to know his secretary very well and she was always very polite, very nice. But he had no reason to take my call, so I said, "You know what? He's not going to ever take my call. I'm just going to sit down and I'm going to write him a letter." I sat down over the weekend and I just put my life on a page. It wasn't blasting anyone. It was just simply stating my intention, that I wanted come back, that I went to umpire school four times, that if you give me this opportunity to come back, I'll go to umpire school a fifth time if that's what I have to do.

I wrote this letter and at the time my sister was working at the Hilton in Short Hills, New Jersey. Over the holidays, she said, "Listen, why don't you come and work at the hotel? They're going to hire extra people for the holidays anyway. I think you would like it." I said, "I don't want to work in the hotel business." My sister, knowing that I was kind of depressed and that this thing had just been going around for 2 ½ years, she made me feel a little guilty and reluctantly I took the job. I was going to be a concierge and they were going to put me in the VIP lounge upstairs. That's what I did. It was OK. I enjoyed it. My goal was still to get back into the game.

Talk about divine intervention. The weekend that I wrote this letter, I brought it to work with me for my big sister to proofread it. I worked in the evenings, like 3 to 11. The lounge closed at 11. As I'm walking down the hallway to the lounge, walking toward me was the director of sales or…I don't remember what his position was…we just said hello and kept on walking, and then he had an afterthought after we passed and he said, "Oh, Phil, by the way, I think you know this VIP who will be coming in this evening. It's Len Coleman, president of the National League." I said, "You're kidding. Of course I know him." I'm thinking to myself, I've been trying to get ahold of this guy for six months and now he's coming to my hotel and I have the letter that I've prepared for him with me. What are the chances?

I called down to the front desk and said, "I understand you have a VIP coming. His name is Len Coleman. Can you call me when he arrives?" It was probably about 10:30 in the evening when I get a call from the front desk. The girl says, "I have a note here to call you when Len Coleman checked in. Well, he just checked in. He's in the gift shop buying a newspaper." I asked what room he was going to be in. There were two floors for people who were entitled to use that lounge.

I gave him about 15 minutes. I was going to knock on the door, introduce myself and hand him the letter. I would at least have the guarantee that he would read it. If I were to mail it to New York, what are the chances that he would have actually read it? Maybe. Who knows?

So I knock on the door and like many plans that don't go as you think they are going to, I hear him in the shower. He yelled out, "Who is it?" I didn't want to tell him my name. He knew my name but he didn't know what I looked like. I said, "Mr. Coleman, I have a letter for you here." He said, "A letter?" He sounded kind of surprised. He said, "Just slip it under the door." I said, "Would you mind if I just come back and deliver it?" He later told me he just thought I was a bellman and that if I had to slip it under the door, I wouldn't get the tip.

BN: Of course.

PC: He said, "Yeah, give me 15 minutes and come back." That was a very long 15 minutes. I probably gave him 20. I go back and I knock on the door. No answer. I thought, "Don't tell me he knows it's me and he's not answering the door." You think all crazy thoughts.

I put my ear next to the door and I hear him snoring. He fell asleep. So what do I do now? I thought, "Well, if I pull the fire alarm in this hotel, I know that he'll have to come out. He'll have to go down the stairs. I could give him my letter then and tell him whatever I had to say." I thought about that for the first five seconds and then I thought, "That's probably not a good idea."

BN: No, probably not.

PC: But I thought, what I will do, I will slip the letter under the door and I know he'll get it. I'll find out what time his wake-up call is and I'm going to come back. And that is what I did.

That was a sleepless night. Long night. I went back at 6 o'clock in the morning in my best suit, as opposed to my uniform suit. I hear him rustling around in his room so I know I didn't miss him. The All-Star Game that year was in Philadelphia and it turns out he was there because he was hosting the Japanese league president and his contingent. He lives in Jersey but that's why he was in the hotel. The door opens up and here's Len Coleman. I don't know if you ever saw him but he's a big statue of a man. He's a big man and he's got this big smile on his face, and he sees me standing there. He didn't know who I was. He said, "Good morning!" I said, "Mr. Coleman, good morning. Pardon the ambush, but I'm Phil Cuzzi." The smile dropped off his face. I said, "No, it's OK. I work here. Did you have the opportunity to read my letter?"

He said, "I did read your letter. And I know your story. I've received more phone calls about you coming back, more calls than I've ever had before." He said, "I've read your letter. Walk with me." He had to go downstairs and he had to meet the Japanese league president. So I had the opportunity to walk with him. He said, "I do know your story. You've been to umpire school four times. Why would you want to go back a fifth time?" I said, "I don't want to go back a fifth time, but I want to come back to work. I shouldn't be working here. I should be working for you."

I said, "Mr. Coleman, remember the movie *Heaven Can Wait*?" He said, "Yeah." I said, "Well, do you remember when Warren Beatty just knew that he wasn't supposed to be there? I'm not supposed to be here." He listened to everything I had to say and he said, "You know, when the season is over, I will give you a call." I thought that he was just giving me the very polite brush, so I pressed him a little bit and I said, "Mr. Coleman, you're certainly much more busy than I. This is more important to me than it is to you. How about if you give me a time and let me call you?"

He said, "No, no. No. I'll give you a call." I said, "Mr. Coleman…" and he stopped me. He looked me square in the eye and said, "Phil, I told you I'll call you. I'm going to call you." I said, "Okay." I had such a sense of peace, because even though I didn't know what was going to happen, there was nothing else I felt I could have done. I said everything I wanted to say. He read my letter. Really, I just had such a sense of peace. I said, "It's really out of my hands now. I did everything that I could have done in an attempt to come back."

And sure enough, just a couple of days after the World Series that year, Len Coleman calls me. He said, "You know, I am going against the advice of every attorney that works for the league, but I think it's a feel-good story and I'm happy to be a part of it. I'm going to give you your job back, but you're not going to go back to Triple A. If you accept these terms – and you will have to sign something saying so – you don't have to go back to umpire school, but you will have to go back to the evaluation course."

After the umpire schools meet, the top percent – based on how many jobs they expect to have – they go to this evaluation course that is run by Minor League Baseball.

"You will have to go back to the evaluation course and you will then have to spend a year in A ball, a year in Double A, a year in Triple A. No guarantee. The only thing I'll guarantee you is that you'll be treated fairly."

I said, "Where do I sign?"

When I got off the phone, my wife said, "What? What?" I told her the terms and she said, "You want to go back to A ball at age 40?" I said, "Yeah." That was my only chance.

That's really how it came about.

BN: It's something like ironic that by the time you worked your way through those three years, that was the year of the mass resignation.[4]

PC: Yeah.

BN: Oh, no! This is happening again.

PC: Yeah. In all of that, that I just described, which was my life, that was the gray cloud over the silver lining. That was not the way…actually, when I got the phone call…that year that I came back to Triple A, that was just the beginning of interleague play. As a result of that, there were more umpires that were needed. Long story short, I get called to go to Atlanta with Jerry Crawford's crew – at the time, he wasn't even a crew chief. He was like an interleague play crew chief. They needed extra guys for everything. That was the start of him becoming a crew chief. They put me with his crew. Baltimore was playing in Atlanta. Jerry said to me, "I'm going to give you a choice. There's a Saturday afternoon Fox game and there's a Sunday night ESPN game. Which one do you want to work?" I said, "I'll work the Sunday night game." That was the game that Cal Ripken hit three or four home runs. I don't remember. It was a really lopsided game. [Phil's third game in 1999 was Sunday night in Atlanta on June 13, 1999. While Phil was working the plate that night, Ripken homered twice, drove in six runs, and the Orioles beat the Braves, 22-1.]

That was the start of me coming back and then when all of the labor issues with the umpires started, I got a phone call. I was back in Norfolk – Tidewater, working the Mets' Triple A – and I got a phone call at the hotel. It was long before cellphones. Len Coleman was offering me a position, a full-time position. I knew what was going on. I didn't know all the details, but I knew there was this mass resignation. I don't know what Len Coleman thought when he called me but the first thing I said to him was, "Mr. Coleman, I'm not sure about everything that's going on, but if you're offering me a job to bust the union, you know what I've been through but I can't take it. I can't take the position." I think he was a little bit surprised. I thought, I have to buy some time – and talk to Crawford and talk to my wife and find out what's going on. I said, "Mr. Coleman, I have to talk to my wife about this." He said, "Listen, this ship is sailing. And I'd like you to be on it." I said, "Can you just give me a little bit of time?" I'm thinking tomorrow. He said, "I'll call you back in 15 minutes."

Now I'm scrambling, to try to get ahold of Crawford. Fortunately, I did reach him. I said, "Jerry, I don't know if you know what'd going on but I just got offered a job from Coleman." He said, "Take the job." I was shocked when he said it. I said, "Wait, you're telling me that there's guys who have resigned and they're not coming back and you're telling me take the job?" He said, "You have to take it. If you don't take it, somebody else is going to take it." At the time, they were only offering, I think it was four jobs. Four, as you know, turned into 22. I said, "Jerry, are you telling me that if I take the job today, tomorrow I can join the union and be a part of the union?" He said, "Absolutely."

So I didn't like the circumstances, but I was more at ease with the fact that I called him and he told me that.

BN: I had heard that from a couple of other umpires that were in a somewhat similar situation. Guys who were veteran guys told them to just take the job.

PC: The whole thing was unfortunate. Am I thrilled that for the last 20 years I've been working in the big leagues? Absolutely. But do I wish it didn't happen that way? For a lot of reasons, I wish it had never happened that way.

I don't mind that I was released and had to fight to get back, and ran into Coleman. I don't mind that. I'm proud of that really. But the fact that guys lost their jobs and that's how 22 other guys…that's the difficult part to take and I wish that that had never happened.

BN: Now you must have passed the 2,500-game mark.

PC: You know, to tell you the truth, I don't even know.

BN: At the end of 2017, you'd worked 2,428 games. Assuming you've worked 72 games this year, you've hit 2,500. {His total after the 2018 season was 2,543 major league games.]

PC: How many games do we have under our belt now?

BN: It's been about 110 or so. Even if you had all your vacation time already, you must have hit it, or be very, very close,

PC: I've had two weeks of vacation. I've had two weeks in replay. I'm close if I haven't passed it.

BN: You ought to work it up. It's a day to celebrate.

PC: Bill, every day in the big leagues is a day to celebrate. But I hear what you're saying.

BN: You've worked three no-hitters.

PC: Two behind the plate and one on the bases, yeah.

BN: You were the third-base umpire for Jonathan Sanchez, and then behind the plate for Bud Smith and Cole Hamels.

PC: For Bud Smith's, I was coming off vacation. The game was in San Diego. St. Louis at San Diego. I was flying across the country, the day of the game and I was thinking, "I've got to fly across the country and work the plate." I didn't know – until Bud Smith came up to bat in the ninth inning – that he had a no-hitter going. I heard somebody yell from the stands something like, "Bud, don't worry about all those zeroes up there!" I look and thought, "Oh my gosh. I didn't even realize it. The kid's throwing a no-hitter." With Cole Hamels, in Chicago, I didn't know until the last out that it was a no-hitter. It was a crazy fly ball hit to left field and it was a circus catch, and all of a sudden I see everybody charging the mound – his teammates – and jumping around. I knew they were talking about trading him. I thought, "They can't be cheering him because he's traded. You know what? I think I just worked a no-hitter." I look up at the board at Wrigley and I see zeroes. That's the first time I realized.

BN: You might have been the only one in the park who didn't know.

PC: (laughs) You know what, I'm glad I didn't know.

BN: Of course. It's better. Better not to know. I've talked to umpires who say that an hour and a half after a game, they might be in a restaurant and somebody asks them what the score was, and they can't remember.

PC: That's very true. But some guys remember. It's like playing golf. You play a round of golf, and then you're playing with some guys and they say, "You know, that shot of the seventh…you came out of the sand on the seventh. Then you came back…" I don't remember those things. You're right. I can't remember the scores oftentimes, either. We always joke because inevitably when you see a player…It was Jedd Gyorko last night. I'm working third, here in Kansas City, and he's playing third and says, "Where'd you come from?" I said, "Uhhhhh… we came from…uh…" I had to think about it. We had a day off in between. Finally, it hit me. He laughed, because he knows. It's the same for them as well.

BN: Sure. They just travel in a bigger pack.

PC: Yeah. Yeah. And a little more conveniently. With charters.

BN: You guys always aim to get the very first plane out, I imagine.

PC: The nicest thing for us is when we have a day game and go out of town. Like tomorrow, we have the Sunday day game and then if all goes well and I make the flight that I'm hoping to, I'll be in Chicago 8 o'clock tomorrow night.

BN: As long as the weather cooperates and you don't have a 14-inning game.

PC: All the above, right. We do have to take early morning flights when we have a night game out of town. I'm only speaking for myself but I know I'm not alone. We're not built to wake up at 5 o'clock in the morning. We work night games and then we wake up when we do. Not to say I wake up at noon, but today I think I woke up at 9:30. But I didn't have to set the alarm to wake up. I just never get a good night's sleep when I know I have to wake up early in the morning. Even if I have to wake up early, I'm still not going to sleep early. You work a night game and you're still charged up. It's like a guy coming home from work at 5 o'clock in the afternoon and saying, "I've got to be in bed by 6:30." It just doesn't work.

BN: Of course not. No. I should let you get on to other things here. I did notice that you said you first got interested in umpiring by going to a game with some friends at old Yankee Stadium. But I notice you also worked the first game that was ever played at the new Yankee Stadium. First base. That must have been kind of fun.

Umpires room door, Yankee Stadium, May 2018.

PC: Yes. It was exciting, because I grew up there. And I worked the All-Star Game in old Yankee Stadium. We used to go to Shea Stadium as well as Yankee Stadium. We'd go on bus rides with the school or whatever. The first time I worked the plate at Shea Stadium, I was a Triple-A umpire. Before the first pitch came in, I just put up my hand and called Time. I just stepped back. I grew up coming here and now nothing is going to happen until I put my hand down and tell the pitcher to pitch. It was a really surreal feeling.

I feel really blessed. I feel really blessed.

BN: I like the new Yankee Stadium in that it looks like the old one.

PC: It does. You're right. The scoreboard's bigger and the lights might be a little brighter.

BN: You can see the trains behind right field and all that.

PC: Yes. Same façade that's up there. The neat thing that was better about the old place was that the…we would come in the same gate that the players did. We parked in the same lot that they did. When you first came into that press gate, the first little doorway was down the stairs and to the clubhouses. The hallway was so narrow that if you were walking with somebody else and someone was coming the other way, somebody had to move aside.

BN: And for fans, the concourses were much narrower, too. It seemed more exciting to me. Some ballparks the fans have more passion than others. Yankee Stadium's one of those places.

PC: You're walking down this little cement corridor that turns and bends and you're thinking, "You know what? Babe Ruth walked down this hallway. Lou Gehrig walked down…Mickey Mantle…" They had to walk down the same hallway. We had to walk past the Yankee clubhouse in order to get to our room. That was always a neat feeling to think about all the history.

BN: Well, whenever you come to Fenway Park, you're working on the same field where Babe Ruth once pitched, and started to hit home runs.

PC: That's true. That's true. And for the first time when I was there Sunday night a week ago, I went into the Green Monster.

BN: Oh good. I worked two games in there. Just helping out. Hanging up the numbers.

PC: I don't know what the temperature was like when you worked there, but it's hot in there. I felt sorry for the two guys that were in there. Sunday night was hot. But it was neat. It was neat.

BN: I wanted to ask you about the 2017 World Series. You worked Game One as the plate umpire.

PC: Yes.

BN: That was like a 2-hour, 20-minute game at Dodger Stadium, Kershaw versus Keuchel. You worked right field in Game Two, and then you ended up as the replay umpire by Game Seven.

PC: Yeah, I went into replay after Game Two.

BN: How did that feel? You're out on the field and you're the plate umpire the Game One of the World Series. You can't ask for anything better than that.

PC: Every umpire's goal is to work the World Series.

BN: Then you're in a much more sterile environment. I've been to the Replay Center. You're definitely far removed from the actual action.

PC: Honestly, it was disappointing to have to leave the field. The consolation was the honor of working Game One.

Before they changed that system, and before the implementation of replay, I never thought that I would ever…that's every umpire's goal: to work the World Series. And if you work the World Series, you certainly want to have a plate job. But up until not that long ago, the only guys who worked Game One and Seven were the crew chiefs. So I said, I'm never going to have a chance to work Game One or Game Seven. Then they changed that.

Was it a letdown? Some guys will say, I was just happy to be there. I was thrilled to be there, but I was disappointed to have to leave the field. But to be able to work Game One was the biggest thrill of my career.

BN: It's not like you had to go home. You were still working the World Series – just at a distance.

PC: There were no calls overturned, but I think there were two plays that were reviewed and the calls stood or were confirmed – I don't remember – but I know that nothing was overturned.

The flip side of that was that Mark Wegner, who came onto the field when I went off of the field, had the thrill of his life by working Game Seven. And he worked a great Game Seven. But I think he would say that he was disappointed to have missed the action of the opening of Game One of the Series – even though he worked the first game in Houston, the second city, which had all of the same [excitement] to Houston as Game One. But Game One is Game One.

BN: When did you get #10?

PC: My first number was assigned and it was 55. I was happy with that number because…

BN: You had a number!

PC: My wife and I were both born in 1955, so it had some meaning to me. When they combined the American league and National League, of course there were duplicate numbers. They allowed the senior man to pick – if there were two number 4's, 5's, whatever – they allowed the senior man to retain his number, and then they allowed the guy who lost his number to pick any other number that was available. So Angel Hernandez and Dale Scott both wore #5, Dale in the American League and Angel in the National League. Dale was senior. He kept 5. Angel, for whatever reason, said, "Well, I had 5, I'll just take double 5. I'll take 55." So he got my number.

I was able to take any number that was available, any number of anyone to whom I was senior. I said, "You know, I'm not going to take anyone's number." I wasn't crazy that I lost my number so I wasn't going to do that to anyone else. But there was really no number that was available that meant anything to me. So I said I'm just going to take the highest number. I'm going to take 99.

So I wore 99 for a couple of years. Then Tommy Hallion, who lost his job in the resignation, his number was 20. After a couple of years of me wearing 99, the number 20 became available. Out of all the guys who might have wanted 20, I was the senior guy. I told Tommy, "I'm going to take 20 to hold it until when you get your job back, and I'm going to give it back to you." So I wore 20 for a year. After that, 10 became available. That was John McSherry's number, so I'll be proud to wear that. That's how I got 10 and I just stuck with it because I thought it was a good number. [Tom Hallion was rehired in 2005.]

BN: They're all good numbers. You're fortunate to get one, right?

PC: That's right.

BN: Most umpires can spend 10 years working and waiting for it.

I understand that a friend of yours died from ALS and his daughter goes to school or maybe just graduated from Harvard, right down the street from me? Dominique.

PC: Dominique. She followed in her father's footsteps. The story goes back to 2001. I was working with Tim McClelland and I was home on a day off. I went into my local deli and got a call from my buddy Robert [Luongo]. Robert and I weren't blood cousins, but we were like cousins because his mother's sister married my mother's brother. We had the same blood cousins. We grew up together. We were the same age. We went to junior high together. Even before junior high when we went to two different grammar schools in the same town, we were always at the same family functions - picnics, barbecues, things like that. We were always very close.

He called me and said, "Something's going on with my hand. My hand just keeps going numb. I feel like it's starting to go up my arm a little bit. I said, "Well, Rob. Go to the doctor. What are you waiting for? Whatever it is, before it gets worse." He was a Harvard grad. He was actually an all-state linebacker for Belleville High School, our hometown. And then he went to Harvard. He played his freshman year. He was just like a big brute of a guy. After he graduated from Harvard, he was working for the 3M Company and then he went on independent projects. He didn't have insurance was the bottom line. He says, "Well, I'm going to wait and see what happens." Fast forward a little bit, he was diagnosed with ALS – Lou Gehrig's disease.

I saw what this disease did to him, the progression. He was living in Florida at the time. All that time when I was in the minor leagues and especially when I went back to work, my first league was the Florida State League. Robert was the kind of guy who'd jump in a car and show up anywhere unannounced.

After he was diagnosed, he lasted about five years, which is kind of the average amount of time. Some a little longer, some far less. He lost every ability to move – every muscle, his voice, except the movement of his eyes. The last time I saw him alive, I said to him, "Rob, listen. I never want you to worry about Dominique's education. I will tap the baseball community and our friends in town and we will raise money to send her to wherever she wants to go." [Dominique was 9 years old at the time.]

It started out – we were actually on a family cruise and it turned out to be one of these disaster cruises that you hear about on the news. We got stranded on this little island where they had just stopped for like a barbecue. Long story short, they offered us another cruise. They paid for that cruise and they offered us another cruise and my wife and I said we're just not cruise people. We're not going through that again. I asked them, "Would you allow me to raffle off my cruise to a charity?" They said Yes. What I did with that money was I bought a computer for Robert – it was in the infancy of the technology, but it was a computer with which he was able to type using his eyes. I've seen them with other ALS patients now and they're far more advanced than what Robert ever had. And don't forget, back then computers were new to all of us anyway. Not only did he have to use this technology that wasn't all that great to begin with, he also had to learn to use a computer, period.

That was the beginning of what I started as the Robert Luongo ALS Fund. I don't remember exactly how much the computer cost – it was probably something like $8,000 – but we raised enough money to pay for the computer, I didn't want to have leftover money and have people say, "He sold this many tickets and that's this much money..." I didn't want to get into any of that. I wasn't looking to be in the fundraising business. But the response, just from our community, was so overwhelming that I did have extra money. I said to him, "Rob, we're going to raise whatever we have to so she can go to whatever school she wants. Because I had this leftover money, I had to legitimize the whole thing so I applied for and received a 501(c)3 from the Internal Revenue, and that's how it began.

I'm just so proud to say that this is our 14th year and it's become a big deal in our town. We have 600 of the same people come every year. Once a year. Because of my position in baseball, I've had great guests. Tommy Lasorda was my guest speaker. Joe Torre. I have mostly Italian Yankee fans, so we had Joe Pepitone. Bucky Dent. We had Goose Gossage. Bob Costas has been there three times. Lou Piniella. We do it as a mystery guest, just for fun. People are always, "Come on, tell me who it is." The word gets around. "I hear this year it's..." "Where'd you hear that?" No one's ever right. Last year we had Willie Randolph. Tony LaRussa came one year. It's been a lot of fun. It's been a lot of work. We raised a lot of money. The money goes to patient care and research. Last year we made a donation for $50,000 for research. We put in countless ramps and chair lifts. It's been a very rewarding experience for me.

BN: Did she graduate, or is she about to?

PC: She graduated last year from Harvard. Yes, she did. It was really nice to see. [After a bit of other conversation]:

As an umpire, it's funny to walk into the ballpark among fans that are going to the game. Maybe they were there the night before. They're complaining about the strike zone, and they have no idea [who's walking right beside them]. There was a funny story yesterday. We were going into the ballpark in Kansas City. There's a gate you walk in and then we take an elevator down. The club seating right behind home plate, they would also take the same elevator down. We're there, and here comes an old-timer. He has a St. Louis jersey on. I guess it was his son with him, who's maybe a little younger than me. And I guess his kids. We're waiting for the elevator and he says, "You from Kansas City?" I said, "No, no, I'm actually from Jersey." So he said, "Oh, so you live in Kansas City now?" I said, "No, no. I still live in Jersey." And he said, "What are you doing?" I said, "I'm just passing through. Here to see the game." We get in the elevator and we go downstairs and, sure enough, when we go out to the home plate meeting, that guy is sitting like in the second row by the on-deck circle of the Cardinals. He sees me and he points to me and he starts laughing, like to say, "It's you! It was you in the elevator."

BN: And you could have gone over and said, "I told you I was here to see the game. I'm going to get a really good view, and so are you."

PC: Yeah. I didn't think of that, but you're right, that would have been a good one.

—end

2

Ed Hickox

Ed Hickox told another story of perseverance. I had met him briefly at the Wendelstedt School in January 2016. We caught up and talked at Fenway Park that June.

Interview with Ed Hickox at Fenway Park on June 23, 2016

Ed Hickox (picking up on something said): There's been times I've walked up to the plate and forgot my shin guards. Or my mask.

Bill Nowlin: A major league game?

EH: Yeah (laughs). I didn't get all the way onto the field, but to the end of the tunnel and said, "Oh, shit. I forgot something!"

BN: You're also a detective with a police department? You wouldn't want to go out unprepared there.

EH: That's right. I certainly want to have my firearm ready there. You never know.

BN: Let me go back to the beginning. How did you first get interested in becoming an umpire? You played baseball in high school…

EH: I played baseball in high school.

BN: What position did you play?

EH: Outfield - center field, left field. I got a scholarship at St. John's River, a community college in a little town called Palatka. I played there for two years. I was 18 years old and I knew I wasn't good enough to play professional baseball so I said, "You know what? I want to go to umpire school. Give it a shot." I lived in Deland, Florida which is right

Ed Hickox has been a full-time major league umpire since 1999.

near Ormond Beach and Daytona Beach, which is where one of the professional umpire schools was – the Wendelstedt School. I went there, saying if I don't make it I'll go back and finish up my college, but I ended up making it.

BN: And doing very well.

EH: Actually, that was the largest class ever. There was 230 students in 1983. Only 13 of us got jobs that year.

BN: Jobs at any level.

EH: Rookie ball. And then I worked my way up. When I first went to umpire school, I can remember the first day – everybody had to stand up, say their age, where they were from, and how much experience they had. There were people saying, "I've done two College World Series…" I said, "I'm 18, from Deland, Florida – about 18 miles away – and no experience." I called my dad that day and said, "Listen, Dad. It's not too late to get your money back."

BN: What kind of work did he do?

EH: He was a factory worker. He worked for Sherwood Medical, which is a hypodermic needle factory. He says, "You know what, Son? You want to do it." He gave me the money to do it. So I did it. I went out there and I just got better and better and was lucky enough to get a job.

BN: If you lived that close, did you commute?

EH: No, I did not. I actually stayed there. My dad talked me into staying there because he said, "You know what? You want to get the feel. You want to study with your partners and stuff like that. Don't worry about coming home." He knew this is something that I wanted to do, so he told me to go for it.

BN: Is he still around today?

EH: No, I lost him in 2011. Which was neat because he got to see me make it to the big leagues – twice. And he got to see me work the All-Star Game in 2011. I worked it in July and he passed away in October.

BN: I was hoping he got to see you make it.

EH: Oh yeah.

BN: I did want to ask you about making it twice. If there's anything uncomfortable that you don't want to talk about, just don't say it.

EH: No.

BN: You were hired as an American League umpire in 1999.

ED: That's right. In 1990, I started work as a part-time fill-in and I worked 10 years to get four openings and I finally got the opening. Don Denkinger retired in 1998, at the end of that season. Marty Springstead and Dr. Budig called me and said, "On January 1st, you're hired full-time." I was just so happy, you couldn't imagine.

And then I went to my first union meeting, at the All-Star break, of 1999, and that's when we as a union decided to resign our jobs. It was my first union meeting, and me being the newly-hired one, I was sitting in the back of the room, saying, "You know…" I was just listening – if it was good enough for everyone else, it was good enough for me.

BN: You also want to go along, because most of them did resign.

EH: Right! Everybody in that room, that day decided to. There were some people who rescinded their resignations, and I wasn't one of the ones that did that, so I was one of the 22 that lost my job. I was on the street from September 1999. It took me all those years in the minor leagues to get there.

I had umpired professional baseball. I only had a two-year college degree. Nothing to fall back on. My wife was a stay-at-home mom. We were making [as of 1999] six figures, and we went from six figures to no figures. The kids had to come out of private school and go to public school. We had to put the kids in Medicaid. We were hurting. What I did is I went to the police academy and became a police officer. I figured that's a trade I could go for six months, come out, and get a job making 15 bucks an hour, which was more than I could make anywhere else. Plus, it's a worthwhile job. If it was something I had to do for the rest of my life, it was a meaningful job. My wife went back to school, and went back to work.

We gutted it out. Years went by and years went by. One day, around 2003, I looked at my wife at dinner and said, "You know what, honey? I made it one time on my skill and merit. And I didn't lose it on my skill and merit. I lost it because of a union labor/management dispute. What if I went back through the minor leagues and gave it a shot again?" I said, "I didn't get fired because I was not good enough." And she says, "Honey, if you want to give it a shot, go for it."

So, with her support, I went back all the way to the minors...I can remember when I was 18 years old, I spent nine days in rookie ball, in the Gulf Coast League. Somebody sold – an umpire got caught stealing baseballs and he and got fired, so I was promoted – at 18 years old – to the Florida State League, which is a low A. Now at age 40, I spent the entire season in rookie ball. It was humbling, to say the least. But I did it. I did it for my family. They didn't deserve, due to the decisions that I made...

BN: Did anyone else go that route?

EH: I was the first one to do it, and after I did, Bob Davidson and Tom Hallion saw what I did and they went back to it. We're the three out of the 22 that made it back. [Some of the 22 were hired back, but not by having to work all the way back.]⁵

BN: It's hard enough getting there the first time.

EH: It's very difficult getting there the first time, and to do it two times is quite an accomplishment. But you do what you have to do.

BN: Going through it the second time, did you feel that you were branded in any way?

EH: Well, you know what? It was made very clear to me by Baseball, there's no guarantees. You're doing this on your own.

BN: But they gave you a fair shot?

EH: Yes, they did. Oh yeah. I'm very, very grateful. For them to even let me come back through the minor leagues, and giving me the opportunity to come back to the big leagues. Believe me, I'm very grateful.

It was funny. Coming back through the minor leagues, I was working with people half my age. And working the plate every other night. So physically, it was very demanding. And mentally, it was very demanding because if you made a good call, they would say, "He was a major league umpire. He should make a good call." If you would make a bad call, they would say, "No wonder you're in the minor leagues."

They didn't know the situation that led to it. But I've got to say that the minor-league establishment really treated me with a great deal of respect. The managers, the players – if the players even thought about saying something, the manager would jump all over them. "No, don't." Not that I asked for it, but they respected that I was a major league umpire and on the way back trying to work my way up. It was humbling, though, to say the least.

BN: Right now, you've got to feel good about it.

EH: Of course! At the end of the day, it's all water under the bridge. It'll be one hell of a book one day. (laughs)

BN: You've got a degree in Criminal Justice now.

EH: I do.

BN: Was that at the two-year college?

EH: No, when I was out of baseball, once I became a police officer I went back to college and I got a criminal justice degree. In our particular department, if you want to be a sergeant or lieutenant or go up in the rank, you have to have a criminal justice degree. Looking into the future, not knowing I was going to get back into baseball, I wanted to explore every opportunity to progress in the career that I was in. I got a two-year associate's degree back when I was 18, and then when I was 40-something, I got the criminal justice degree.

BN: And you do work now, in the offseason.

EH: Yeah, when I got my job back in the big leagues, I went to the chief. I put my badge and gun on his desk and said, "I have to resign. I can't be in a traffic stop and lose a six-figure job." He says, "Tell you what. Why don't I promote you to detective and when you're home in the offseason, you've been a great worker and we love you around here…" I think he liked saying that he has a major league umpire on his staff.

BN: Sure! Of course!

EH: So I go in when I am home in the offseason, two or three days a week. Make my own schedule. Say this week I can only work Tuesday and Thursday. This week, I can work Thursday and Sunday. It's nice because…they give me my own cases. Property crime cases, stuff like that.

BN: Current cases, not cold cases.

EH: No, we've had some cold case murders that I've helped work out. Usually, I go and help with my partner, interviewing, we'll dust fingerprints, process a scene. They keep me active. Give me my own desk. It's really neat how they take care of me. It's a lot of fun. And it keeps my certification active. In the State of Florida, if you let your certification lapse – if you're not hired by somebody for a certain period – I think it's two years – then you have to go through the police academy all over again. So it's an opportunity to keep my certification active and still keep my badge in my pocket.

BN: And as you said at the beginning, you're able to feel you're doing something worthwhile.

EH: Oh, yeah. I feel good to this day to be able to take bad people off the street. Try to help out the community. It's great. And, listen, there's still risk. We do search warrants and we make arrests and there's a risk of getting hurt. That risk is still out there, but being a detective is not quite as risky as being a first responder right on the scene. Any time you carry a gun, you have a chance of a bad guy not liking who you are. But that's something I really, really enjoy doing. It's a great department.

BN: And it's Daytona Beach Shores. That's a different community from Daytona Beach.

EH: Yes, it's just south of Daytona on a little peninsula. I think our city's six miles long and a quarter mile wide.

BN: You were also a first responder for Homeland Security?

EH: I have my commercial instrument pilot's license, and my own plane. During the earthquakes in Haiti, I flew my plane and picked up passengers and transported them to Miami. And I also fly for Angel Flight, a nonprofit organization where pilots donate their time and their airplane to transport sick children or sick families to better hospital care around the country. That's kind of like my charity, what I do. It makes you feel good, transporting people who can't afford to get good care. A part of that, too – I did take a course – I am signed up with Homeland Security. If there's a disaster, they'll call on us to transport medical needs or whatever is needed.

BN: You have been an instructor at the Wendelstedt School?

EH: For 33 years now. I went to school there in 1983 and Mr. [Harry] Wendelstedt hired me in 1984 to start teaching, and I've been there every year since.

BN: Including the years you were…

EH: Including the years I was gone, yes. He was very loyal to me and kept me there and gave me a paycheck. I'm really, really grateful to him, and his family.

BN: This guy sitting at the table with us [Mike Estabrook], he was one of your students.

EH: He was. Matter of fact, Greg Gibson was a student. [Pointing to Dana DeMuth] He was not a student; he was one of my fellow instructors. He actually taught me.

BN: You passed him [referring to Mike].

EH: Oh, no. I don't always make real good calls, but… (laughs)

Mike Estabrook: They got it right in 1999. They actually knew what they were doing.

BN: When you got the call, Ed, the second time around, did you know it was coming?

EH: No, actually, I didn't. The union negotiated a new agreement, and they agreed to wear microphones and to hire us three back – me and Tom and Bob. But I didn't *know*. We heard rumblings that that was a possibility but I wasn't waiting by my phone. I was kind of surprised. The first time I got hired…Denkinger, he didn't let anybody know he was retiring until it happened. I just got a call, and that was a surprise. Both of mine were really out of the blue.

BN: A happy day, though.

ED: Oh ho! I think the second one was happier than the first one. Just the accomplishment of going and going back through the minor leagues and doing what it took to get back.

BN: You've worked seven no-hitters and a cycle – at least one at every base?

EH: Yeah, I've worked one at each base and I did two behind the plate and I had one this year – that's the seventh one, yeah. I've been very, very fortunate.

ME: I think the record is 11.

EH: There's been people that's worked 30 years that's never had one. You know what was interesting? Last year, I had Alex Rodriguez's 3,000[th] hit.

After the game, a reporter came in and he asked me, "Ed, do you know where you were on...?" I don't know the exact date. Like May 25, 1994. [It was July 9, 1994.] I said, "I don't even know where I was last week." He says, "You were at Fenway Park. Alex Rodriguez was playing for Seattle and he got his first hit. And you were working the plate. And you worked the plate on his 3,000th hit." That was 21 years later. What are the odds of that happening?

BN: The last thing I wanted to ask about is, you've had a lot of injuries.

EH: I have.

BN: And some pretty serious injuries. You wear a different kind of mask now. I saw Greg [Gibson] was wearing a similar type of mask.

EH: Yes. Yes. Hockey helmets. Mine is modified, with extra padding and stuff. Unfortunately, I've had six or seven head concussions and two of them were serious. So, yeah, that's a constant concern.

It's an umpire hockey mask. They call it a hockey mask, but I have extra padding and stuff in mine for extra protection. Knock on wood, we won't have to worry about that anymore, but it's certainly in the back of my mind.

BN: There's not too many umpires that wear them yet.

EH: No, but a lot of the guys who have had prior concussions wear them. It really protects you if you get a backswing and get hit on the back of the head. For my sake, any new technology or anything that can help keep me safe out there is, I want to...

BN: As we've learned, the effect can be cumulative.

EH: It's certainly something that wears on you. It's always in the back of my mind. But I have to go out and make a living and do my job.

BN: Listen, thank you for making the time.

EH: Oh, no. It was a pleasure. Thank you for coming in and asking.

—end

3

How This Book Came to Be

Both accounts – Phil Cuzzi and Ed Hickox – show a real determination to pursue the profession, and how dedicated they each were. There are only 76 major league umpires at any given time. You don't get to the top of a profession as exclusive as major league umpire without hard work, commitment, and perseverance. From the very first interviews I did, it was clear to me that these umpires deeply cared about their work and that it troubled them if they thought they had underperformed on a given day – even if no one but them really knew they had perhaps been subpar.

How was it that I started on this project?

The first time I had interacted with some umpires – and learned a lot more about umpiring – was during SABR's annual convention in Boston in 2002. I organized a panel on Thursday afternoon during the convention. The panel included Dave Anderson, Chair of SABR's Umpires and Rules Committee, and included official scorer David Vincent, Umpire Observer Kevin O'Connor, and former National League umpire Bob Long.

In July 2013, I interviewed Randy Marsh about his work umpiring in the 2004 American League Championship Series. That was for the book *Don't Let Us Win Tonight: An Oral History of the 2004 Boston Red Sox's Impossible Playoff Run* (with Allan Wood.)

Late in 2013, I began talking with Larry Gerlach about working together on a book that became *The SABR Book of Umpires and Umpiring*. We worked on gathering a number of historical pieces, written by a number of various SABR authors, and began to plan out the book. In the book we included biographies of each of the 10 former major league umpires who have been inducted into the National Baseball Hall of Fame. Various SABR authors contributed biographies of another dozen umpires, including Yanet Moreno of Cuba, the first woman umpire in any country's major league. There were a lot of articles about umpiring, as well.

In mid-December, I wrote to umpire supervisor Steve Palermo inquiring about writing his biography for SABR. Just after noontime on Christmas Eve 2013, he wrote back and agreed to an interview. It was August 2014 before we got around to it. I met him at Fenway Park where over the next couple of years, we sat in the same row of the press box that year and spent a little time together. One of his brothers visited a couple of times as well.

Umpire observer Kevin O'Connor, who had been on the SABR convention panel back in 2002 and is often assigned to work at Fenway Park, was always friendly and has been very helpful throughout the SABR book and this one.

By the time the 2015 season got underway, I was ready to start learning more about contemporary umpires and the work they do. I was ready to ask to interview some of the current working umpires.

I wasn't sure what reaction I would get. Would they be reticent? Suspicious? That wouldn't have been unreasonable. If umpires engender any reaction from the crowd at a ballpark, it's not cheers or applause. It's boos and catcalls. If someone in the media wants to ask them a question, it's usually because of a disputed call or an incident on the field. In 2019, there is really only maybe one umpire who would be recognized off the field – Joe West. It didn't take long to learn that umpires relish their anonymity. As Phil Cuzzi said, it can be kind of fun to walk into a park amongst all the fans and not be recognized. And if an umpire does a good job, they're not noticed. A game without controversy involving umpires or umpiring is, for them, a good game.

I wondered what reaction I would get. I lucked out.

4

Ted Barrett

The first conversation I had with Ted Barrett was on the telephone on April 30, 2015. I caught up with his crew in July when they came through Boston, but first we spoke on the phone. He was in Oakland at the time.

Interview with Ted Barrett on April 30, 2015

BN: You're from the State of Washington. I don't know if you grew up there, too.

TB: No, my dad was in the Navy and I was there until I was about a year old. I grew up in North Tonawanda, New York, outside of Buffalo. After 10th grade, I moved to Mountain View, California and finished high school there. I went to Foothill Junior College and Cal State Hayward.

In high school, I played football, basketball, and baseball. At Foothill, I played football and basketball. At Hayward, I played football and I also boxed.

BN: So baseball wasn't your main sport by the time you went through the whole thing?

TB: No, it was probably my third or fourth sport but I always enjoyed it as a spectator. One of the coolest things about moving to the Bay Area was being able to go to Giants and A's games. In Buffalo, we never got to any games. In my early teens, we lost the Bisons. Around '81, they came back in the Eastern League. There was a gap there. By the time I got to California, they went back to Triple A.

BN: What kind of work did your father do in the Navy?

TB: My dad was a radioman and then – the reason we were in Pasco – he became a recruiter. My mom was a nurse. She grew up in Spokane, Washington. There were four boys, after my youngest brother got out of kindergarten, she went back to school and became a nurse and she was a nurse until she retired.

BN: So you had a bunch of brothers?

TB: Three brothers – and a big St. Bernard. No sisters. We all grew up playing sports. My dad played high school football and track, so he encouraged us to play sports. Most of us played hockey and getting up at 4 in the morning to get ice time, and being an expensive sport and everything, my dad kind of steered me away – "You want to play basketball, don't you?"

BN: How'd you first get into umpiring?

TB: When I was 14, I had a buddy who had umpired the year before for the Little League and he asked me to come on out. I did. Umpiring is one

Ted Barrett with his Carlucci chest protector, Fenway Park, August 24, 2016.

of those things where you either love it or you hate it, and I loved it. I started doing Little League games – no real training, I just went out there and did it. When we moved to California, in addition to everything else that was going on…

BN: Did you get paid a couple of dollars a game or something like that?

TB: My first game, I remember, if you worked the plate you got two dollars, if you worked the bases, you got a dollar – but you weren't given cash. You were given credit at the snack bar. So that was my pay.

A couple of years later, we ended up getting cash. I think my last year in New York we got three dollars for the plate and two dollars for the bases.

BN: That makes you a professional.

TB: I guess I was a professional. At age 14. I don't think I paid taxes, though.

BN: Taxes come along later, I guess. You maybe don't have to pay taxes on snacks at the snack bar. How did you decide to do it as a full-time thing?

TB: When I was playing football at Hayward, I would go to park up on the baseball field and after practice one day, I was walking up and they had a Fall League game and I talked to some of the umpires. I said, "Hey, look, I want to start umpiring." I explained to them I had done some. They told me to go to a meeting of the local high school group and I started doing high schools in the Bay Area. It was a great job. I think they paid like $47 a game back then. This was the mid-80s. It beat working at a job, like a lot of other guys.

A couple of guys in that group were actually minor-league umpires and they saw me and they said, "Hey, you need to go to umpire school."

I did, after graduating college I went to Joe Brinkman's Umpire School in 1989 and started my career from there. In '89, I worked in rookie ball in the Northwest League. In '90 and '91, I was in the California League. In '92 and '93, I was in the Texas League and then the Pacific Coast League. In '94, I went to the big leagues for the first time. I went up and down there, doing vacations and injuries until I got hired fulltime in '99. I got some back-time – credit for some games I'd worked before I got hired so this is my 19th year toward the pension.

BN: If all you were doing was filling in for others taking holidays and stuff, you worked 127 games in 1996…

TB: Yeah. The American League staff was older and back then in '96 we had a lot of guys hurt, so it was great for guys like me and Fieldin Culbreth and Brian O'Nora. I think we all had over 100 games.

BN: You had 64 the first year, but then down to 30 in your second. In your third year, you worked 127 games.

TB: What happened on that, the first year in '94 I went up and I stayed up 'til the strike on August 11. When the players went on strike, I went back down. In '95, obviously the umpires hadn't worked from August 11 all the way until into the middle of April – you had some replacement umpires that had worked – so they were all healthy at that point and they all stayed healthy, so there wasn't a lot of time for a lot of us who were filling in then. In '95, we didn't have as many games.

BN: It was mostly July you worked in the majors that year.

TB: Yeah. I was working in the Pacific Coast League.

BN: One thing I was curious about, you were an American League umpire through 1999 and then there were no separate leagues…you became a Major League umpire. Did you have any sense of loss involved with the change? Did you have any kind of esprit de corps or a friendly rivalry with the National League umpires?

TB: Yeah, we did. We definitely did. That's pretty much gone away. Some of the old-timers, you'll still see that. With my generation guys, with the labor unrest we had in '99, we tried to be kind of peacemakers – bridge-builders – and part of that was kind of getting rid of the American League/National League divide that we had. It wasn't exactly a healthy rivalry that we had going on. Now that that's dissolved, it's actually a little better.

BN: It's just human nature, if you're in one group and there's another group…I mean, you wore different colors at that point, right?

TB: Yeah. Yeah.

BN: I just figured there must have been at least a joking rivalry between the two groups.

TB: Now it's more of a joking rivalry. Back then, there was some bite to it. I'll put it that way.

BN: These days, you get the schedule for the whole year in advance, right?

TB: Yeah. In the past, we got it up until August but they give us the whole thing now.

BN: Then you have to wait and see how the postseason sorts out.

TB: Right. The postseason, they don't let us know until the very end.

BN: Do your hotels get booked for you by MLB, or an agency that works with them?

TB: No, we book our hotels and we prefer it that way. In the minor leagues, the guys stay wherever they're put, but in the big leagues, we book them. We have the freedom to stay wherever we want. The flights are booked through a central agency, and that's convenient. That's changed. We used to get tickets, open tickets, ourselves and did our own flight arrangements. It's a lot easier now. We just call the travel agency and they book us.

BN: The agency has an arrangement with Major League Baseball.

TB: Yeah.

BN: Do you tend to travel together?

TB: We try to, but it doesn't always work that way. Some guys regionally try to stay on certain airlines to build up their status, which is really kind of a survival thing to kind of get in and out and get the perks that come with it. But, yeah, we try to stay together when we can. Of course, a lot of guys as they get an off-date, they'll go home and…

BN: Different people live in different parts of the country.

TB: Yeah, exactly.

BN: Do you tend to stay at the same hotels?

TB: Yeah, for the most part, but not always. Sometimes we're in different hotels. Some guys prefer Marriott. Some guys prefer Hyatt.

BN: You usually try to avoid staying at the hotel where the visiting team might be staying?

TB: Yeah, we do, for a couple of reasons. Not seeing the players and them not seeing us. That's good. But also the players' hotels also tend to have a lot more activity going on. They've got fans waiting in the lobby. They get busy. We try to stay away from any hustle and bustle.

BN: Of course, if a fan sees a typical umpire walk through a lobby, they wouldn't know.

TB: Exactly. They would have no idea who we were. We can move pretty much anonymously.

BN: Maybe a dozen years ago, I talked to a couple of umpires and they said in a place like Boston, they'd often just take the subway since they wouldn't be recognized. Your local transportation, does that get reimbursed? Would you actually save money by taking the subway in a place like Boston, as opposed to taking a cab?

TB: Everything gets reimbursed, so it's just kind of a matter of convenience. Years ago, it wasn't that way. It's probably why they were taking the subway.

BN: One last question today. In 2005, you ejected 10 players in just the one year.

TB: When you see inflated numbers like that, it's from a brawl usually. [Indeed, there were six players ejected on April 24 – Boston vs. Tampa Bay]

—end of April 30 interview

5

Laz Diaz, Chris Guccione, Cory Blaser, and Clint Fagan

The first group that I sat down with, interviewing them around the table in the umpires' room at Fenway Park, was on July 3 and 5, 2015. The crew chief for the series was Laz Diaz. Crew chief Jeff Nelson was on vacation, so Laz Diaz served as crew chief for the three games. The Houston Astros were in town. Chris Guccione, Cory Blaser, and fill-in umpire Clint Fagan were the other umpires on the crew. [Note: this conversation was originally printed in *The SABR Book of Umpires and Umpiring*.]

Conversation in the Umpires Room at Fenway Park on July 3 and 5, 2015

Bill Nowlin: You guys answered one of the questions I had as you walked in just now. I wondered if you brought your gear with you.

Laz Diaz: DHL. They pick it up at the ballpark where we're at – we were at the Mets. Yesterday, Citi Field. It's waiting for us. Our clubhouse guy, Dean [Lewis], he opens it up. Whatever's underneath, we have in a bag, our dirty clothes. He washes all that and hangs it up here. He does our shoes and has everything ready once we get in.

LD: If you've got real fanatic fans, the ones that study baseball and study the umpires, they know who we are. But the regular Joe Blow, they won't know. I've gone with my friends at Wrigley and the first couple of times they came to Wrigley, I've taken a shower and gone and hung out at some of the bars around Wrigley, right in the neighborhood. Walk in and have my beer and hang out with them. They [other patrons] don't know who I am.

Chris Guccione: I think I've been recognized twice ever, having dinner or having a drink after the game. Once or twice.

BN: That's because you were wearing your face mask.

CG: Yeah, that's what it was. I had all my gear on.

BN: [to Clint] You're a Triple-A umpire right now?

Clint Fagan: Yeah.

BN: How does that work? You worked like 110 major league games last year.

CF: I really don't know, ranking wise. You're given assignments. You're put on a list for callups.

BN: Mostly you're filling in, like for Jeff Nelson tonight.

CF: Yes. I fill in on replay, injuries, vacation.

BN: That's as many games as most regular guys work. You worked 119 games last year.

CF: I don't know the exact number.

LD: We're on our four weeks' vacation, where he goes first and gets his week [indicates Cory Blaser], then I got my week, then Jeff Nelson, and next week he goes [indicates Chris Guccione.] So he'll fill in [Clint] for the whole month for us. After he leaves us, Sunday, in Cleveland, when we have the All-Star break, there'll be another four guys, another crew, having their four-block, so he might go there and work with them for the whole four weeks. Yeah, he'll work maybe even more than what we work.

BN: You're the crew chief tonight?

LD: For the whole week.

BN: While Jeff Nelson's away.

LD: Yeah. These guys have been trembling the whole time.

BN: I imagine! It's a dictatorship, right?

LD: It's a dictatorship.

Cory Blaser: I was in his spot [Clint's] for four or five years and just recently got hired in January of last year, 2014.

BN: Did you all come together here just now, in a taxi or something?

LD: We have a car service that we use. We flew in last night, the car service picked us up at the airport, took us to the hotel. This morning, we did whatever we wanted to do during the day.

BN: Does MLB select the hotels for you?

LD: No, we pick our own hotels.

BN: You tend to stay together at the same hotel? This crew, anyhow?

LD: Yeah, we tend to stay at the same spot. We're all Hyatt guys; we like Hyatt. There's some other crews that like Marriott.

BN: If you get with one of their programs, you can build up points.

LD: Exactly. We're paying for our hotels, a daily per diem rate. Out of your per diem rate, you pay for your own hotels, so if you want to stay at Motel 6, you can, or you can stay at the Ritz.

LD: And when you're home, like when they're home in Denver [Guccione and Blaser are both from Colorado], of course, they don't use their per diem. It's real nice to be home and open the refrigerator.

CG: Like this city here, different cities have car services that we use – Toronto, New York, San Fran, Oakland, Chicago – both Cubs and White Sox, maybe that's it. All the rest, we get a rental car.

BN: One guy I talked to maybe 15 years ago, he just took the subway here. Which you could do if you don't get recognized.

CG: People don't recognize you.

LD: The only thing they see on the field is a black shirt.

CG: You know, it's funny, a lot of guys are staying at hotels and there's a lot of fans at the hotel. We'll leave the game and many times we're standing right in the same elevator. They're talking, "Oh, man, that was an awesome game. This and that." And we'll say, "How was it? Who won? How'd the umpires do?" or something like that. And they're all, "It was great. They did this or that…"

BN: I wondered if you ever might have said, "Did you see that call at third base? What a…" You've heard it, but did you ever just goof on them?

CG: Oh yeah.

LD: I have, yeah. In Chicago, with a couple of guys that came see me, there was this one guy "Oh, the Cubbies won! The Cubbies won!" He was so happy. I said, "Yeah, but that second-base umpire" – I was working second base that day – "he blew that call." He said, "Yeah, he did" and he'd start to get all upset. I told him, "Listen, let's make a pact. If we ever see that umpire again, we're going to punch him right in the mouth, okay?" He said, "OK!" And all my buddies standing around me, they're all looking at me like, "You're crazy, man."

They don't know who we are.

BN: This room we're in is fairly new. You used to be up over the Red Sox clubhouse, right?

LD: Dean, how long we been here?

Dean Lewis, umpire room attendant: This room's been here since 2004.

BN: More than 10 years. A long time, now. When you go around the league, are most of the facilities relatively similar these days?

LD: The new ballparks are…

BN: Bigger than here?

LD: Yes. In the newer ballparks, but in San Diego – which is a new ballpark – that locker room is smaller than this one. Wouldn't you agree?

CG: Yeah.

Cory Blaser: But like Minnesota, that's enormous. Our dressing area, our living room area, the bathroom, everything…

LD: Philly's huge.

BN: What's the worst one?

LD: Wrigley?

CG: Wrigley's not bad, because they re-did that one also.

LD: I think the smallest one is San Diego.

CG: A lot of times when they build these new ballparks, they forget. At the last minute, someone will ask, "Where's the umpires room?"

CB: Miami's is not that big, either.

LD: Personally, what I look for is – especially in this area here [where the lockers and equipment trunks are], where we get dressed, to have enough room.

BN: Not bumping in to each other.

LD: Not bumping into each other. Stretch. The one in Miami is very small. You could probably touch his hand. Where you are in front of me, that's how close we are.

BN: But they're similar enough these days. There must have been some really bad ones, 20, 25 years ago.

LD: Milwaukee.

BN: County Stadium?

LD: County Stadium was bad.

CG: Didn't that have a dirt floor?

LD: You had to lift up your trunk, because if it rained, the clubhouse would get flooded. [There was a little talk about Cuba. I mentioned seeing umpires walking in to the park from the neighborhood around the ballpark.]

LD: I'm hoping to be in one of those games, if they have a spring training game next year. When I first heard of it, it would be 2017 but they've been pushing it for next year. [Diaz was the third-base umpire in the Tampa Bay vs. Cuba game at Estadio Latinamericano on March 22, 2016 in Havana.]

BN: Are you Cuban by ancestry?

LD: My dad came over in '61 and my mom in '62. They were already married in Cuba, and then when they got here, they found each other. I was there last week, to see my mom and dad's home town, in the north central part of the island. Where Livan Hernandez is from. Yuniesky Betancourt. That area.

Umpire's room at McCoy Stadium (AAA), May 6, 2018.

BN: When you leave here to go to the field, do you go through the edge of the visitors' dugout?

LD: Yeah, we go through their dugout.

BN: Is that usually the way it is, through one team or another's dugout?

LD: It depends where we're at.

CB: Very rarely. There's maybe only three spots where we go through the dugout, right? It's usually separate.

BN: A lot of them are right behind home plate, right?

CB: Or a section right over from the dugout, where we go through a different tunnel.

CG: Just here and Toronto, really.

CB: What about Wrigley?

LD: Wrigley.

CB: There's only three, maybe four, that you still go through the dugout. A lot of them are right next to the dugout, but a separate tunnel.

BN: The positions you're working tonight, do you make that up, as the acting crew chief or does that come from New York?

LD: When the season starts, the crew chief will always have home plate for the first game. The #2 guy will have first base, #3 guy second, and #4 guy at third base. And from that rotation, we just go. The whole year.

CG: It doesn't stay like 1, 2, 3, because like right now, let's see, it'll go him [Cory], he's the three guy now, then it'll be me, I'm at first – I'm the two guy, then it goes Clint. With guys leaving and everything, it gets mixed up. You keep the rotation pretty much intact. It might get a little bit skewed throughout the year but it stays pretty consistent.

BN: You get feedback from New York on a regular basis? Or from Kevin [O'Connor] upstairs?

CG: Kevin's a regional observer. There's supervisors and then there's regional observers.

BN: How often do you get feedback? After every series?

LD: After every series.

CB: Almost every day, you have video stuff to go over for calls that you had on the field. If New York believes that it's a close call – close enough – they'll put it in the system that's reviewed by a supervisor and put into a system that we log onto that says "Correct. Correct. Correct. Incorrect." They'll let you know. Obviously, if you go into replay and you get one overturned, it'll say "Incorrect" but there may be a lot of comments on positioning stuff.

BN: Do they do that with balls and strikes, too?

LD: We have what they call the ZE system.

CG: ZE. I don't even know what it means. [The technology (called Zone Enforcement, or ZE) that was implemented in 2009 provided all home plate umpires a report after each game, showing them the accuracy of all of their ball and strike calls.]

LD: My game last night is posted, and all I do is log on and it'll tell me my percentage – raw – and then you'll have pitches that the catcher maybe butchered, and stuff like that. It might say my percentage, raw, in 93, and with adjustments, 94.

BN: So you have a grade every day?

LD: Whether you're on the bases or on the plate, yeah.

CB: We get graded on everything. You know, a lot of times in the media you hear, "The umpires need to be held accountable." They have no idea. Every pitch and every play you have on the bases is graded.

BN: And promotions are tied into that.

CG: Sure. And postseason.

BN: It's a physically demanding job and you don't see – any more – umpires who seem to be as out of shape as some of them looked 20 or 30 years ago. Do you guys end up working out on a regular kind of basis?

LD: He runs like six or seven miles every day.

CG: I just ran eight miles today. Go for a jog. I work out usually...try to do at least six, depending on travel. Sometimes five.

BN: Hotel gyms?

LD: That's one of the reasons we like the Hyatts. They have a pretty nice gym. This one has a nice gym and a pool. Minnesota has a real nice gym, big gym and a pool, and a basketball court and a boxing ring.

CB: Twenty-five years ago, they didn't have a medical director. We have a medical director, Mark Letendre. If you have a head blow, if you take a foul ball off the mask, you have a text message before you even get off the field, and you have to call and check in.

BN: For concussion.

CB: Concussions. Any time you have any injury, you have people from the ballpark who will stop by and check on you. They'll have different physical therapies for you. And the nutrition part of it's changed, I think night and day from 25 years ago. In the ballpark, most of the time it's healthier foods. Postgame meals, I think, are healthier. In the offseason, too, they'll have outfits if you're overweight and you need to see somebody – a nutritionist – they'll take care of all that. They want us to be healthy and in shape.

BN: It can be dangerous if you're not. And it also maybe doesn't look as good.

LD: There's also Mackie Shilstone out of New Orleans, who's kind of our guru nutritionist guy. In January, we go to a retreat. He has a place in

New Orleans and if you need to go, you can stay there for a week. They have a hotel or something and you go through a training process and an eating process. And you can take your wife and you'll get up and you'll go through your different work exercises. Then you'll have a good breakfast, and a snack, and have a good lunch and then some more exercise. You get your routine, along with your wife – meals and exercise and all that, so that way when you get back home, you continue that same process. He's got several books out. He's trained boxers…

CG: [Tennis pro]Venus Williams.

LD: A lot of athletes go to him to get into shape.

BN: Did you ever work in the same ballpark in back-to-back series?

LD: Every series you're in a different park. We used to do that in the minor leagues, but not here.

CB: The only time would be if we're working San Francisco, Oakland. We won't work in the same park.

LD: Maybe we'll have a three-game set here and Monday will be a day game where they'll start a four-game set – Monday, Tuesday, Wednesday, Thursday. Let's say the Yankees are coming in and they're playing an afternoon game on Monday at 1, and the crew that's coming in for that four-game set is not able to make it, we'll stay for that one game and then we'll leave for wherever we're going to go for Tuesday, Wednesday, Thursday.

CG: It's pretty rare that you will see the same team even within the next two weeks. We won't see Boston for at least two more weeks; we might not even see them for the rest of the year.

BN: This is the second time you've been here this year and you might be back…

CG: This is it. We're not coming back to Boston.

LD: We miss seven stadiums this year. We miss Wrigley, Yankee Stadium, Philly, Tampa, Houston, Atlanta, and DC. We miss those seven stadiums this year.

BN: I'm surprised you're missing that many.

LD: Usually, it's not that many. Usually it's three or four, but this year we miss seven.

BN: You guys all go to New York for replay?

LD: Yes.

BN: As a crew?

LD: As a crew.

BN: When you're there, will all of you be…

LD: In the room together?

BN: Or maybe just or three of you.

LD: There's two crews in there. Every Tuesday and Wednesday, Friday, Saturday, and Sunday, there are 15 games.

BN: There's a lot of games, and there's East Coast games and West Coast games.

LD: Mondays and Thursdays are usually travel days/off days. But Tuesday, Wednesday, Friday, Saturday, and Sunday, everybody plays. I'd say Tuesdays and Fridays are the most hectic days in there because everybody starts to play.

CB: We work in shifts, four to five hours. Or if you're working the West Coast…I call them the graveyards, they're start at 10 or 11 and you go 15, 16 innings, you're in there until 4 in the morning.

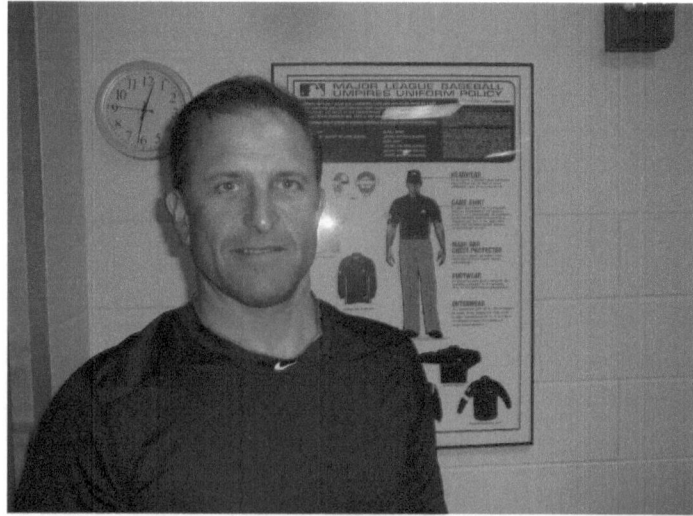

Chris Guccione in Fenway Park umpires room, July 5, 2015. Behind him is a poster illustrating Major League Baseball's Umpires Uniform Policy.

LD: We're in Miami Labor Day weekend, and we go in to replay Labor Day Monday. I've already talked to the people at replay. I'm driving home from Miami to Orlando and I'm going to get up at 6 o'clock in the morning and catch the first flight out to be there for 1 o'clock, because there'll be a lot of day games. I told them already, I'll take the West Coast games, the late shift. That way, I can get up at 8 o'clock, 9 o'clock.

CG: Here's the whole schedule for the year. [Displays schedule.]

BN: I'm not supposed to see that.

CG: After the first night, they know you're in town anyway.

LD: Sometimes they post it anyway, right on the scoreboard.

CB: Minor leagues.

LD: Umpire hotel sponsored by…

BN: [to Laz] You started as an American League umpire. [to Chris] And you started as a Major League umpire.

CG: The first year, 2000, through spring training, I worked National League and American. That's the year they combined the two.

BN: You talked about wearing a black uniform. What's the last year you actually wore blue? American League umpires were wearing red jackets for a while there.

LD: We wore dark blue and red, in the American League.

BN: You always hear people yell, "Hey, Blue!" And I'm thinking, yeah, maybe 20 years ago.

LD: We still got the blue… [indicated shirt hanging in locker]. We always wear black. I remember being at first base one time and, "Hey, Blue! You missed that call." I look at him, like, "I missed the call?" "Yeah." "You say I'm blind?" "Yeah, Blue, you missed it." "You're one who's blind, because I'm wearing black." After that, they don't say anything.

OK, now, can we call them black?

BN: Well, you don't want people calling *you* black, because that causes another problem.

LD: If they're going to call me Blue, but I've got a black shirt. There's some guys that are, "You know what? You're right. Hey, Black, you missed that call!"

BN: What made you first get into umpiring? What made you choose this as a profession?

Clint Fagan: I went to a college umpire camp because I wanted to learn how to umpire. I played high school ball. I started doing it through college as a part-time profession, just to help pay bills and tuition. I ended up running into a major league umpire, Eddie Hickox, and David Rackley. They asked me if I ever thought about going to umpire school. I said, "No, I'm just graduating college and I don't know what I'm going to do." I said, "Sure, I'll go." I got a business degree from the University of Houston. After that, it was all downhill. They gave me all the information. I graduated in December and I went the next month, in January. 2005.

BN: When you say it's all downhill, then there's a long uphill. One you're still going through right now. And I guess, Cory, you say you spent like five years or so doing what Clint's doing now?

CB: Yeah, I spent 12 full years in the minor leagues. In his position, four or five years. [Before that] lower minor leagues, working your way up.

BN: When you're here working in the major leagues, you get the same per diem everybody else gets.

CF: Yeah. The per diem rate is the same across the board.

BN: What about when you're in the minor leagues?

CF: Different. It's a different contract.

BN: When you first came up and joined a major league crew, was there any kind of hazing or anything? Here you're a tighter and smaller crew than on a ball team.

CF: No. No type of hazing. You get your chops busted a little bit because you're the young guy, but no hazing. It's all in fun.

BN: What do they do to bust your chops? You don't wear pink backpacks or anything like that.

LD: Mostly talk. In here. In years past, the young guy…they're supposed to get all the towels. So if there's a young guy here, one of us will go get all the towels. "Don't worry about it, I'll get the towels." Then the other guys will say later, "You let the crew chief go get the towels?"

That was a big thing back in the day, especially in the National League. In the National League, the young umpire had to go get the towels. The young umpire was the last one to shower. The young umpire was the last one to sit at the table and eat. Routine. Not so much in the American League, but in the National League.

BN: That's one of the things I want to talk with Ted Barrett about next weekend, what it was like between the two leagues. I guess there used to be some rivalry between the two leagues. It almost doesn't make sense.

LD: It used to be.

CG: That's called pride.

BN: But basically you find that the more senior umpires are really helping you learn the ropes.

CF: Absolutely. Absolutely. There's no way you can work in the big leagues without getting advice from the guys who have been here. You wouldn't survive.

BN: You'd go to different cities you hadn't been to before, so you'd just sort of tag along and go where people suggest.

CF: Absolutely.

BN: And you're working in a brighter spotlight, too.

CF: That's true. Very true. It's a lot different than working in Triple A. Absolutely.

BN: What are one or two of the ways you say it might be different?

CF: I'd say the play is better. There's not as many mental mistakes that the players go through, or the manager. As to yourself, you don't want to make those type of mental mistakes. The physical is the same, but the mental aspect of the game is more…captivating. You've got to be on every pitch, every play. You can't drop a second while you're out there.

BN: And every game is televised, which probably isn't always true in the minor leagues. I guess it depends on the level.

CF: I think Triple A they have a video on every game, but it's just for in-house. It's not broadcast nationally, or regionally.

BN: Have you already worked some games in the minors this year?

CF: Yes, I worked a couple.

BN: And you may work another few as things progress?

CF: Yeah, I kind of move around.

LD: Hopefully not!

CF: Yeah, hopefully not, but sometimes you're switching crews and there's breaks and stuff and sometimes you just go down for a while. It's part of the system.

When you go down, you work twice as hard.

BN: Why?

CF: Because you set an example for young guys. You set an example. This is a profession that's seniority-based. You don't want to come down and "big-league it" or anything like that, so you work twice as hard when you go down.

BN: That makes a lot of sense. There are guys who have never been up.

CF: Exactly. And you want to teach them the ropes and give them the opportunity, and pass down what was passed down to you.

LD: And shame on the guys who go down to Triple A and don't do that. A lot of guys when I came up, they would go down and would not pass on the information, being that they were probably uncertain of themselves or whatever the case might be.

BN: Well, going back in history with ballplayers, the veteran ballplayers would almost always freeze out the young guys because they were afraid of having their job taken. I was wondering about that here, the way you get graded on everything. You're all trying to get better. They want you to get better, or stay at the level that works for them. But with the grading system, do you find that some people don't get promoted?

CB: Are you talking about from the minor leagues to the big leagues, or up the big-league ladder?

BN: I'm talking about actually once you're in the major leagues and you're being graded. Or if you're filling in and being graded. What happens if you get bad grades? I know what can happen in other jobs.

LD: A bad grade for us, when you average it out, is still a 96 or a 97. Doctors aren't that good.

Somebody's got to be at the bottom of the barrel. And if you're at the bottom of the barrel with a 95, it's kind of hard for them to say, "Hey, you're 95. You're going to get fired." If you're 85 and the next one above you is 93, then there's a gap. But when you've got 95.2, 95.3, 95.7, 96, 97, and the highest one is 98, and you've got 76 of us…

BN: So there's not that many guys who wash out, because that would have happened well before.

CG: There's never been an umpire fired, ever, within the recent…for performance.

BN: That says a lot for getting to this point. Let me ask you, Cory, how you got started umpiring.

CB: I was 14 or 15 when my dad said, "If you want to get a car when you're 16, you've got to get a job." So I got a job at Target. I was working at Target, working eight-hour days or more and making very little money after taxes. I was working inside, and didn't really care for it. My dad was a longtime high school umpire in the State of Colorado for 20-plus years and he asked why I don't umpire. I said I never really thought about it. I took a course and got into umpiring and I was 14 or 15, working Little League games. I worked eight-hour days there and made a heck of a lot more money doing that. I really liked the job. The next summer, I started getting into high school ball, in the summer leagues. I promised my dad two years of college before I decided to go to umpire school or not. I wanted to go right out of high school but he said, "Go to college for a couple of years and make that decision." I went to Colorado State University and then two years later went to umpire school in 2002, and here I am, 14 years later.

BN: It worked out.

CB: Yeah. Luckily.

BN: Economic questions can be kind of touchy sometimes. If you don't mind, what is the per diem you all are getting? Are food and hotels separate?

CB: No, it's four something, but we get taxed.

LD: 52% of our per diem is taxed. Let's say we get an even number of $400 a day. Fifty-two percent of that is taxed, which is $208. So we get $192 cash money and the other money is taxed.

CB: It sounds like a really large number, but after tax we get close to 4. It's the high 390s, I think. The first night here, we stayed at this hotel, with us working out that multiple people would be staying here…$299 for the first night.

CG: $340 with taxes.

BN: That's pretty close to break even, then, with food and all.

All: Yeah.

CB: It sounds like a large number and people think you're going to pocket some of that money, but in the bigger cities – Boston, New York…it evens out. You may go over your per diem.

BN: It's the same per diem regardless of the city.

All: Yeah.

CB: So you may have a little extra from Cincinnati and St. Louis but then when you come to bigger cities, you're paying more than your per diem. It evens out. You don't really make any money off the per diem.

LD: Any umpire that thinks he's going to make…you can, but you're going to be staying at a Comfort Inn, a Holiday Inn Express, places like that.

CB: Another thing. We pay the clubhouse guy. We pay him between $60 and $100 a day. Per guy.

BN: That's a pretty good job.

CG: Real good pay.

BN: He was telling me how he brings in food and all that, all on his own dime. He pays for all that himself.

CB: You're making $300 a day or more. Up to $400, depending on the service.

BN: That's why he's been doing this since 1990, I guess.

CG: Yeah.

BN: You've got these chairs [pointing to chairs in the room, each of which has the Red Sox logo on their back and on the seat cushion], with the team logo on them.

CF: I didn't notice that.

BN: I just wondered, why wouldn't they have neutral chairs in here?

CB: We don't care. It's just a chair.

LD: They probably just order a whole bunch.

BN: Sure, but I thought MLB might frown on it.

LD: MLB doesn't have to pay for it. These chairs are paid for by the Red Sox. They [MLB] don't care where we sit.

BN: It's just the visual, seeing team logos. I realize that…I've talked to a few umpires who, if you ask them after the game is over, it might take them a moment to remember which team won.

CB: Yeah. We don't care.

LD: You come in here after the game, you take a shower, you go back to the hotel. You might sit at the hotel bar for a minute and the bartender… the bartender probably didn't see the game, and he'd ask, "Who won?" Who did win? "What was the score?"

CB: It's funny, too. We'll get to the next city and you'll get asked, "Where are you guys coming from?" We'll all be looking at each other. We can't even remember what city we were just in.

LD: We know more where we're going next than where we just were.

BN: Your pay now is much better – maybe even double – what it was when you were starting off [asked of Laz]?

LD: When I started, it was 75 [thousand] for a first-year guy. 72. I don't know what it is now. One something [Over $100,000].

BN: So when you're working in the major leagues and you were working in the minor leagues, that's a big jump?

LD: Drastic.

CB: Probably quadruple.

CG: What would a Triple-A umpire, if you worked every game at Triple A...

CB: $3,400 is the max you can make a month.

CG: Times April, May, June, July, August, and a little bit of September.

Triple-A crew at Pawtucket on July 22, 2017. L to R: Shane Livensparger, Ryan Clark, Scott Costello, Roberto Ortiz.

CB: You don't get paid in the winter. It's just the months you're working.

CG: $15,000.

CB: Yeah, it's like, max.

CG: And you get a per diem of $40?

CF: You max out at $55.

LD: My last year at Triple A was $34.

CB: And Triple A is the highest you can go in the minor leagues. We all started out in rookie ball.

BN: That's when *you* pay *them* per diem!

CF: Ed Hickox told me that when you reach the majors, it's kind of like you're getting back pay.

BN: So, let me ask you, Gooch – how'd you get started? You told me a little before.

CG: I grew up in a small town in Colorado. We didn't have much baseball. We didn't have any baseball in high school. Our last year of baseball was like a Babe Ruth at age 15, but in between then, I was already at the ballpark anyway with my brother, who was four years younger than me. I was umpiring Babe Ruth baseball even into high school. I was already there because my brother was playing and it was easy money. It was enough to buy fishing lures or fishing poles or whatever else garbage I could buy. So I did that for a lot of years. My best friend in high school, Chris Carson, his dad said, "Why don't you guys go to umpire school?" I'd never heard of umpire school, didn't know what it was about, never knew where it was. So he and I and his brother C.P., we all ended up taking a bus 52 hours from Salida, Colorado, to Kissimmee, Florida. That's kind of how I started umpiring. The shorter version.

BN: You probably get asked this question a lot, but I better ask it. Sometimes you guys are out there four or more hours a night. What happens if you've gotta go?

CG: You leave. You just leave. You just run off. It takes you longer than the inning goes, you wait 'til the next half-inning. And you work three-man. Very rarely, but it's happened. You just wait out the half-inning.

BN [to Laz Diaz]: I wanted to ask you about the town in Cuba, if you could spell it for me.

LD: La Panchita.

BN: Are your parents still living?

LD: My mom is. My dad passed away three years ago.

BN: Did she go with you?

LD: Yeah. I was 15 years old the first time I went back. Then I joined the Marine Corps and I didn't dare to go back until…

BN: Not in uniform anyway.

LD: Until now. This is the fourth time I've been.

BN: You're fluent in Spanish.

LD: Yeah.

BN: What did your parents do before they came over here?

LD: My dad worked the sugar cane.

BN: Cutter?

LD: Yeah.

BN: That's about as tough work as you can get. [Shows on Google Maps where his parents grew up, and even finds a baseball field.]

BN: You like going back?

LD: I like it. There's nothing to do. Your day consists of waking up and having a coffee, having breakfast, going on the porch and having a cigar. Then in the afternoon your cousins, they all come over from work or wherever they're at. My uncle's retired now so he'll come by. You go to the little store that's nearby, you buy a case of beer and bring it back to the house, you sit on the porch and have another cigar and tell stories and drink a couple of beers.

Havana's about four or five hours away from my mom and dad were at. We used to fly to Havana. Now we fly into Santa Clara, which is an hour away.

BN: You mentioned Mackie Shilstone. He seems to cater to all sorts of athletes, but does he offer some umpire-specific programs?

CB: Fat camp.

LD: I've never been but from what they tell me the place he has is immaculate. They have a kitchen area. They've got cooks that can teach you and your wife how to cook. You just go down for a week, maybe 10 days.

BN: Mark Letendre who you mentioned, does he travel?

LD: No, he sees most of the crews when they go through Phoenix. He used to travel more but he slipped and fell and had a head injury. He had trouble with his equilibrium so he's not traveling as much.

BN: It kind of impressed me. I went to look him up and I got onto an MLB umpires page and I saw the list of people, from Joe Torre on down, there's a long list of people. That's quite an investment they're making to make sure that umpires are on the field and doing their job well.

LD: Mark Letendre has his hands full. When we get sick or we get hurt, they're going to try to put us back on the field. When we're not able to do that, they're going to bring up minor-league guys to replace us, which dilutes the staff a little bit. They'll keep pushing – "Hey, you need to get Clint on the field? What's wrong with Cory?" He's constantly calling – "Cory, how's your knee? Have you been going to rehab? Have you been taking your pills?" He's constantly calling Cory trying to get him back on the field. He's getting pressure from the top to get him back on the field. He's got a very difficult job. He's between a rock and a hard place.

BN: Tell me how you got started.

LD: Well, I played high school ball. Played college ball, and I played in the minor leagues, with the Twins organization. Shortstop/outfield. In '84. I got released at the end. In '85 I tried out with the Cardinals. Got hurt and left. Sat out '86. In '87 I went to spring training with the Yankees. They let me go and I said, "OK, I'm done." That's when I started umpiring. One of my best friends that I played baseball with, he was going through a divorce and he needed to make some extra money so he said, "Why don't we do umpiring?" We were good friends. I said, "OK, we'll go umpire." We started with slow-pitch softball. We did beer leagues on weekends. Then we got into high school ball and from high school we got into college. When I got my divorce, one of the guys who helped after I was going through my divorce said, "Hey, now that you're divorced, you don't have anything holding you back. Why don't you go to umpire school?" And like Gooch, I didn't know anything about umpire school. Didn't know anything about nothing. I knew there was one in Cocoa. Joe Brinkman School. And the Harry Wendelstedt in Daytona. I knew what Cocoa was all about because that's where there was minor-league spring training for the Twins. There was nothing there. No way I'm going back to Cocoa. It's closer to Miami than Daytona, but you know what, if I'm going to go do this I'm at least going to have fun.

So I went to Daytona. I got lucky and blessed and came out of there as one of the top students and got a job, worked my way up, and here I am.

BN: How often do you go to replay?

LD: We go twice. We went in May and now we go in the middle part of September. There's some crews, they go…

CB: Max is three weeks. When you go, it's a week at a time. The crew chiefs can bid on what ones they want, by seniority. Some of those have three weeks. Some have two. One or two have two and a half.

BN: Now you three guys were on the same crew – were you on the same crew last year?

LD: No. I was with Jeff Nelson last year. He was the crew chief. Gooch, who were you with?

CG: Hallion.

CB: I was with Jimmy Joyce.

BN: And is that…can you assume that next year, you'll all be on different crews?

Laz Diaz with photo of his father in his equipment trunk.
Photograph by Chris Guccione.

CG: You can assume that. We could all four be back together, but it's highly unlikely.

LD: Yeah. He'll [CG] probably be a two-man somewhere. Most definitely, he'll be a two-man somewhere. With his skills and everything, he'll be a two-man somewhere.

Cory Blaser with baseball, July 2015.

BN: You're a number three right now.

CG: Yeah.

LD: Last year Mark Carlson was number three and now he's a two man on another crew.

BN: They probably want to mix it up anyhow.

CB: Yeah.

LD: See, that's one thing sometimes I don't understand. If you've got a crew that gets along and you do well off the field, on the field, unless you're going to promote him from three man to number-two man, why don't you keep the same crew together?

If we're gelling, we get along on the field, we get along off the field, we have fun, and we're a good crew.

BN: The only reason I think they might want to do that is that they thought you might get stale somehow, or that there'd be some funny business going on. There was a thing with someone selling memorabilia some time ago.

LD: No, trust me, with Cory around, nothing gets…

CG, pointing to his chest protector: This is kind of my thing here. These are all the patches for people who have passed that have been umpires. Frank Pulli, Harry Wendelstedt, Marty Springstead, Wally Bell…

BN: People you worked with at one time or another.

CG: No, I never worked with Frank. I never worked with Harry. I never worked with Marty. Never worked with Wally. Shag Crawford, Sammy Holbrook.

LD: Those are just people who passed. [Points to the inside top of his trunk.] That's a picture of my dad there, a patch for Wally Bell. And that patch used to be for Harry Wendelstedt. It's upside down, because Michael Hirschbeck passed away last year. John Hirschbeck and I… worked with John together for so many years that I know his family very well, been in his house. So I looked at the patch and I turned it around. HW – MH. That's a tribute to Michael Hirschbeck [John's son]. When I went around the league last year, I asked all the clubbies if they still had Harry Wendelstedt patches, which they did. And I shipped them to…

CB: [talking about posing for a photo] I'll get one rubbing a baseball.

CG: (laughs) You haven't rubbed a baseball since Double A.

CB: Shall I do one with my mask on, since I usually work the plate?

BN: Fine with me! Fool around. You can take one in the shower. No…

LD: Sitting on the pot.

BN: Yeah, right. Thank you all again.

—**end**

Note: Though Clint Fagan had worked 522 major league games from 2011 through July 30, 2017, he had not been hired full-time and he decided it was time to seek another career. As of 2019, he is raising a family in Texas, working as a Farmers Insurance agent, and is working toward a law degree,

6

Ted Barrett, Angel Hernandez, Chris Conroy, and Pat Hoberg

About a week later, on July 11, Ted Barrett's crew came to Boston. The crew was comprised of Ted Barrett, Angel Hernandez, Chris Conroy, and Pat Hoberg.

Conversation in the Umpires Room, Fenway Park, July 11, 2015

Bill Nowlin: Mainly, I wanted to talk to you about being a crew chief. Your last crew, you had a couple of different people than now.

Ted Barrett: We're on our individual vacations now, so Pat's in for Scott [Barry]. And in Chicago, they brought in a guy to assist us with the doubleheader. Tom Woodring.

BN: Marcus Pattillo?

TB: Marcus was there because Angel had to cover another crew. Someone was out so they had to beef up the crew so they took Angel.

BN: So your normal crew is you three and Scott. He's on vacation now. [to Pat] This is your first year now?

Pat Hoberg: Second.

BN: [Pointing to photographs on the wall of the Fenway umpires' room] In this room, you've got all the Hall of Fame umpires. Most of the rooms you go to around baseball, is there some kind of historical recognition, or is it kind of hit and miss?

TB: Hit and miss, yeah. Detroit's got plaques of every one of them. Interesting story on that, there was these pictures of old ballplayers in Oakland, back to the Philadelphia A's, and Ernie Harwell would always come in the umpires' locker room and say hi. There were no captions, so I had no idea who these old players were. He's looking and saying, "That's Ed Rommel, and..." he's going on and on. I thought Ernie's losing it. He looks at me and says, "You know why these are up here" and I said, "Yeah, they're the A's and we're in Oakland." He said, "No, these are players who became umpires." I thought that was kind of cool. Last one was...the guy whose son played in the National League.

Angel Hernandez: Kunkel?

TB: Yeah, Bill Kunkel.

BN: You've been a crew chief for a while now?

TB: This is my third season.

BN: Obviously, you've got to put in a few years to get there.

TB: Yeah, it's seniority driven.

BN: (to Angel) I was wondering how that works. You started a few years earlier than Ted, but have you been a crew chief yet?

AH: I have no recollection of it. I don't really follow those things.

TB: He's a crew chief a lot of times when crew chiefs go, and he fills in. Bob Davidson is the other one.

AH: When a crew chief goes on vacation, the #2 guy basically just runs the crew. He's the intern.

BN: What do you do as a crew chief?

TB: Basically, it's just – probably the biggest thing is when it rains. That's the biggest thing, is trying to coordinate with...

BN: Dave next door? [David Mellor, head groundskeeper]

TB: Yeah, and the ballpark personnel. Even now, with the technology. Other than that, it's just on the field. Replay's brought a whole new dimension to it.

BN: There's two guys who go on the headsets.

TB: Always the crew chief and the other one's the calling umpire. If that's me, then the two-man, Angel, would go with me.

BN: If you were the calling umpire.

TB: Yeah.

BN: And the other two stand around.

Chris Conroy: Make sure everybody's…

TB: There's actually a lot of responsibility. They're doing a lot. There can't be any conferences, changes, and they also are thinking through what happens if a play gets flipped – what's the count, what are the outs, where are the runners? When we come off the headsets, there's a lot of information. If there's something wrong, the runner's in the wrong spot, or the count's wrong on the board, I rely on these guys to come over, "Hey, wait a minute, wait a minute…" before we start.

BN: It's a whole new world, I guess. I don't know how you feel about it. Some of the fans…it used to be kind of fun to see a good argument.

TB: Baseball purists, from the feedback I'm getting, they don't like it. But it seems like our society's so tech-driven now that they love it. And they want the machine to call balls and strikes, and I think eventually that's going to happen.

BN: Well, if they get it just right, in three dimensions, it probably could.

TB: I think they would rather have it in its present state than us. But people who been around baseball a little more appreciate what we do a little more. I think this younger generation doesn't…

BN: Did the crew chief used to handle things like hotel and flight arrangements?

TB: Not since I've been umpiring.

BN: There's an agency that makes the arrangements for the flights, but you all make the arrangements with the agency?

TB: Yeah, we all individually do that. We have a guy – Chris handles our hotels. There's a lot of leg work and Angel helps him. They're on the phone constantly. Even on the way over here today, we were talking about our future reservations.

When I came up, the crew chief was a little more domineering. We would always get two rental cars and he would always take one that was at his disposal. You couldn't take the chief's car. The old-timers tell me that you didn't answer the phone when it rang in the locker room. Only the crew chiefs did. The real old-timers – the chief showered first. These seem like ridiculous rules; that's all kind of out of the window. We're all really respectful of the crew chiefs, but there's no more of that domineering stuff going on.

BN: Do you get paid a little extra?

TB: A hundred dollars a game. So when I'm gone, Angel will get the hundred dollars. It adds up over the course of the season.

BN: Are you guys all staying at the same hotel?

TB: This time we are, yeah.

BN: Do you think the role of the crew chief has changed over time? I'm not talking about what you already addressed, but umpiring on the field, or anything at all.

TB: I think, especially for younger guys – people like Pat – when Angel and I came up, the crew chief was the one who would really critique you, who would give you advice. Now, it's more the supervisory staff. And we really almost have to stay out of their way because as we transitioned into that, we would tell them some things that might be counter to what they [supervisory staff] were saying. Then we're just messing them up. So we try to stay out of their way and be a kind of support system.

BN: Do you hear directly from the umpire observers, or from the supervisors?

TB: The observers we don't hear from. We get evaluations through the computer, from the observers. But the supervisors we'll hear directly from. He'll hear [indicating Pat] directly from the supervisory staff. We have a supervisor assigned to us. For our crew, it's Ed Montague. So if we have an issue, we call him or he calls us. Our supervisor will look at the observer's reports, and we'll get them, too, but we don't have any contact with him.

BN: But what he puts on the computer, you'll see the exact same thing.

TB: Yeah.

BN: You don't filter any of that information, as crew chief. It's just there on the computer.

TB: Only in the case of somebody like Pat, somebody that is filling in. They might call me and say something like, "Pass this on to him" or Work with him on this." But not with these guys [points to Chris and Angel]. They would contact them directly.

BN: [to Chris] Are you officially a major league umpire now?

CC: Yes.

BN: And you're a minor-league umpire [Pat]. That would be the dividing line.

TB: Yeah. There's some crew chiefs that might maybe be a little more hands-on with that, but for me with on-the-field stuff, these guys are so good that…

AH: In my opinion, he's a major league umpire when he's here. Because that's what he's doing. He's working a major league game.

BN: And he's getting all the benefits of being a major league umpire, too, while he's here.

AH: And that's exactly why they called him, because otherwise they wouldn't have called him.

BN: [to Pat] How many games did you work last year?

PH: 120-something.

BN: That's about as much as almost anybody works, right? So you're basically just paying your dues, so to speak.

AH: This is his chance. He's getting his exposure. That's how everybody started. Vacation or injury, they'll call the next guy that they're looking at – a prospect. You're looking at one. He's right in front of you.

BN: What do you call them – "fill-in umpires"?

CC: Up-and-down umpires.

AH: Fill-ins. Call-ups. Prospects is what I say. The future.

BN: You were born in Cuba?

AH: Havana. I left when I was 11 months old. Yes, sir.

Angel Hernandez, before a game in Boston.

BN: I was just there a few months ago. Have you ever had occasion to go back at all?

AH: I never have. [Hernandez was selected to serve as the first-base umpire in the Tampa Bay vs. Cuba game at Estadio Latinamericano on March 22, 2016 in Havana. That became his second trip. In the 2015-16 offseason, Angel joined Ted Barrett on a mission to Cuba.]

TB: I've been there. I was there last year.

BN: International umpiring?

TB: No, actually on a mission trip. Religious visit, but then I ended up hooking up with the umpires through that.

BN: They have a woman umpire there, and one up in Canada, too. Yanet Moreno in Cuba – I didn't get a chance to meet her.

TB: I did. She came to the clinic that we did. She did a good job. You know what, they didn't have uniforms and last year when we went, we took them pants and shirts. Now they match. They were wearing…one had a blue shirt and one had a black shirt. One had a jacket.

BN: I think I saw five games this last trip and everybody I saw was in uniform.

TB: Maybe that's the uniforms we took them.

BN: Could be. Actually, I noticed that some of them had something that looked like MLB logos on them and I wondered where they got them from.

TB: Yeah, we brought a lot of our extra old shirts.

AH: But I am not the first [Cuban umpire]. The first was Armando Rodriguez. Mr. Richie Garcia was born in Key West, in the States. And Laz Diaz as well. Armando was the first. For the record.

BN: It's all black and gray now pretty much, right?

AH: They kept the light powder blue color for hot games. So we still have them. For hot games, it's needed.

BN: That could be tomorrow.

AH: I will be wearing it. You can assure yourself. [Indeed, game time temperature on July 12 was 86 degrees and the crew all wore their blue shirts.]

BN: Are you working the plate tomorrow?

AH: God willing. If He will allow me to, I will be, yes.

BN: You [Ted] were an American League umpire, and you [Angel] were a National League umpire before they came together. I asked you [Ted, on an earlier phone call] if there was kind of a rivalry between the two leagues, even though there was no interleague play until 1997, so you hardly would see each other. You said, yeah, there was, and I said something like just a joking rivalry, and you said sometimes it had a little bite to it.

TB: Yeah.

BN: And I was wondering, what's that all about?

TB: I don't know. I never understood that myself. I think it was just kind of a pride thing. I'd always kind of equate it to my son's in the Army and the other's in the Air Force, and they tease each other.

BN: Sure.

TB: And if anybody knows a Marine, they tease the other three mercilessly.

BN: Right.

TB: I thought it was like that, but there were occasions that I think it carried into a little more of a prideful thing. That's gone now, now that we're all together.

AH: Look at the history of it. They were really different. American League umpires wore the balloon, the outside chest protector. The National League umpires never wore that. They always wanted to be different. And they were different.

BN: And of course since the DH. You'd only meet each other in the off-seasons, postseason, or the All-Star Game.

TB: Union meetings.

BN: Did people really say stuff like, "Our league's better?"

TB: Yeah. There's stories of fist fights.

BN: You were a boxer. Nobody's going to pick a fist fight with you!

TB: By the time I showed up that was kind of gone, but there was still the teasing.

BN: Maybe one or two people were a little too thin-skinned?

TB: Back then, it was so different. Like Angel said, with the uniforms, the equipment, philosophies…

AH: Higher strike zone, lower strike zone because of the positions they worked with the different equipment. When we'd get together, there'd just be arguments about different rules and theories.

TB: Our way's the right way.

BN: Obviously there weren't brawls all the time, but once or twice somebody hit somebody?

TB: Yeah.

AH: The DH versus the no-DH, why the American League games were longer, why the National League games were shorter. Just discussions like that.

BN: The pace of game has come down some this year, but I don't think it's due to replay. I think it's due to the clocks between innings and on the relievers and…

AH: There's really no data for that yet. We'll see at the end of the season. You've got to love all the changes that they're making. They're trying to make it better for the fans as well as the game and for everybody to enjoy. The beauty is, the gate's always open for you. You pay to watch entertainment. If you don't like it, you can always leave. You pay to go watch a movie. I'm a big moviegoer, but if I don't like it, I leave. It's entertainment.

BN: With the comings and goings throughout the season, you get into a working rhythm if things are working right. Is it a little disruptive, in a way...though you only typically have one person gone at any given time.

TB: Usually that's not too bad when you've got one guy coming in. it's when you have massive turnover – you look at some crews, they've just completely blown out. Injuries.

BN: On top of vacations.

TB: Yeah. And that can be disruptive. But when you just have one of our guys, like Pat, slide in for a few weeks, that's usually pretty seamless. It's refreshing to get a young guy in and try to help him out, too.

BN: Maybe it helps you guys, too, in a way. I mean, you all came up once, too.

TB: Yup.

AH: To give back, exactly. We remember, like I do, our first game. Excited. You never forget your first game. Where it was at, who you worked with, the score, et cetera. That's a memory-filer, for sure.

BN: You guys who are major league umpires, when's the last time you actually rubbed up a baseball?

CC: It would have been back in Double A. You get to Triple A and the teams – ball boy, or whoever, start doing that. Double A was the last time I remember rubbing up a baseball.

BN: Was that your experience, too, Pat?

PH: Yeah.

TB: I did it until about the late 90s.

AH: Special mud. It's really special.

BN: You've got some of it right over there inside that cabinet.

TB: I don't miss it. You get tired of it. In the minor leagues, it wasn't bad. It's a couple of dozen and it's kind of your routine. In the big leagues, there's so many. You're rubbing up seven or eight dozen and it'll take a while.

BN: Dean [Lewis] says he does 12 or 14 dozen.

TB: Yeah, he probably does.

CC: When I was in Double A just four or five years ago, we were doing seven or eight dozen.

AH: Back in the day, and I don't go that far back, the pitchers would be upset if the catcher…[many people talking at once] they would toss that ball out. Now you see it where every ball gets thrown out. Even take notice of the ball the catcher will throw to second and is short-hopped. The hitting coach is yelling at you, "Hey, change the ball!" So just to save time, we don't even wait for them – we know it's coming, so we go to the catcher, "Here's a new one." It's such a habit that when they're throwing it around to the third baseman, as opposed to tossing it to the pitcher, he's throwing it to the third-base coach or throwing it to a kid.

BN: It's good for the fans.

AH: It's very costly, when you think of it.

BN: Working with the groundskeepers – and that is you, primarily, as the crew chief…?

TB: Yeah. He'll usually stop in and give us the lowdown, what's going on, and then if there's a delay I'll go over to his office to look at the radar. [Groundskeeper Dave Mellor's office is immediately adjacent to the umpires' room.]

BN: [pointing to the closed door behind which is the home run replay equipment] Do you use this home run thing anymore?

TB: That's in case of emergency. That's a backup, if the system goes down.

BN: If the current replay system goes down.

TB: Yeah.

BN: But you used to use that for a couple of years.

TB: A couple of years, yeah, for home runs. We call that The Legacy. The techs refer to that as The Legacy.

BN: Nobody uses it anymore.

TB: No. If the system completely crashes down there…

BN: Has that ever happened yet?

TB: No.

BN: Let me ask the other three of you. [To Angel] How'd you first get interested in umpiring?

AH: My dad. Credit my dad for everything he did. He came from Cuba. He brought us up…I have five brothers…he brought us up playing baseball. He loved the game. Long story short, when I was old enough to start umpiring, I wanted to hit the streets, but in his mind there was no way I was going to hit the streets and catch up with my friends. Hialeah, Florida. Near Miami. So he started a program for umpires in the Little League organization. There's where I started to umpire.

BN: What age?

AH: 14. Over 60,000 kids played there.

TB: How many major league players came out of there?

AH: A lot. A lot of major league players. Alex Fernandez. Ricky Gutierrez. Johnny Cangelosi. [Rafael] Palmeiro. That's where it started, and I can thank him for that.

BN: Did you ever play ball, too?

AH: Just high school. My brother was a first-round, eighth pick in the nation, for the Brewers. Nick Hernandez. But he just basically quit. [Catcher out of Hialeah High School, in the 1978 draft.]

BN: Did you ever, at any level, happen to work a game he was in?

AH: No, that was before I went to school. I went to school in '81.

It's happened. We have an active umpire who umpired while his brother was playing, but they would change him. They would change the cities for him. It's a no-win situation. Jim Wolf. His brother is Randy Wolf.

TB: When I was in A ball, one of the guys in the league, his brother was the pitching coach for the Angels. Another guy's brother played on an independent team. But the story I always tell when it comes to managers, there was an umpire in Triple A in the Coast League named Zack

Bevington. His brother was Terry Bevington. He would do his games and everybody thought that… but as it came out, they hated each other. They wouldn't talk. He ejected him one night. "You've always been a butthole." They just quit talking.

AH: As a matter of fact, that question came up at umpire school. I went to Bill Kinnamon Umpiring School. One of the umpires asked me, "So, if you get a chance to call your brother out on a strike…" I said, "I would have to be doing my job, so hopefully that would happen one day."

BN: [to Chris] How about yourself?

CC: I can remember back when I was playing Little League baseball as a kid. For a reason I can't explain, I can remember being fascinated and my eyes being drawn to what umpires did on the field. I thought it was neat. I thought the uniforms were cool. I thought the way they made calls…I used to find it amusing how different guys had a different kind of strike mechanic. From that point on, it always stuck in the back of my head that it looks like it would be something neat to do. I maybe worked a handful of games as a teenager just because I maybe happened to be going by the Little League field and nobody showed up and it was like, "Hey, could you help us out?" I liked doing that but I didn't do a ton of it.

Then I was in about my mid-20s and I was single and just one day, I was like, "You know what? If I'm ever going to give this a shot, now's the time in my life to try it and if it works out, great, if it doesn't, then I tried and I know and I'll move on with my life. I got in, and here I am. I was 25 when I went to umpire school.

BN: Which one?

CC: I went to Evans. I went in 2000.

PH: My dad was big into Little League. He did a little umpiring, so I started when I was 12, 14, somewhere around there, doing Little League games. I actually played basketball in college. My summer job was umpiring high school and college baseball, four games a day Monday through Friday. I decided when I was a sophomore in college that I wanted to do it so I did the research, graduated, and then went to umpire school. Grandview University in Des Moines.

BN: [to Chris] What were you doing until you were 25?

CC: I went to college. Graduated there in '96. I had a couple of jobs when I first got out of college. I was working for a YMCA. Then I spent a couple of years back in my hometown working on a youth recreation center. I was like 23, 24, making like 30 grand a year. It was OK for me but I just wanted more. In the back of my head. It was a time in my life I was just like if I try this now, it only impacts me. I'm not married, I have no kids. It's as good a time as any to try it. They gave me a leave of absence from the job to go five weeks to umpire school. It's all worked out OK.

AH: It's the best experience of my life. I went at 18 and it was like a boot camp. Set up like a boot camp. They had lots of umpires there, trying to get into the game. And I never thought I would be one. Very competitive from the start. I remember calling my dad on a rotary phone back then, a pay phone, and he says, "Son, you're young, so if you don't get a job…" I said, "Dad, I'm up against men here. I shouldn't even be here." He said, "Give it the best you can." The instructors were all major league umpires and that was a phenomenal thing being in the presence of these guys. It was overwhelming – the experience and everything you learn. Besides the rules, they taught you positioning. You didn't even really need to have umpired when you went to umpire school. They literally taught you everything to know about the game.

BN: It's a pretty small percentage of people who go to umpire school and actually make it to the major leagues.

AH: Oh, yes, sir. The percentage is very low.

CC: I can remember the first day, you're sitting in a big room with 120 or 150 other guys and they'd say, "Statistically speaking, in this entire room, one, maybe two, will be a major league umpire someday."

AH: And then you've got to endure the years in the minor leagues. I've worked with a lot of really good officials in the minor leagues. The opportunity was just never there for them when they were around, and they had the years in so they just passed them over, but they were quite deserving of working as well. I've worked with a lot of good umpires, guys who would go out there and work the job day in and day out.

Then there were the guys who found out it just wasn't for them. The loneliness, the travel, the heckling. When you missed a call, back then they taught you, you never admitted it. The game's changed a lot there now. It's different.

BN: Did you enjoy the heckling sometimes?

AH: No. And it kind of scarred you. It made who you were. Those years in the minor leagues is what made you who you were. If you endured that.

There was a spectator in the Carolina League, and he called us all "muleheads." You wanted to laugh but you couldn't laugh. I wanted to grin and I had to bite my teeth together. He was hilarious.

[On the other hand, AH talked about anti-Latino slurs being thrown his way.]—**end**

[*This interview was also published in* The SABR Book of Umpires and Umpirin™g.]

As I was starting to leave, something came out in parting conversation that I couldn't let go. I learned that Ted Barrett had a doctorate.

Conversation with Ted Barrett, July 11, 2015 at Fenway Park

BN: So you're Dr. Barrett?

TB: Reverend Doctor.

BN: Reverend Doctor!

TB: So the guys call me Reverend Doctor Crew Chief.

BN: That's like three titles in one. So you're an ordained minister.

TB: Yeah.

BN: What denomination?

TB: I was ordained in the Southern Baptists, but I'm in a non-denominational church right now. In Arizona. I live in Gilbert.

BN: The SABR office is in Phoenix these days. We moved it there from Cleveland a few years ago.

TB: My undergrad was in kinesiology; that was in '88. Then after a few years I decided it was time to go back to school and get a theological degree and I got my master's degree in Biblical Studies, from Trinity, which is a seminary in Newburgh, Indiana. They were big in the early days of distance learning. They also dig regional seminars and I was able to go during the winter. You could go for a four-day thing and meet the professor, which was great then as we talked back and forth. My dissertation is on the life of umpires. I had to do a lot of filler, as you know, so I went through the day-to-day life of it.

Two years ago. 2013. Trinity Theological Seminary. It's a four-year college as well as a seminary – Trinity University as well as Trinity Theological Seminary.

[I asked but he didn't know if he might be the first umpire to be in the ministry at the same time as being an umpire. He may be the first.]

TB: I found some who went into the ministry later in life. Dan Bellino actually had a J.D. I don't know if that's equivalent to what we have or not.

BN: There might be the possibility of an interesting article coming out of your dissertation. Maybe you yourself could summarize it into an extended abstract, or I could write up something.

TB: Yeah. There's some more sensitive things in there. Everything's anonymous but there are some things that maybe we wouldn't want…the general public.

BN: In the dissertation?

TB: Yes.

BN: You shouldn't have put it in there if you didn't want it to get out!

TB: It's all anonymous but it talks about some of the negative behavior in the past. Even as I wrote it I knew that if the general public got ahold of it, so everything's protected. Nothing's really secret.

BN: You were probably talking about him, right? (point in jest to Angel Hernandez, who came over)

AH: Any of us – not just the ones in this room – any official's toughest call, whether it be baseball of any sport, is his next one.

BN: Why do you say that?

AH: Because they're all tough.

TB: People ask you, what's your hardest call? It's the next one.

AH: The reason we don't miss a particular call on this crew, we're out there for all of them. And God's with us. He takes care of us.

—**end**

After the conversation, I obtained a copy of Rev. Dr. Crew Chief Barrett's dissertation. To provide grounding for his dissertation, Barrett began with the words "It is said the job of the umpire is to start out perfect and get better." And yet, under all the stresses of the job, it is not surprising that in their personal lives "some umpires fall into destructive behavior patterns." Reading the dissertation and talking more with Ted about his research made for an interesting article, which was submitted to the National Pastime Museum website, but also ran in the SABR book.

As a scholar and an interviewer himself, and with an open personality, he was perhaps more receptive than many other would have been, right off the bat. It helped to have interviewed umpires such as Laz Diaz, Chris Guccione, Ted, and Angel Hernandez at the beginning of my research. Not all umpires were as immediately receptive.

7

Jim Joyce, Greg Gibson, Chad Fairchild, Carlos Torres

There was a third crew I interviewed as a group in 2015 – Jim Joyce's crew. They were quite receptive, too.

Interview with Jim Joyce, Greg Gibson, Chad Fairchild, and Carlos Torres at Fenway Park on September 26, 2015

Bill Nowlin: I notice that a lot of umpires have family photos on the inside of their trunks.

Jim Joyce: Absolutely.

BN: You joined the major league staff in 1989, I guess. Was that a tradition which goes back that far?

JJ: Oh yeah. Every bit of that. You bring your family on the road. We're on the road so much that you bring your family with you. We have these little cutouts that usually sit on top of our clothes and a lot of times we'll use that and just do a collage. I have pictures going back to when I started. I keep those on there just to remind me where it all came from. Like I said, we bring our families on the road with us.

BN: It's a tough life, obviously. You don't get to play half your games at home.

JJ: Exactly. And every time we walk in here, that reminds us of, really, part of the reason we do this.

BN: Well, if you make it this far, you begin to make a decent living but it's the years you put in to get here that are the biggest struggle.

JJ: Without a doubt.

BN: That's one of the things I wanted to ask you about. You went to the Kinnamon School?

JJ: Yes, I did.

BN: What is it like today…do you go back once in a while to instruct, or look in on one of the schools to visit?

JJ: Never have. Gibby [Greg Gibson] has, in the past.

BN: I'm just curious how different it is. The curriculum is probably relatively similar, but presumably more refined. More use of video, certainly, and digital media.

Greg Gibson: Hunter Wendelstedt took over the school from his dad. Hunter and I have been friends. I've worked for Harry. I sat at the feet of Harry Wendelstedt for 10 years. One of the things about it, you want to get a real perspective of where we all get started, you should call Hunter – he's at umpireschool.com – and make a trip down to umpire school to see. Because one of the things we do, we treat – even if a guy…there's been lots of times we get a guy with experience, and then we get the 18-year-old kid that he doesn't really know what he wants to do and mom and dad don't want to waste money on college. Three grand is a better investment to see if he wants to do that. They treat everybody [the same]. He starts with the basics. Obviously things change and you have to teach the system that is sent down from Umpire Development as far as coverage and things like that. Things change with the way they want to do things, depending upon who's in charge.

The basic fundamentals that they teach at umpire schools is one of the things that I remind Triple-A guys when they get here. What's your first responsibility? Fair/foul, catch/no catch. The things that we teach from day one are the things you build on no matter what level you're at. One of the things that I enjoy going back is to be around not only the kids who want to learn but the kids who teach. When you go to umpire school and you're an instructor, most of the staff is made up of minor-league umpires with the supervision and help of…Hunter will bring in…Jerry Layne's always there. David Rackley's still there. Eddie Hickox is still there. Jordan Baker comes down. Kids that have went through the school as instructors, made it as major league umpires. I haven't been down for three years now.

BN: One of the things you said you'd heard of umpires who had to sleep in their cars when they were starting off.

JJ: Oh, yeah. Actually, the way I got started is that I was a player and I wanted to stay in the game. I got hurt and I couldn't play anymore. There was a guy back in Toledo, Ohio by the name of Tom Raveshear who was a long-time minor-league umpire. He worked for the Toledo Recreation Division and I was 16 years old and I used to listen to his stories about umpiring while I was playing. When my playing days were over, I went back to him and asked him about it. He told me how tough the life was and everything, but you know what? It was still professional baseball.

BN: You played in college.

JJ: Yeah. Bowling Green State University. The Falcons. I was a pitcher.

BB: One thing I thought was interesting was that three of you on this crew were all born in Ohio. On this particular crew.

JJ: Yeah. On this particular crew.

BN: And one from Venezuela. Only you [to Carlos Torres]. You missed.

JJ: By a few miles. And a few countries.

BN: There seem to be little clusters. There's a group of umpires that came from Connecticut. A group from Ohio. Michigan.

JJ: We were talking about that the other day. Chad was talking about how many guys are from Ohio. I don't know how many we ended up coming up with, but there were quite a few. It's kind of funny. We all kind of placed somewhere else, though. We met our wives or whatever.

BN: Your dad worked at Jeep? What kind of work did he do?

JJ: My dad was in charge of payroll. He went way back. He started back when it was still Willys Overland after the war when they built the Willys Jeep. Then it went to Kaiser Jeep, then it went to American Motors, and then it finally ended up Chrysler. He put in like 36 years. My mom actually worked there, too. And so did I.

BN: I knew you worked there. Greasing tie rods or something?

JJ: Yes, I greased tie rods. I worked in the press shop. I worked in the paint shop. The body shop. My dad would always get me in during spring break or summer breaks in college. Over at least five years.

BN: And fulltime for at least six months or so.

JJ: Yeah, yeah.

BN: I read your book, that's how I knew that. You also have a special interest in Christmas lighting?

JJ: Absolutely.

BN: You put up one of those monster displays at home?

JJ: Absolutely. Absolutely. And my son has developed a knack for it. To this day, I'll put up – well, we live in a different house now, but at my second house, I was putting up over 30,000 lights. This house, it's scaled down to about 10,000.

BN: Your father did some umpiring?

JJ: Yes, he did. He was an amateur umpire for a while. I would follow him around a little bit. I don't know if he just lost the interest in it or whatever, but he abruptly quit. Just quit doing it.

BN: You had already started by that time?

JJ: No, no. This was when I was just in high school ball. I never umpired until I went to umpire school. I never umpired. I just watched him. It was kind of interesting. It was a way to stay in baseball. That's the reason I pursued it.

BN: You just decided to go to umpire school and they thought you were good enough, and you got the bug a little bit.

JJ: Yeah. That's exactly how it goes. I spent 11 years in the minor leagues.

BN: In the early years before the leagues united, I heard that there was some real rivalry between the National League umpires and the American League umpires.

JJ: It was kind of funny because we all became – in 1982 is when they did away with the outside protector. I always wore the inside, anyway. I think it came from that. The way the two different leagues developed. American League umpires were considered high-ball umpires and National League umpires were considered low-ball umpires. When we went to the inside protector, uniform all the way across the board, there became a friendly rivalry between the American League and the National League. They were always called the Senior League. When I came up, we were a much younger staff than the National League and it was a competitive drive a little bit to show that the American League was just as good as the National League. And the National League never believed it.

BN: And the AL had the DH, too.

JJ: Exactly. That was a big thing, and it was a big thing only because with the addition of the designated hitter, the American League games increasingly started getting longer and longer. There was more offense. The National League always had the belief that their games were always shorter. I was an American League umpire for 13 years and one of our arguments was that our pitchers don't hit and we have more offense in the game. The National League always claimed that their game was better without the DH.

We all came from the same place, though. We all ended up in the major leagues. And we're all doing the same thing. I like to think it was more of a friendly rivalry.

BN: You actually saved a woman's life one time.

JJ: Yes, I did.

BN: Jayne Powers. Do you keep in touch with her?

JJ: All the time. It's been three years now. What was it? 2012. August 20. I just saw her three weeks ago.

It's really strange. There's a lot of eerie coincidences. Her birthday and my wife's birthday are at the same time. We're all of us very Irish. She had a vision that she was going to have a heart attack. The day before, we left late to the ballpark and I told my crew the next day that we're leaving 20 minutes earlier because we were a little bit late. If we hadn't left early that day, I wouldn't have been walking down the tunnel.

She actually had a heart episode, not a heart attack *per se*, that only five percent of the people survive even with CPR. Everybody should know CPR. Everybody. Tanner, Chad's son, could do CPR. You're going to be 13? He's going to be 13 and he could do it. I think it should be a prerequisite in school. I'm pushing for that in Oregon.

BN: I do have one question that I guess is kind of the obvious one. I would suspect that you wish that there had been replay at the time of the Galarraga game.

JJ: It would have been very beneficial. It would have spared me a lot of death threats.

BN: You really had death threats.

JJ: My whole family.

BN: I didn't realize it had reached that point.

JJ: I've said ever since the incident, it was my worst day in baseball but it was also my best day in baseball. Actually, in my life. I always look at outcomes. I always look at things done for a reason. I still don't know the reason, but a lot of good has come from it. More good than bad.

BN: Besides becoming a published author. Before that time, were you in favor of replay at all, or just really not that interested?

JJ: Probably not that interested. At that time, we already had the replay with the box for boundary calls of home runs and stuff. I think we all knew that eventually replay would evolve into what it is today. And I'll be honest with you – I'm a fan.

BN: I think we know that the technology exists that could even call balls and strikes.

JJ: If that happens, I'm not so sure that you'll need us.

[some interruption that prevented continuing to talk to Carlos Torres]

BN [asking Greg Gibson]: When you first joined the major league staff, was that a result of the big transition that occurred in 1999?

GG: I'd rather not answer questions about that.

BN: OK. But that's when you first got your opportunity.

GG: My first opportunity was when I went up in '97. But I got hired in '99.

BN: I mentioned to Jim before that it caught my eye that three of you guys were born in Ohio.

GG: I was born there, but I was raised in Kentucky.

BN: OK. Well, part of Ohio is just across the river. I notice you were involved in a couple of replay firsts.

GG: The very first one, with Frank Pulli. [May 31, 1999, in Florida, Cardinals versus Marlins] Cliff Floyd hit a ball that went off the wall;

Plate conference, Fenway Park, September 27, 2015, Baltimore vs. Boston. Home plate umpire - Carlos Torres. Other umpires: Chad Fairchild, 1B; Jim Joyce, 2B; Greg Gibson, 3B.

Frank called it a home run. I went to the minor leagues with Cliff Floyd and I was at second base. Cliff got to second base and he said, "Gibby, that was a home run." And I said, "No, the ball hit the wall." Cliff ran right to Frank. Frank was working third. Frank whistled (GG gestures the circular motion indicating rounding the bases) and gave a home run.

Well, there's kind of a thing in the umpiring world where everybody comes out of the dugout and starts yelling at you – chances are, you might have missed it. This was back in the days before replay or anything. Frank was an old National League guy, and you just didn't huddle. You made the call, that was the call, and that was it. We huddled.

BN: Frank overruled you?

GG: No, it was Frank's call. It was Frank's call all the way. But Cliff got to second base and he talked to me. Cliff and I had known each other since A ball. Cliff and I had been together for eight years, every level up through.

Cliff ran to Frank and Frank called it a home run. So we huddled. Frank was big on seniority and Greg Bonin had the plate. He said, "What have you got, Peewee?" "Ah, I don't know, Frank." Ed Rapuano was at first base. "What have you got, Eddie Rap?" "I don't know, Frank. I'm not real sure, Frank." Frank called me Hoot. Hoot Gibson. Frank had a big

Italian…"Hoot, what have you got?" I said, "The ball hit the wall, Frank." "*What?*" I said, "The ball hit the wall, Frank." He said, "Where?" I said, "What do you want me to do, go out there and climb it?" I remember it like it was yesterday. I said, "What do you want me to do, go out there and draw you a big X on the scoreboard?" I said, "It hit the scoreboard."

He said, "There's only one way to fix this. And, with that, he turned and he started walking toward the Marlins dugout, with Greg Bonin. And I looked at Eddie Rap and I said, "Is he going to do what I think he's going to do?" And Rap said back to me, "Like you're going to stop him?" (laughs)

So Frank goes to the Marlins' first-base dugout and he literally asks one of the technicians to turn the camera and around and give him the look. Well, some photographer is trying to take pictures of the whole thing. Greg Bonin grabs the guy's camera and slams it to the ground. Breaks this guy's real expensive camera. Anyway, it was just a mess, the whole thing was just a mess. That was the first use of instant replay.

John Boles was sick and not there. Fredi Gonzalez was the bench coach and actually the fill-in manager for the Marlins. And I had gone through the minor leagues with Fredi as a manager. So we're getting ready to go and Fredi comes out and goes, "I want to protest. I want to play this game under protest." We huddle again and Frank looks at me and he goes, "You're the rules guy. What have you got?" "There's nothing to cover this." I said, "Frank, you're using technology. There's nothing to cover this." Anyway, Frank marks up the protest. We can't even get off the field. Runge was the supervisor. This was back and I was the only guy who had a cellphone. The first year I had a cellphone. Let's just say it was a major, major, major…it was a big deal.

BN: You had two other firsts.

GG: Well, we had replay come into effect on boundary calls [in 2008]. I was with Charlie Reliford. Brian Runge had the call. Jerry Layne was at first base and I was at the plate. Tropicana was weird; they had these two…lines. (gestures toward roof) We huddled. Charlie looks at me and says, "What have you got?" and I said, "Brian got it right, but we've got it. We might as well use it." And Charlie was like, "Okay." So I stayed on the field, and Jerry and Charlie and Runge went off the field and used it.

And then last year, I was the infamous one. I was with Ted Barrett and kicked the crap out of a call at first base. I was the first guy to get overturned.

[March 31, 2014 at Miller Field, Braves vs. Brewers. Bottom of the sixth: BREWERS 6TH: Braun grounded out (third to first); Braves manager Fredi Gonzalez challenged the call at 1B when Ryan Braun was ruled safe; the review overturned the call, which was the first time a call was changed in the newly expanded replay system.]

So I hit the trifecta. What I want to point out is this: I was 2-for-3 with all the firsts on replay. As Meatloaf said, "Two out of three ain't bad." Well, that's been me. I got two out of three right.

BN: Do you know who was in the chair at the replay center?

GG: Brian O'Nora. Mine was the first one flipped. People know I had the first one overturned but they didn't know that I also had the first unofficial and the first official and I had both of them right.

BN: And probably 99% of all the other calls you've made, too.

GG: Well, they only remember you for the ones you miss. They don't remember you for the ones you get right.

BN: You did work behind the plate for Randy Johnson's perfect game.

GG: I did.

BN: That must have been quite a thrill in a way.

GG: Well, it's one of those things that you really don't think about it until it's over.

BN: And you worked Kershaw's no-hitter, too.

GG: Kershaw's no-hitter, yeah.

BN: Some guys work their whole career and never have a no-hitter from behind the plate.

GG: A lot of guys.

BN: Mexico City. World Baseball Classic. Was that a different experience?

GG: Just the culture. It was fun to go and do that. The World Baseball Classic, there's three major league umpires and four amateur picked by the international committee. So that's fun. You get to work with those guys and they enjoy being around us. It's a lot of fun.

BN: Those are all the specific questions I have for you right now. Maybe I can catch up with the other guys another time. I know it's running late.

GG: I'll be honest with you. One of the most important things – and one of the things I enjoy most – is playing cards before the game.

BN: When you go to replay, do you usually show up there about an hour and a half before the games?

GG: No. Thirty minutes.

BN: At least you don't have to change beforehand.

GG: It's a nice break. It's intense, though. It's one of those things where you might not have anything going on and then all of a sudden you've got something going on over here and something going on over there. It's a break, but when they come to the headset and they're needing info, it gets intense. We are all about getting it right, whether we're on the field or off the field. Our job is the integrity of the game and our job is to get it right.

No matter what a fan thinks. As a fan, you can look at a replay and I can look at a replay and you can have your opinion and I can have my opinion. But at the end of the day, what our guys do, we get it right.

BN: Chad, I wanted to ask you one question. You're #4.

CF: Yes.

BN: Do the numbers mean anything to people?

CF: Some people, they do; some people, they don't. Me, they don't.

BN: That was Tim Tschida's number.

CF: If I had a number to pick and everything's available, I'll take 24. Other than that, I have no…I don't care what my number is. Is that Jerry Layne?

JJ: Yes.

CF: So if he retires and I'm able to, I'll take 24. Other than that, I don't care what my number is.

[A further interview with Chad Fairchild was conducted on April 20, 2016.]

Interview with Chad Fairchild on April 20, 2016

BN: I wanted to ask you about the season you worked umpiring Venezuelan baseball. Was it one season?

Chad Fairchild: I worked one season in Venezuela, yes.

BN: I went to a couple of games there, in Caracas. How was that different?

CF: Oh, it was very different. The game on the field, you have to manage it differently. The personalities are a little bit different, but I had a great time down there. I loved it. It was a great learning experience. More than anything, I loved my time off the field, too, just learning about the culture, new foods…

BN: Did you know any Spanish at all?

CF: Very, very little. Unfortunately for me, I had people with me who were bilingual and so many of the people – no matter where you travel in the world – they speak English. So it's tough to pick up other languages. Everywhere I'd go, they speak English. I would like to be forced to pick up a little more Spanish.

BN: You went to various cities.

CF: Yes. Gosh, it's so many years ago now, I can't remember how many teams were in that league. I was there in the 2002-2003 season. Our home base was in Caracas, but I was rarely there. I had a couple of series in Caracas. At that time in Venezuela, the living conditions were very poor. The hotels that they put us in were just downright…there was many a night where we spent our own money to stay in another hotel. I've heard it's gotten better. That was one thing I did not appreciate about the Venezuelan League at the time, and I'm not afraid to say it. We'd check in at some places and the glass would be broken out. A couple of the guys got mugged and beaten up. We finally said we'll go spend our own money and stay in something that was livable. But other than that, it was great.

I did a couple of spring training games this past season in Mexico. I've been to Puerto Rico and worked a few games. So I've got to travel a little bit with baseball, seen a few different cultures. It's been nice.

BN: When you did the WBC…

CF: That was in Puerto Rico. I did round one and two in Puerto Rico.

BN: I saw Cuba vs. Puerto Rico there in 2006.

CF: I probably had that game. [He was the first-base umpire for the Dominican Republic vs. Cuba game on March 13, 2006, and home-plate umpire for the Venezuela vs. Dominican Republic game on March 14.] Marvin [Hudson], who's on this crew normally, has gone to Cuba the last couple of years with Teddy [Barrett] on that mission.

BN: A question that was raised to me – when you umpire behind home plate, do you sometimes wear sunglasses?

CF: Day games, I always do.

BN: Do most umpires wear them?

CF: I don't know if most do. I know a lot do, but I also know there's some who do not.

BN: Is that because of the glare on the ball as it may sometimes comes out of sunlight into shadow?

CF: For me, I always wear sunglasses when I'm in the sun. If I don't, I will squint and get a headache after about a half an hour.

Shadows are something in every park when they have those later afternoon games, coming across the batter's eye and that's a time sunglasses will [word indistinguishable, may have been "go."]

BN: I just wondered if they helped moderate or even out the view of the ball.

CF: I don't think so. It's just one of those things you have to battle through.

8

Tim Timmons

As we have seen, Phil Cuzzi worked his first World Series games in 2017. As he said, working the World Series is every umpire's dream. It's the culmination of all the time the aspiring umpire put in during umpire school, the long years working their way up in the minor leagues, the uncertainty of knowing when there might be an opening in the majors, and then years of working in the major leagues – still being evaluated – before being selected to work in a World Series. Phil Cuzzi had his starts and stops as he persevered in his efforts to become a big-league umpire, and remain one. From the night he worked his first game in the majors (June 4, 1991) to the night he worked the plate in his first World Series game (October 24, 2017) was more than a quarter-century – some 26½ years. Now he has a memory to savor that no one can ever take away from him.

The very next year, Tim Timmons worked his first World Series game. It was on October 23, 2018. He worked the plate, at Fenway Park. The next evening, he worked the right-field line. From the point on, he was one of the umpires at the Replay Operations Center in New York. For Tim, it had "only" taken 18½ years to realize the dream. I was able to talk with him just after the first couple of games and before he settled in to work replay. The first game he worked Replay was the 18-inning game, finally won by the Dodgers at 3:29 AM Eastern time. There were no calls challenged in the Series games he was at the ROC.

Interview with Tim Timmons on October 26, 2018, a telephone interview as Tim walked from his hotel to the Replay Operations Center in New York.

BN: Congratulations on working your first couple of World Series games.

Tim Timmons: Well, thank you. I really appreciate that. It was a nice call to get.

BN: You're going to be working Replay tonight for Game Three of the World Series and as many games as remain.

TT: After a couple of nights with so much adrenaline in your system, it's going to be more relaxing.

BN: You're not going to have to stand outside in wet and 39-degree weather.

TT: Oh God, it got cold in the sixth, seventh, and eighth.

BN: You're just lucky to be able to get both games in, with the rain.

TT: Oh yeah, absolutely.

BN: I'm kind of curious, if you don't mind my asking, you've had 19 or so years working at the major league level. You worked the Japan Opening Series in 2008 – I was there for that, too – and you worked the China Series that same year. But you've worked all these years and you're just getting into your first World Series. That seems like a long time.

TT: Yeah, well, there were a lot of guys hired. There were a few guys who were younger guys. I understand that. I'm on the back end of my career. I think it's important to get young, strong umpires experience. There's a reason for everything. All I can tell is that when it came, I felt like I was well-prepared. I was comfortable being out there. It was a great, great experience.

BN: And you got to work home plate for the first game, too!

TT: Yeah.

BN: That's an honor itself.

TT: It was. Absolutely.

BN: And you got to see two big strikeout pitchers, too. Sale versus Kershaw.

TT: Yeah. Great pitching.

BN: I heard some commentary afterwards saying that they thought you had a tight strike zone, but that it was fair to both parties. You don't need to comment on that. Obviously, the consistency is what people look for.

TT: You want to be below the radar. The less people who know who's umpiring, the better.

BN: You know, I saw a quote you made. You said, "You want to be absolutely perfect, and we all know that's impossible. As an umpire, the excitement is when no one notices you."

TT: Absolutely.

BN: The word "excitement" kind of stood out at me there.

TT: Yeah. When people go, "Wow, you were out there? I didn't even notice you." That's a really good feeling. It just is a really good feeling. You want to protect the game. You don't want to be part of it.

BN: Now you're going to be working two-to-five games in Replay, depending on how long the Series goes.

TT: Correct.

BN: Will there be other umpires there? I'm sure there will be some supervisors there.

TT: Yeah. there's another umpire. And I bet there will be probably 10 to 12 other folks in there. Have you been?

BN: Yes. Not during a game, obviously, but I've visited the center a year or so back.

TT: It's like walking into the NASA Control Center.

BN: Yeah. Mike Teevan met me there and showed me around.

TT: It's really quite impressive.

BN: It's a great break for you during the course of the season, but during the World Series…

TT: (chuckles) Well, you know, even during the season, it's sort of like you can work the plate and then people who don't really understand it think you've got the day off. That's no way to approach anything in a baseball game.

BN: I'm just talking about your feet, your knees, your legs, you know…

TT: Oh yeah, absolutely. That definitely is a break for your body.

BN: And it's climate controlled.

TT: Climate controlled (laughs). That's true! I hadn't thought about that, but that's true. I'm not going to standing there with hand warmers in my pockets, in my socks, in my gloves, in my hat.

BN: In terms of being out of the limelight, you'll get as close to anonymity as you can get.

TT: Bill, this conversation sounds more and more like the kiss of death.

BN: No, no, everything's going to be fine.

TT: (still laughing) I know it is. Umpires a little bit superstitious.

BN: I was just thinking of your not wanting to have anybody notice you. Well, if you're sitting in Replay, there's no fans going to be noticing you.

TT: The thing is – just like anything else associated with umpiring – nobody notices you until they notice you. Believe me, if you have something strange or quirky, they'll notice you. It's like the first-base coaches and the third-base coaches. Some of those coaches aren't on the pension, and for the guys who aren't on that full pension – which is a shame – if they send a guy or don't send a guy, yeah, I say to them, "They don't notice you until they notice you. That's the reason you should be on the pension as well." Everybody out there has a role to play. You have to be conscious of it and conscientious about it every single pitch.

BN: Of course, we saw Joe West in the fan interference call in the ALCS when Altuve hit the ball to Betts. I guess that's one of the last positions you ever want to be in.

TT: That's the thing. You work 130 games or so from first base and you look at it from that angle and now [working down the right-field line, as West was] you've got really the best angle you could possibly have, being out on that line, and when you take everything into consideration, it's a completely different look.

BN: Even growing up, working two-man crews and three-man crews, you were never out there.

TT: It's a different look.

BN: It's only the playoffs that someone is out there.

TT: Right. Which is why they're out there.

BN: How come you're not further down the line? I always wondered.

TT: Especially in Boston, if you get closer to Pesky's Pole or the Wall, the last thing you want to do is to get into a position where you're looking up. You want a good look at a fair/foul, to be back enough so that you have more of a reference as far as where it is spatially. With Pesky's Pole, you could get a little further down but then the fans are so tight and in that corner you have no frame of reference on the fair/foul on that wall. The pole sits further back, almost a foot and a half, or two feet back. The closer you get to the fair-foul on the right-field line in Boston, the more that the actual line on the wall "disappears." There's a reason that guys do that.

BN: Yeah, I remember some time several years ago there was some incident that happened around that pole and Randy Marsh actually came up from New York – it was about five or six years ago, I think – he came up from New York and they had a conference a few hours before a game and they were all standing around looking at that line on the wall.

TT: Yeah, it's a different animal.

BN: When did you hear that you were assigned to this year's World Series? When do the postseason assignments come in?

TT: I think it was the last day of the LCS, or the next to the last day. I got a phone call from Joe Torre. I said, "Hello?" He said, "Tim, it's Joe Torre." I said, "Hi, Joe, how are you doing?" He said, "I'm doing well. How are you?" And I said, "Well, you tell me." He said, "Well, I'd say you're doing all right."

That's the same exact conversation I had with, I think, Ralph Nelson who called way back when to hire me. I said, "Well, you tell me" and he said, "I think you're having a pretty good day."

BN: So you didn't know you would be working the World Series until near the end of the LCS?

TT: At the end of the LCS, yeah.

BN: Really? I thought you would have known even before the Division Series started.

TT: No, no.

BN: So you were sitting at home and you got a call saying that in a couple of days, you'd be working the World Series.

TT: I was sitting in front of my 1970 914-6 Porsche engine, disassembling it. I have a Porsche habit.

BN: I saw that, someplace or other.

TT: I think they're pretty awesome machines. Fifty, sixty-year-old machines that you take apart and the engineering's like nothing that you see today. It's just high-quality, sturdy craftsmanship. Hopefully, like most umpires. (chuckles)

BN: Right, yeah. How'd you get into that?

TT: When I was 13, I mowed lawns. My older cousin, on my mom's side, he worked at the golf course and he did the maintenance on their machinery. Every year, my dad and I would put our lawnmower in the back of my dad's car and we'd take it up and my cousin Mark would tune it up. Well, in the fall I had seen him with a flatbed truck and three was this wreck – I knew what a Porsche was, and this had the 911 shape. When you're a kid – 10 or 11 years old – and you see something that's all rusty and all, you think, "What a piece of junk!" But I knew it was a 911. I also knew that he worked at a golf course and I thought, "Well, he's probably grabbing some parts to sell, or something." That was in September or something. In late April or early May we go over there. The little one-car attached garage, the door goes up and as it starts to go up I see this ivory-colored…the most beautiful Porsche you've ever seen in your life. At that age, it came up to me just below my chest. I knew that he worked at the golf course as the maintenance man and the mechanic superintendent. I knew he didn't have enough money to have a Porsche, so I go, "Whose is that?" He goes, "It's mine." I go, "Where'd you get it?" "Do you remember when you saw me in the fall?" He showed me the pictures of how he restored it. That was the biggest mistake Mark could have ever made. From the time I was 13, until I went to school, I was over there constantly. I was absolutely hooked.

He just showed me everything. Then I got into umpiring and I didn't have any money for a long time. I met a girl. I had a couple of cars and they were stored out at my sister's. Just a little 914 poor man's Porsche. We got married. We found this piece of ground. It had a kennel on it. My two cars showed up. She's like, "What are those?" I went, "Well, there's this kennel and I'm going to make it a shop." Then I restored a 1969 912

Porsche, which is a 911-looking thing with a four-cylinder engine, a 356 engine. My sons helped. That was a seven-year process. I did absolutely everything myself. I painted it twice, and then I figured that there was definitely more art to it than I could muster so then I had it painted. I still have that car.

I do quite a bit of charity work during the offseason, and then I do the Porsche stuff as well. Once again, I think it's like umpiring. I went to the... like last night, I went to the Philharmonic for the first time. They played Tchaikovsky's Fourth. Everybody asks, "Are you a baseball fan?" And I go, "You know, I'm a fan of mastering your craft." Like working that game a couple of night ago, you couldn't have asked for a better situation – two great pitchers, great catching, just awesome teams. And to work 30 years – damn near – to get there to that spot, you just appreciate the mastery – guys mastering their craft. It takes all that time to get to the point where you maybe, just maybe, have a clue about what is actually going on and what's going to happen and how it's happening, and you can appreciate it.

BN: You played baseball yourself as a kid.

TT: I did.

BN: What position did you play?

TT: Catcher.

BN: OK. So you were behind the plate.

TT: Yeah, which I think helps as an umpire. That's my opinion.

BN: I would think so. What kind of work did your parents do? I saw something that maybe your father umpired a little bit.

TT: My dad is actually in the Ohio High School Hall of Fame for officiating. [Jack Timmons was inducted in 2006, into the Ohio High School Athletic Association Hall of Fame] My dad worked in a factory at Borden's – Columbus Coated Fabrics. Two weeks before he would have had his 25 years and gotten his full pension, they fired him. They did that to a lot of guys.

BN: Two *weeks*?

TT: Oh yeah. That's how they rolled. They fired a number of guys. My dad was out of work for a solid year. I remember him telling the story years later – he was going for a job interview and he went to get a haircut.

He opened his wallet and he had like 12 dollars. The barber said to him – they'd been talking and he'd said, "I'm tapped" – so the barber said, "Hey, Jack, this one's on me." My dad said, "Nope. Something good's going to happen. We pay our own way. I wouldn't take money out of your pocket. That's not what we're going to do." So he paid for his haircut, and tipped him. And he got hired at Stewart and Silver, which is a concrete block company. When he started working for them, in the mid-'80s, he worked there for 10 or 12 years. I never wanted for anything. That guy could sell a ketchup popsicle to a woman wearing white gloves.

He worked for them for 10 years or so. He went to another concrete block company and that company had one plant. By the time my dad finished with them, they had three plants.

BN: What kind of work was he doing there?

TT: Sales. When he quit, within two years they had closed two of the plants. He was really quite good at what he did. Still to this day, back home I'm "Jack's boy." I'm not Tim the umpire, I'm Jack's boy still. The guy just knows everybody. He was unable to come [to the first couple of World Series games at Fenway Park] for health reasons. He watched it at home. I'm glad that he's still here when I worked it.

BN: Over the years, he's seen you work games in person, I guess.

TT: Oh yeah. He had a couple of strokes a few years ago. He never has been afraid to let me know how I did via text. (laughs)

BN: When we met at the park a couple of weeks ago, I remember you said you'd got this call that your father had had some bleeding.

TT: Yeah, that freaking guy, he's like the Energizer bunny, he just keeps on. I'll tell you what, the sonuvabitch, he can eat. They moved into an independent living place, he and my mom, probably six years ago – my mom has since passed – I go, "Don't they feed you over there?" He said, "Not like this." He's eating crabcakes and a steak.

BN: Did your mother work?

TT: My mom didn't work until…I was in Columbus and they started busing when I was going into sixth grade. We were Methodist and somehow my dad – I don't know how – got me into the local Catholic school. In order to pay – it was a lot of money, private school – my mom went to work at activities director and nurse's aide at Wesley Glen, which was a retirement center. That was right at the top of the street. I'd ride my bike to school and then on the way home, I'd stop because they always had ice cream and cookies and that type of stuff. It was a great experience for a kid in the sixth, seventh, eighth grade to interact with older folks and to realize that older folks are just younger folks that have gotten older. Between that and the Catholic school service work requirements – when you have an adversity in your life, and this is not going right or that's not going right, if you're able to get out of yourself and give to somebody else, it makes your life a hell of a lot better.

BN: One of the charities you work with is Life Care. What kind of work does that do?

TT: Life Care Alliance is a community outreach program for Central Ohio. They organize outreach for the medical bus that goes around, they have tutoring in reading and math. I do a lot of work with them. I've delivered Meals on Wheels for probably 15 years. You have to fill out a questionnaire and they do a background check so I filled it out. It was maybe three or four weeks after I began delivering meals that a guy called me and he says, "Hey, it says here that you work for Major League Baseball." His name was Chuck Gearing and Chuck went to St. Charles, which was an all boys' school, and he said, "After you have done with your route today, can you stop over to the office? I want to talk to you."

I said, "Sure." So I went over there and he asked, "What do you do for Major League Baseball?" I said, "I umpire." He said, "You *umpire*?" And I said, "Yeah." He said, "I've got a meeting. Have you ever done any fundraising?" I said, 'No." He said, "Well, just come with me." So I went with him and we're talking. Guy's a huge baseball fan. Chuck said, "Well, we want to get X amount." Toward the end of the conversation, the subject comes up and he says X amount. I said, "Well, instead of 5 grand, how about 10 grand?" He said, "No problem." So for a number of years I did black tie events for their fundraising. I did a package – an evening with an ump.

People don't realize that umpires have mothers.

Once again, it's sort of like you don't want to be noticed, and at the same time I am absolutely shameless about using that uniform to help people.

It's amazing. People always want to [word unclear] an umpire, but when you sit down in front of them for a cup of coffee, they're fans of the game. They're not fans of this team or that team. They may think they are.

People might think, "I hate the Yankees," but…they don't. They love the game.

BN: Some people get a little obsessed. Some of it's good humor. Between the Red Sox and Yankees, it used to be really bitter – but not anymore. I don't know if you even noticed, but in the top of the ninth inning of Game Two, the Dodgers had one out and there was nobody on base. And the "Yankees suck" chant came up.

TT: Yeah, they did it the first night, too.

BN: They did. The Yankees weren't even playing. They'd lost out two series earlier, in the Division Series, but it's almost like a ritual. It has no real bite to it anymore. It used to, before 2004 when the Red Sox finally beat them and won it all, but…

TT: Yeah. Plus 9/11 changed a lot of things in this country. That was my most memorable moment in baseball. Even having had the World Series now, still to this say that first game after 9/11 – I was out in Seattle. It sounds corny, but people need baseball. People need sports. But the country needed a damn baseball game after that happened.

People always ask me, "Doesn't it suck? People yell at you and boo you." Hey, they're yelling at the uniform. If somebody's had a terrible day, or they're going through something, and getting agitated with the umpire is going to make them feel a little better, go for it. It's better than them going out and getting in a fistfight with somebody. It's just a great game.

BN: Most of them don't even know your name. It's just, "Hey, Blue!"

TT: Oh yeah. Nobody does.

BN: There's really only one umpire that people recognize these days, and that's Joe West.

TT: The rest of us mopes, we're just pressed shirts.

BN: You could walk along the street in Manhattan and no one would even recognize you [Tim was, in fact, walking along the street in New York during the interview, heading from his hotel to the Replay Operations Center].

TT: It's very, very rare that I'm recognized. Very rare.

I'm on the board with the union. We were on a conference call this summer and Joe said, "I think I've got 41 years now." I go, "You've got that many years?" How many years does he have?

BN: Well, he started when he was 23 years old, for one thing, which I don't have to tell you doesn't happen anymore. You're putting in eight to 10 years before you get to the majors now.

He's up there, well over 5,000 games. I think in May or June 2020 – if all goes well – he'll pass Bruce Froemming and Bill Klem for the most games ever.

TT: That's absolutely unbelievable.

BN: I'd heard that he tries to get out of Replay in favor of games on the field.

TT: Well, they don't let him anymore but he did the first couple of years.

Tim Timmons working home plate.

BN: I don't know why Replay games don't count as games worked.

TT: Well, they should.

BN: They should, yeah. You're working the game.

TT: They should, but I think historically it would be an asterisk, so…

He'll get it. He'll get the games.

BN: What do you think you would have done if you hadn't gone into umpiring? What got you into umpiring in the first place?

TT: It was my dad. Plus, I played in high school and college. I did want to play, but I figured out real quickly by the time I got into college once you get to that level, that pool of experience, OK, that's not going to happen. From the time I was 13, I played and I always wanted baseball to be part of my life. I just thought it would be coaching.

I studied history. I did sell some real estate when I was in the minors. I probably would have either sold real estate or taught. I would have done some charity stuff. I've always enjoyed that. I don't think I ever would have gotten into the cars like I have. It's expensive to get in.

I majored in history. I probably would have just taught grade school or something. I'm no mental giant.

BN: But your father was umpiring while you were growing up.

TT: When I was little. So I'd go to…I remember going down to O.U. [Ohio University in Athens, Ohio]. I think Mike Schmidt played down there for them when he was in college. I can't remember. But I'd go. He'd get dressed in the back of the car and pull out his lawn chair and have a little Beech Nut and some Juicy Fruit. I'd go sit in the press box. He worked out in Ohio State all the time. I just grew up around it, and I just thought it was cool. You know, when you're in high school and you can go to a weekend tournament back then and work six or seven ballgames and get 150 or 180 bucks, that's pretty good money for a young guy.

Ny buddy Scott Dunning and I…actually, he posted something on Facebook – a picture of us – and he always said, "I'm way better than you" so he was obviously one of the first guys I called. I said, "Just so you know, it's official." He said, "What?" I said, "You're a big-league World Series quality umpire." He goes, "Did you get it?" I go, "Yeah." He says, "Hell, yeah. World Series, I'd have been there before you." He posted a picture on Facebook and it's he and me walking back from a weekend tournament. We had worked the weekend tournament and we weren't scheduled to work the championship game. We both had our girlfriends. We were going out. It was a Saturday evening. The guy comes to us and said, "Hey, we need you to work the championship game tomorrow." We're like, "Ahhh, we got plans. We're going to go down to…" He goes, "Name your price." I looked at Scott and said, "Fifty bucks a man." He says, "Done." Our eyes got as big as saucers. He gave us each a fifty-dollar bill.

I worked first and had like 17 just whacker plays. He had one play at third, kicked the hell out of it. I go, "What in the hell is going on? You got one play and missed it. I got 17 and parents are ready to kill me."

BN: I noticed one thing. Did you have cause to eject anyone this year?

TT: I don't know if I ran…yeah, I think I ran maybe one guy.

BN: I noticed you had zero last year.

TT: Yeah. Well, Bill, I'll tell you, the older you get…I don't have much hair. And it's white. Either they just look at me and say, "Oh, that poor old guy just got confused" or they're just, "Ahhh…maybe he's right." I don't know which it is, but it just seems like the older you get…

It's like they know you. That's the thing.

BN: I thought maybe you were mellowing out or something.

TT: That may be part of it.

BN: I'm just kidding. Obviously, circumstances happen. Of course, with Replay there's not as many ejections as there used to be.

TT: No. No, there aren't.

BN: It's kind of disappointing, in a certain way, from the fan's standpoint. It used to add a little extra excitement. But it's better to get the call right, or as right as it can be.

TT: Absolutely. I've had some wins and losses over my career. It's a terrible, terrible feeling. Once again, you don't want to be part of the game. You just want to be sure the game is protected.

BN: I did have a chance to talk with Jim Joyce, the last year before he retired. It has to be about the worst experience.

TT: Yeah, yeah.

BN: Of course, he did write a great book about it, the two of them together. {The book is *Nobody's Perfect*, by Armando Galarraga and Jim Joyce. It tells the story of how Galarraga had thrown a perfect game in 2010 – until Jim Joyce called the runner safe on what would have been the final out of the game. It was a call that Joyce quickly saw was incorrect, once he had the opportunity to see it on video. The call was one that gave considerable impetus to the installation of the current replay system.]

TT: Yeah.

BN: That was very impressive, to see them come together and do that.

TT: Yeah, yeah. Absolutely.

BN: You said you're on the board of the union. I understand the current contract is up at the end of next year.

TT: Yeah, they're typically five years.

BN: I guess we'll see how that goes.

TT: That should be fine. I think they believe we do a good job. We try to do the best thing possible for Major League Baseball, and protect the game. I know that we have some concerns, as they do, about this gambling issue. It's really…I think it's dangerous. The integrity of the game becomes…it's always important, but with this…you have to be very, very vigilant about who's making certain that the game is protected.

BN: Well, you should be in alignment on that.

TT: Oh, absolutely.

BN: It's not like management and labor are going to have a different viewpoint on that. I'm shocked that it's gone as far as it has.

TT: I am absolutely shocked. I would agree with you. That's the correct word. To think that somebody could sit behind home plate and wager on whether or not the next pitch is going to be a strike…

When you're out with a crew after a game and something has happened, or something hasn't happened, and somebody says, "Hey, aren't you guys the umpires?" It's either, "Hey, buddy, we're not in our umpire uniforms" or, typically, the one that shuts them down is, "What are you, a gambler? Did you lose some money on the game?" And they'll leave.

Now, with the legalization of it, it's a different animal.

BN: You co-founded the Association of Minor League Umpires?

TT: Yeah, I was the first. I went through the NLBR process and I was the first president of that group, yeah.

BN: Was that something that Minor League Baseball was…was fine with?

TT: Pleased about? No, not really! (laughs) I don't think I would use that word.

BN: Well, it could be that it was better for them to go one way than another way.

TT: No, they did absolutely everything they could to impede that.

BN: Well, then you were putting yourself in a very risky position there.

TT: Yeah, but it was the right thing to do. That's what we do every night. It could have been me or any other of the 239 umpires that were there and more than willing to step into that position. I felt like I had some tools that made me uniquely capable of dealing with a number of different entities that we had to deal with and I was glad to serve everybody in that group.

BN: It could have either blackballed you, or put you in a slightly better position because if they're going to fire somebody, they're not going to fire the president.

TT: Yeah, well, they definitely didn't hire the president in '99. I don't think the word "helped" would be the correct word. And that's OK. I wasn't doing it for any reason other than it was the right thing to do.

When you went through the minor leagues, you never knew where you were ranked. They never shared that with you. I can remember being in Double A and being seen one time that year. We put them in a position where they had to disclose the rankings – where you were ranked – and there are supervision minimums now. You'd have to room with a guy until you were in Triple A. Guys get their own rooms now. We've got more umpires. The biggest thing that needs to happen is that Major League Baseball needs to take that whole system over, because you're in a situation where guys aren't getting hired to the big leagues until they're 30, 32, 35 years old. You're not having a guy like Joe West hired at 23. And the money is not good enough to identify the best prospects.

BN: You lose a lot of people who can't afford to wait eight or 10 years.

TT: You lose people who don't even come in the door. They look at it and go, "There's no way. I'm going to go work in the NBA." Or "I'm going to get my accounting degree or juris doctor and work in the NFL. Or I'm going to work in the NHL, where there's an identified process." You should know from the day you come out from umpire school that you are an actual prospect and if things go right you should be working in the big leagues in four to five years. There's no reason you shouldn't.

BN: So nowadays, minor-league umpires are informed where they stand in terms of ranking.

TT: Yes. Absolutely. You know exactly, and that happened…it sort of worked a different way. You have the known knowns, the known unknowns, and then you have the unknowns. One of the things that's happened is that virtually everybody now under that system makes it to Triple A. That didn't used to be the case, before we knew the rankings, but now they've got a legal issue where they have to disclose who's what.

I think they just move them through. I'm hopeful that that's going to change.

BN: How would it change?

TT: It would change with Major League Baseball taking the whole system over. I would like to see them actually reduce the number of professional umpires. Grandfather guys in over a three- or four-year period. Work guys out, and then only have a certain number of professional crews, so that you have less guys who are in that system, who are making a livable wage, who are covered as far as their insurance, and they're getting supervision and input 10 or 20 times a year. Every couple of weeks, you're being seen. And not by minor-league supervisors, but by guys who have worked in the big leagues and are coming in and literally working with you to get you to that next level.

BN: Well, I've taken up enough of your time. Are you still walking along the street?

TT: I'm at the shop now, so if you've got any other questions, you could call another time.

BN: I'm good. I'll always have more questions. I had a couple here about travel, but they're not that important. Ever miss a flight?

TT: No, I've never…knock on wood, I've never missed a flight. I've had flights canceled. I've been on flights that have been sitting on the tarmac and we've had to call the office. A couple of years ago, we had a Red Sox-Yankees series and our crew was sitting on a Southwest flight, because it was the earliest one. We were at about an hour-and-a-half, and I said to Kellogg, "Should I call?" He said, "You better call." You're stuck. That's a hell of a thing, when the umpires don't show up because they're stuck on a commercial flight.

BN: It wouldn't look good to be catching a ride on a team charter. [Not that they'd be seeing the same team back-to-back anyway.]

TT: No, it wouldn't, and that's not palatable. For anybody. You don't want to make them uncomfortable. That's their time. A time to unwind, not to have any kind of agitation.

BN: Next year, the Red Sox and Yankees are going to be playing two games in London, England. Will crews put in for that?

TT: Yeah, that'll be picked by crews, I think. It will just be in your crew schedule, I would imagine. When they turn out the spring training thing, you can request an assignment there. I put in for Tokyo [in 2008], but we'll just see what happens on that. That was a great trip. Japan's a great trip. People ask, "How was the sushi?" You can't explain how much better the sushi is. This isn't sushi in the States.

BN: Well, thanks for taking so much time this morning, Tim.

TT: Thanks a lot and we appreciate what you do.

–end

I was joking, of course, about the umpires catching a flight on the team charter. But in fact, it has happened. Before Hurricane Irma struck Miami in 2017, Paul Emmel explained that the crew he was working with had gotten out of town the quickly after the game at Marlins Park on September 6. "We hitched a ride on the Washington Nationals' charter last Wednesday night from Miami to D.C. I did it once before when a hurricane hit Tampa in, and if I remember correctly, 2004. TPA was closed so we flew with Toronto after the game to Baltimore where we spent the night and flew to our following assignment the next morning."[6]

9

Tim Welke

Near the end of July 2015, I was able to talk with Tim Welke. He'd begun his career as an American League umpire in 1983. As it turns out, 2015 was his last year before he chose to retire, at the age of 58. When he did, he had worked 4,216 major league games, and four World Series among his 98 postseason games. He worked three All-Star Games as well. One thing that had interested me – I knew Tim's brother Bill Welke was also a major league umpire. That was unusual, of course, and I hoped I would have a chance to speak with both of them. I caught up with Bill a couple of months later, in September.

Interview with Tim Welke on July 30, 2015

BN: Maybe you could tell me about how you first got interested in umpiring.

TW: Sure. I grew up in a small town in Michigan – Coldwater, Michigan. I played all the sports in high school and I realized I liked baseball. I played baseball – I wasn't the greatest at it, but I did play – and in the summer, I enjoyed the umpiring aspect. When I was in high school, it was a way to earn extra money. I knew I wasn't very good about umpiring either. I heard about an umpire school in Florida and I said when I went to college, I'll take a semester off and I'll go to one of these umpire schools. I'll learn how to be a better umpire, and then I'll go home and finish my degree. Maybe when I do high school and college, they'll quit yelling at me.

I had no intentions to be a professional umpire. Here I am, now it's almost 40 years or so and they're still yelling at me.

I went to the Al Somers Umpire School. It was in Daytona Beach, Florida. Being a kid from Michigan, going down there in January and

February for six weeks was appealing to me. I had no idea that they took the top finishers at these umpire schools into the low minor leagues, and then you just work your way up like a player does. I thoroughly enjoyed that. I like the challenge of it, learning to be a better umpire. And to this day, you learn something new every day.

BN: Did you finish college?

TW: No, I haven't yet. But that's around the corner. I'm close to retiring, so that's something I'm going to go back and finish. That's one of my goals.

BN: Ted Barrett's got a PhD at this point.

TW: Sure. Sure. A lot of our guys are diverse. When I went to umpire school, I was 19 years old and I moved through the minor leagues really quick as a young guy. At 25 years old, I was working in the big leagues.

BN: You started in the Gulf Coast League and then the next year to the Florida State League?

TW: Yeah. I spent a couple of years in the Florida State League and then a couple of years in Double A, in the Eastern League, and then when to the American Association where I worked with two guys who were more senior to me at the time and both ended up being big-league umpires – Drew Coble and Tim McClelland. The big-league supervisors would come around to watch them and they happened to see me. Like a lot of life, it's the right place at the right time, and taking advantage of your opportunities.

BN: You said you were thinking about retirement. Is it that you're thinking about it, or is there an age requirement?

TW: There's no age requirement, but I've done this for a long time. I was hired in '84. I worked half of '83 as a fill-in guy. This is my 33rd season. I've worked over 4,000 games. I've had a wonderful and great career, and I'm ready for the next chapter. There's a lot of things to do, and one of them is to get my degree. I'm a husband and a father and a grandfather. That's important to me. This is a young person's job. It's not for people …I don't have the best knees in the world, anymore, but I have a lot of experience, and that helps.

BN: What subject do you expect your degree will be in?

TW: I don't know. I don't know. I've always been fascinated by people. In this job, you travel so much and you see so many diverse people. I don't know what that will lead into, but I know it will lead into something great.

I'm excited about the next chapter. I have a feeling that it's around the corner; I don't know when, whether it's the end of this year or the end of next year. It all depends on my health and that sort of thing. *[See Chapter 30 for Tim Welke after beginning his retirement.]*

BN: When you talk about people, I see similarities with a scout's job. You're on the road all the time, with a very small group – with three other guys most of the time.

TW: You're absolutely right. Your crew becomes your family. You spend so much time together, so you have to like each other's company if at all possible, if you have the same interests. You spend a lot of time together in locker rooms, in traveling, and that sort of thing. And of course the three-plus hours every night when you're on the field spending time together. It's unique. It's different. And I tell people, it's a great job in the winter also. It's a great job in the summer, but it's also a great job in the winter.

BN: Well, you guys keep busy. It's not just April through October.

TW: Correct.

BN: There is work, at least for younger umpires just starting out.

TW: Absolutely. There's winter ball, and I did a lot of winter ball when I was a younger umpire. I worked two winters in the Dominican and I worked Florida Instructional League for four years. That helps give you more experience to get you ready for the big leagues, and then when you come up to the big leagues, you spend the first five years trying to figure it out, especially since I was such a young guy working in the big leagues.

BN: What kind of work did your parents do?

TW: My dad was an engineer. He worked for the State Highway Department of Michigan. He built roads and bridges and at the end of his career he was in charge of the entire department and worked out of Lansing. I got my work ethic from him. I saw that every morning he got up to go to work and that's what I try to do every day. I try not to miss a day. If you don't feel good, or if your knees are sore, you still go out there and you go to work because that's what you do.

BN: That kind of raises a question. Since you've been umpiring such a long time, how would you characterize the change of attention – at this point, from Major League Baseball, but before that, the American League – in their care about health and conditioning for umpires?

TW: I think it's outstanding. About 2000, Mark Letendre came on and he's the Director of Medical Service for umpires. It's improved tenfold. He's done a terrific job at that. The health and welfare of the umpires has just turned into something outstanding. It's a demanding job. The guys are healthier today. He oversees that. He's done a terrific job maintaining people.

In the old days, when you'd get hit in the face mask with a foul ball, you'd just kind of blow it off. Now they're concerned about concussions. And guys' backs and necks and knees and all the components. And quality of life is mentioned that's something that's really important.

BN: You have mandated vacation days now.

TW: Yes. And that helps. I really don't call them vacation because you really don't go on vacation; you get a break. You're off the field. They're called vacation days, but I call them break days. You just get away from the daily grind. In Boston, the Red Sox play half their games at home. The Mets play half their games at home. We have no home stadium. Every three or four days is a new town. You work about seven or eight weeks in a row and then you get a break. It's good. That keeps you fresh.

BN: Back in 1986, you worked 149 games. In '87, you worked 148. There weren't that many games off. Right now, most guys work 120 or 130.

TW: Exactly. Exactly. As we're talking, I'm in New York doing replay. Our crew had three weeks. We had one in May and now we've got this week, and we've got one late in September. With replay, those are games you're not working on the field, although you're watching two games – but you're sitting in an air-conditioned environment, and you're sitting. You're not standing. Those are probably 18 or 20 less games that you'll end up working on the field. You're still away from home. You're still in a hotel. You're still doing what you have to do, but you're not on the field so that's a little more refreshing. It's a lot easier to go to work and home from work after that.

BN: Do you stay near the replay center?

TW: I'm about 15 minutes. It's not that far. Some nights, if it's cool, I'll walk. Otherwise, I'll take a cab. And we get out at different times. Depends what shift you have. Tonight, I've got two 8:10 games, East Coast time, so I'll be there by 7:30 for the 8:10 game and then I'll leave when they're done.

BN: And then there are the people with the West Coast games…

TW: Exactly.

BN: How about your brother Bill? Did he follow in your footsteps, more or less?

TW: Kind of, I guess. I'm the oldest of seven kids and Bill's the youngest. Age-wise, we're 10 years apart. I remember he was going to Western Michigan, and he said he wanted to go to umpire school. It was something that he wanted to try. I said, "Well, make sure you get your degree first." He did. He graduated from Western Michigan and then he went to umpire school and he worked his way up and then in '99 he got his opportunity when a lot of guys got their opportunity.

We had a few years when we worked together as partners, which was good. But I think with young umpires, especially in his case, it's good to work with different people. You can learn things from everybody. Sometimes you learn the wrong thing to do, but then you learn that that's not how you do things – so that's a good thing, too.

He's off to a nice start in his career and that's terrific for him.

BN: So they didn't have any requirement that you two, as brothers, work on separate crews? It just worked out sometimes one way and sometimes another?

TW: Exactly. As a crew chief, you're entitled to put down four or five names of people you're interested in, and that sort of thing. There were a few years there when I thought it would be really nice to work with Bill. We live close to each other. Our families are close, and that would be very nice. So we worked together for a few years and then I just kinda felt that maybe it would be better for his career if he works with different people also, not just see it from his big brother's standpoint but see it from others. Like I did when I was a young umpire. I got an opportunity to work with Marty Springstead, who I would call a mentor. And Joe Brinkman and Rich Garcia, and guys like that. Dave Phillips. Working with different people helps you become a better umpire because you see different ways to do things.

BN: That's good. But you were on the same crew for at least a couple of years there?

TW: Yes, we were. Yes, we were, and it was awesome,

BN: How about Jeff Kellogg?

TW: I never worked a lot with Jeff. Bill's married to Jeff's sister. Her name's Teri. I've worked postseason with Jeff a couple of times. We had a World

Series together and a couple of other events, but we've never been on the same crew. Jeff's also a crew chief, and he's been a crew chief for a while. Crew chiefs typically don't work together unless it's postseason. When he was an up-and-coming umpire, he was in the National League and then when we kind of went together in 2000, when the leagues merged – which has been really a good thing. You go to 30 cities now instead of back then, the 14 cities in the American League. It's a better thing. It really is.

I haven't worked a lot with Jeff, but we live really close together. We live only 10 or 15 minutes apart and I see Jeff quite a bit in the winter or even in the summer if I'm at home and he is, too.

BN: He was born in Coldwater.

TW: Yes, the three of us all graduated from Coldwater High School. Once I got to the big leagues, my wife and I – we married young and had a young child when I was in the minor leagues – we chose to move to Kalamazoo because it's 10 minutes from the airport and it was a bigger city. It just made more sense to be 10 minutes from the airport. Sometimes you can be home for a day or so and you don't want to be spending an hour each way driving to the airport. It's more convenient, and it's a great place to raise a family.

BN: Jeff being six years older than your brother, maybe it was you when inspired him to go into umpiring.

TW: I would think. I would think that he...I know he graduated from Central Michigan and I think he became a police officer for a while. That's kind of aligned. It's similar to being an umpire; you get yelled at for no good reason at all. You get cursed at for doing your job.

I'm sure he became aware of what an umpire was, maybe through me. You'll have to ask him that. It would make sense. It's kind of rare to have a real little city in southern lower Michigan that's got 10,000 people and you've got three active major league umpires from that town.

BN: Absolutely. You mentioned the leagues coming together. You did have considerable experience as an A.L. umpire before that happened. I've asked this of a few people. Did you have any sense of any real rivalry with the National League, between the two groups?

TW: I don't think so. We were all in the same union. We were always together, even back when I started and got in the union in '84. At the union meetings, there were always American and National League umpires together, so guys knew each other. They just umpired in different leagues. And I think that when we merged together, I don't think there was any rivalry. I think it became really good for the profession. Now young guys that came up have no idea that that even took place 15 or 16 years ago.

BN: It's only natural that there would be a certain kind of good-natured rivalry, two groups and all, but I'd even heard of one time a couple of guys got in a fight.

TW: Well, I don't know about that. That was a generation ago and most of that generation is gone. There's a few of them left. Very few. I'm part of it, but I never had a rivalry with people and I don't think, if you asked Gerry Davis who's a senior guy, or Dana DeMuth or John Hirschbeck… Dale Scott, maybe. Joe West. There's a handful of us left. I don't think we have a rivalry at all.

BN: I meant back then, not now.

TW: Back then, you had some hardliners that maybe didn't want that coming. I'm not going to name names but those people are long gone. It's a better thing for the profession.

BN: When we talked about Dave Vincent, when we met, he keeps a lot of data as you know, about umpires, for Retrosheet. This is just coincidence, but looking you up this morning, I noticed – no meaning behind it at all – do you know how many people you've ejected over the years?

TW: I know in the last several years, not many.

BN: No, only one since 2010.

TW: Yeah, and I don't even remember who that was, or what it was for. You know, back when you're a young umpire trying to earn your stripes, people were more aggressive toward you and more derogatory or whatever, trying to test you. But once you become an older umpire, maybe they respect the gray hair a little bit more sometimes?

BN: The last guy you ejected was Joe Girardi. He threw his cap.

TW: Oh, OK. OK. Now I remember that. (laughs) That stuff's not important to me.

BN: Sure.

TW: Yeah, yeah. That's why I don't remember it, because that's stuff's not real important to me.

BN: The reason I brought it up is because I noticed that Bill Welke has 72 ejections and that's the same number you have. You're tied at the moment.

TW: Really? OK.

BN: Now, I'm not urging either of you to break the tie.

TW: (laughs) Well, some of those, I know, are automatic ejections because you issue warnings and then you have fights and that sort of thing. Some of that just happens. Now I hope you don't jinx me Monday when I go back to work on the field. I hope we don't have a throwing incident where we've got to run people or…

BN: I hope neither of you has to run anyone for the rest of the year. It's better that way, right?

TW: Well, it means you're doing your job. Just because you have to eject people…sometimes it's okay for agreeable people to disagree.

BN: Yeah, I've read a couple of books like Ron Luciano wrote quite a few years ago and he'd talk about how Earl Weaver would come out and say, "Ron, you're going to have to throw me out here…"

TW: It's the old Bobby Knight theory of if I get a technical foul, maybe it will fire up my team.

BN: Right. Exactly.

TW: It's the same sort of thing.

BN: I appreciate your taking the time. I guess you're not coming back through Boston this year.

TW: No, we're not scheduled and the way things are going, it doesn't look promising at this point.

BN: No, not at all. It would take a Colorado Rockies kind of thing like they pulled off in 2007.

TW: Exactly. Well, good luck with the book. You've got my phone number and if you need any more…you take care and you have a great day, OK?

BN: Thank you very much.

–end

John Tumpane, John Hirschbeck, Bill Welke, and James Hoye arriving at Fenway Park prior to the September 24, 2015 game.

Over the four seasons that I interviewed umpires coming through Boston, I found that there were crews that might arrive twice in one year but other crews that never came though during the course of a season. With 19 crews – Crew A through Crew S – that's perhaps inevitable. The Boston Red Sox, for instance, had 26 teams visit Fenway Park over the course of the 2018 season, and had 25 teams visit in 2019. Some crews are going to work more than one series, but not many. And, simply due to geography and optimal planning of the schedule, there are crews that don't turn up in a given season.

When I talked with Jeff Nelson on May 10, 2019, I was a little surprised when he said they'd be coming back in a matter of weeks. I expressed surprise at how they would be coming back twice, and that there already had been one crew which had come through twice – while at the same time, there were still one or two umpires whom I had never met over the course of my interviewing. Jeff joked, "It's sort of like the wheel on *Wheel of Fortune*. You never know when it's going to land on 'bankrupt' and you get us."

10

John Hirschbeck, Bill Welke, James Hoye, and John Tumpane

When I did meet Bill Welke for the first time, it was as part of John Hirschbeck's crew. Bill is 10 years younger than Tim, and started umpiring at the big-league level in 1999. John Hirschbeck had started the same year as Tim – 1983 – also in the American League. He worked one more year, and wrapped up his career at the end of the 2016 season. He was the second-base umpire in the 10-inning Game Seven of the 2016 World Series, when the Chicago Cubs won their first World Championship in over 100 years. That may have seemed as good a game as any with which to end a career.

Interview with John Hirschbeck and crew, at Fenway Park on September 22, 2015

The crew: John Hirschbeck, Bill Welke, James Hoye, and John Tumpane.
    (Mark Hirschbeck, son of former umpire Mark Hirschbeck (1987-2003), and John's nephew, was visiting in the room from college.)

BN: (Speaking of Mark) Maybe we should see if we can get another generation going here.

John Hirschbeck: We wish better for him.

BN: All he'd need to do is put in about 25 years and maybe there'd be an opening.
    It did interest me that you and his dad (Mark) were the first brother duo, and now we've got the second one.

JH: The Welkes.

BN: And then there's the Runges that were three generations. There's a few other connections, like Vic Carapazza is married to Rich Garcia's daughter.

JH: Stephanie, yeah.

BN: So there's a lot of connections.

JH: There's a lot. It gets in the family, I guess, you know.

BN: It seems like there's a couple of states – in his case (Bill Welke's), Michigan – that seem to be very well-represented.

JH: Ohio has a lot. Kentucky has a lot.

BN: Tell me a bit about how you got started. You were doing Little League while you were in high school?

JH: Yeah, my senior year in high school, I needed a part-time job. I was looking for money to go to my prom. A guy in town said, "If you umpire in Little League, we'll pay you five dollars a game." I hadn't played baseball since I was 12. I didn't really like it all that much. I thought, "Okay, I'll try it" and I really enjoyed it. The next year, I went to Central Connecticut as a freshman but I joined the local association in Fairfield County and started doing baseball, 18 and under. And I was 18 at the time. I liked it more and more and did it through college, and started wondering – through watching games on TV – how you ever get to do it at that level. I found out about umpire school, so in the middle of my senior year – because it's in January – I went down to Florida and I attended Al Somers Umpire School.

BN: Was there someone who mentored you locally at all, in some way?

JH: Really not. There was one older gentleman – his name was Art Drake – and he had been a long-time umpire in the area and he helped me a lot.

BN: Maybe he told you about the school?

JH: Just from watching TV, I found out about it. Kind of researched it and found out how you got into the big leagues.

BN: So you were making five bucks? Steve Palermo said he was making two bucks when he started out.

JH: Times have changed, right?

BN: You'd probably make a little more today. But it was Little League itself?

JH: Yeah, Stratford Little League.

BN: What had you thought you might have done before you started doing this?

JH: I went to college to become a phys ed teacher. My major was Phys Ed. I loved basketball and I coached for a couple of years at Fairfield Prep. I was the freshman coach the first year and helped with the varsity, and then I was the JV coach the second year, and helped with the varsity. Never lost a game in those two years. I had good kids.

BN: Connecticut does that really well, too – win basketball games.

JH: Then I was offered a science teaching job there. I was offered the head coaching job for the basketball team and a teaching job, but I was in Double A, and still wanted to get to the big leagues, so I didn't take it and continued on with baseball.

BN: And your brother came along…he's six years younger than you, more or less.

JH: Six, yeah.

BN: He first came in about three years after you, in terms of first games in the majors.

JH: Is that what it was? I don't even remember. I was in Triple A, so it might have been three or four years more with me. I was in Triple A and he came on the road with me once and said, "You know, I'd really like to try this." So I said, "Well, go home and umpire and make sure you like it a lot." I think he went to umpire school the following year.

BN: He eventually developed a hip problem?

JH: When he retired, yes. He needed a hip replacement and the operation went bad and it took five surgeries to get things right, or as right as they could be.

BN: You were president of the World Umpires Association for nine years.

JH: We called it the World Umpires Association because major league baseball is kind of the world. It was just a name that the membership chose at the time. This has nothing to do with international; it's just a name we chose at the time.

In '99, without getting a whole lot into the politics – the decertification of the union and everything – I ended up being elected president and I served in that capacity for nine years.

BN: From the beginning of the new union.

JH: Yeah, from the beginning of the new union. Yeah.

BN: I guess after nine years, that was enough.

JH: That was enough. It was time. You know, everything needs a change once in a while. It was time for me to move on, and to get some peace back in my life, because it kept me busy, for no reward other than a cellphone.

BN: There's a couple of other people…Dan Iassogna…

JH: Ed Rapuano, Iassogna, years ago Greg Kosc…

BN: From Connecticut.

JH: I knew Dan since he was about 3 years old. I knew his father. I used to do football with his father. His father Ralph still is a good friend of mine. Back when I was about 22 or whatever – Ralph is just a few years older than me – we were on the same crew doing high school football. When Danny was in college, there were several times that he would come with me and come down to Yankee Stadium and go to games in the city.

BN: Jim Reynolds.

JH: Also from Connecticut. They were roommates in college, yeah.

BN: And there was a guy named Matt Winans.

JH: Yeah.

BN: I just happened to run into him upstairs. He only worked a very few games – eight at each position – and he just didn't think there was going to be any chance for advancement.

Bill Welke: At times, there isn't.

BN: Tell me how you got started.

BW: Well, my story's different from the average kid. Tim's the oldest of seven kids and I'm the youngest. Our folks had seven kids in a 10-year stretch. We're one day shy of being exactly 10 years apart. Tim went to umpire school at the age of 18.

BN: And you were 8.

BW: He left home when I was 8, yeah. I never saw him again for what seemed like a really long time. So from the age of 8 I was more interested in following the umpires than following the teams. I've really been an umpire fan since I was 8 or 9 years old. All I can remember growing up is my mom standing at the sink doing the dishes every night and listening to Ernie Harwell on the Tigers games. Our whole family was intrigued by what Tim did, and followed him. I never grew up being a diehard Tigers fan. I was more of an umpire fan.

When I went off to college, I wasn't sure what I wanted to do. I went to Western Michigan and got a business degree. I was thinking about quitting college to go to umpire school and give it a try. I had done some umpiring around home and I really enjoyed it, so I said something to Tim about it and he said, "If you quit college, I'm not going to help you." It was his way of saying, "You need to finish school." Because the chances of making it to the big leagues is so slim. I don't know what the percentage is, but it's very low.

BN: One in a hundred among umpire school graduates is what I heard.

BW: When you're in the minor leagues, it seems longer than those odds.

So I decided to finish school, got a couple of job offers in the field I got my degree in – business management – but I just had this tugging that I wanted to umpire. I really enjoyed officiating. I officiated wrestling – I was a wrestler in high school. I played a little baseball. I played football. I really enjoyed officiating in general. So I went to Tim and he said, "OK, I'll help you." He gave me a lot of good advice and some used uniforms, and I went off to umpire school.

BN: By that time, you might have gone to a few games with him?

BW: Yeah, when Tim was working with Jim Evans the year before I went off to umpire school, I told Tim to share with Jim Evans – who was running his umpire school in Arizona –that I was concerned with being Tim Welke's brother. I wanted to be my own man. Tim was concerned about it. I was concerned about it. Tim made me ride to old Comiskey Park with him where I visited with Jim Evans and Jim said, "I'd love to have you come and be one of us." This was only the second year of the school. I shared my concerns with him and he said, "We'll address whatever comes up" and he goes, "It's not going to help you. It'll probably put you under more scrutiny. At times, while the advice and being able to pick up the phone is an advantage, you're going to be under more scrutiny."

At the time, Mike DiMuro – whose brother Ray was on the staff…he [Evans] said, "I've got Mike DiMuro coming…" So I said OK and I went to his school and made my way and 8½ years later, I got hired.

BN: You worked together for a while and then he said, after working together for a while, "Maybe it would be a good idea for us to work on separate crews."

BW: Yeah, and we realized that. Actually, I don't think baseball was crazy about it [the two of them being on the same crew], because there were times when we were both out there and I know the bosses had shared with me that at times, there are people who don't know you are two different people. They say "Welke." I remember when I was coming up and a player would ask for my name and I'd said, "Bill Welke." He'd ask, "Are you related to Tim?" And I'd say, "Distantly." He'd say, "Distantly," and I'd say, "Yeah, there's five kids between us."

JH: I always liked that story.

Bill Welke waiting for the first warmup pitch of the game, May 31, 2011.

BW: The first couple of years, I got called "Tim" all the time. After about four or five years, someone would call Tim "Bill" and I knew I'd arrived when they started calling Tim "Bill."

That's kind of how it all shook out. I really enjoyed working with him. It was great, not only for the two of us in our families but for our folks. They could turn on the Tiger game when we were in Detroit and they could see both of us out on the field at the same time, and that was really cool. I really enjoyed it and I learned a lot. I like working with John [Hirschbeck], veteran crew chief. I've learned a lot of good things and a lot of skills.

But I think it was time to move on [from working on the same crew as Tim]. You don't want to be in anybody's shadow. What we do is a very difficult job and the spotlight's on us. You don't want some sort of…a really quick story, I was in Tampa and I had a chopper in front of the plate, the catcher came out to field it, and the batter ran into him and I called interference. Lou Piniella's managing Tampa. He came out and put on this little show. Tim's the chief and Tim walks out. I said, "This is the time for Lou to either get ejected if he wants to get ejected, or leave." So Tim comes down and talks to Lou and tried to get Lou going, and Lou starts and then stops and he says, "Oh, this is bullshit." He starts walking back and then he stops and turns and looks at Tim and I and goes, "I think I'm getting brothered here." And then just walked away.

That was Lou, though. Lou was my first ejection in the major leagues, on national TV. Once you stood up to Lou, he treated you completely different. He treated you like a professional that you could talk to.

There's guys who come at you from this angle, and there's guys who come at you from *this* angle. Lou's was loud and in your face like the managers of the old days. We don't really have a lot of guys like that anymore. We still have a few.

The last thing I'll say about working with my brother is we did an interview with the *Detroit Free Press* years ago, and John Lowe asked, "How do two brothers become major league umpires and how do you deal with that?" This is the best way to sum it up: when we're on the field, we're two umpires who happen to be brothers, and off the field we're two brothers who just happen to be umpires.

BN: You ended up marrying Jeff Kellogg's sister?

BW: Yes, but for the record, I was dating her before Jeff went to umpire school. Small town. The Kellogg family and the Welke family, they had eight kids and we had seven kids. Mr. Kellogg was a longtime teacher/coach and a 30-year A.D. in our small town so everybody knew everybody. Wayne K. Kellogg. I started dating Teri at the end of our senior year and I think that next year Jeff went to umpire school. So my kids are related to three major league umpires.

BN: Have you two [Bill and John] worked together for a long time?

JH: Quite a lot of years.

BW: This is, I think, my fifth year working with John.

BN: I kind of wondered – just as it could be thought to be good for you and your brother to work on separate crews, I wondered if there were two unrelated umpires who worked together for a long period of time, whether Baseball tries to shake it up a little bit.

BW: If I were to work with John for five straight years, that might become "stale" — to a certain extent – on a lot of people's parts, and maybe they'd make a change after three or four years. But my four or five years with John had been here and there. That's not an issue with us. It can be, but it's not with us.

BN: Of course, if the two of you are working together, you're never going to be the crew chief.

JH: When it comes his time to be a crew chief, it would take him away. He wouldn't stay. I wouldn't stand in the way of that.

BW: When John goes on vacation, I run the crew in his stead. Last year, I bounced around from crew to crew and had several opportunities to be crew chief. That's how it works. They give you crew chief assignments in several doses to see how you perform. They give you some feedback and if you perform the way they wanted, you get more opportunities.

JH: Correct.

BW: And then in a year or two when John's gone, or a year or two when Tim's gone…

BN: A year or two?

JH: I'm 61, so I'm not going to be here that much longer.

BN: 32 years now?

JH: This is my 33rd. I actually started my 33rd year on July 1. So I'm in my 33rd year now.

BN: A third of a century.

JH: And another seven in the minor leagues. Sixty-one years in my life and I've been umpiring professionally 40 of them.

BW: I think John has been more years in the big leagues that Tump's been alive. [John Tumpane]

BN: You've still got a while to catch up with Bruce Froemming.

JH: Well, that won't happen. That's not a goal of my life.

BN: John, I don't know much about you because the Media Guide…

John Tumpane: I'm not in there. A picture, that's about it.

BN: One thing I noticed right away, though, you've already worked the plate for a no-hitter.

JT: Yes, I did.

BN: Just a few weeks ago.

JT: Correct. It was in Houston. Michael Fiers for the Houston Astros.

BW: He almost had a perfect game, too.

JT: Two weeks later I had a perfect game into the eighth inning with Madison Bumgarner of San Francisco. It was crazy. Obviously…

BN: Some people that never happens.

JT: Some people wait forever, and obviously it's just the luck of the draw.

BW: No, he's our plate guy for that!

JT: Right place, right time, but obviously a humbling experience to be a part of and a memory that I'll never forget. I've been real fortunate.

BN: Fiers walked somebody in the first inning, so a perfect game was never an issue in that game.

JT: No, but Bumgarner kept it going all the way to the eighth inning and then they got a base hit in the top of the eighth.

BN: Were you aware of it the whole game?

JT: The Houston game, I saw we were moving along well but he had thrown so many pitches and it was like the fifth inning and I'm like, "We got a no-hitter going and it's looking good but I don't think he'll ever get to nine innings at the rate we're going, with the amount of pitches." Obviously, it happened, and two weeks later to be in San Francisco, in the third inning we were moving along, and just coming off of that [in Houston] it's a little fresh in your mind that this could be a possibility. So we were a little more aware of it at that point.

BN: One of things you guys can't do is you can't jump on the pile…

JT: No. No. But as we walked off the field, obviously the team's going crazy and I'd met John [Hirschbeck] at third base and we walked off as a crew. As we were waiting there for everyone to get there, he said, "Congratulations. Now just turn around for a minute and take it all in because this is special." He was right and I'm glad he said something and I got to take advantage of that. It's a memory forever.

BN: How did you get started? What made you decide to become an umpire?

JT: Little League. That's what we did. I used to just hang out at the complex all the time and sometimes the umpires didn't show up and I'd be able to work the bases at a young age. I kept doing it and kept doing it. My father refereed basketball at the time, so I knew about officiating, but he didn't do baseball. Just hanging out at the Little League, I became interested and started doing it. A high school summer job came along to umpire, so I continued. One summer one of the guys I worked with said, "Did you ever think about doing this for a living?" I didn't know you could do it for a living at the time.

I looked into it and sent it for the information, talked it over with my parents, and went to umpire school after graduating from high school. I was fortunate to be able to get a job at 18 and went into the minor leagues.

BN: What did your parents do?

JT: My mother is a nurse and my father's a salesman.

BN: What do you think you might have done otherwise?

JT: I probably – like most of these other guys – would have been a teacher, a coach…try to be involved in sports in some way. I was always interested in that. Then this came along and worked out at 18 and went to the minor leagues and now I'm in my 14th season in the minor leagues, and I'm fortunate, I've worked over 400 games in the major leagues.

BN: I saw you had 302 before the season began.

JT: Yeah, and I've been up pretty much every day with these guys so I've got over 400 now and I'm learning, and hoping that a spot opens up and my name can fall in there.

BN: You never know, I guess. You can't ever know.

JT: No, you don't know. It's been a heck of a run and I'm enjoying every minute of it. Any day you're in the big leagues is a good day. For many reasons.

BN: I guess you get some credit afterwards; it's not 100% credit but…

JT: Yes, for every so many games you get a year's credit, so if you get hired, you can come in with a certain amount of years. That's good to have.

BN: So you're enjoying it.

JT: I'm loving it. Loving it. John's like a mentor to me, actually, and I'm fortunate to work this long with him. And these guys as well, James and Billy.

BN: You've been on different crews.

JT: Yeah, over time, yes, but for the last few years I've worked the majority of games with John's crew. It worked out. There was a spot on this crew and I kind of got a long-term fill-in.

BN: How did that work out?

JT: Sam Holbrook, his wife passed away. He was supposed to be on this crew, but by the time Sam came back there was other spots where they needed Sam so I was fortunate to be able to stay here.

James Hoye: That's a nice story.

BN: So what's yours?

JHoye: I don't really have much of one. I'm still trying to get my first no-hitter and he's just had so many accomplishments…

BN: You're just one of these umpires that comes up out of the ground?

JHoye: Just come out of the ground, yeah. Disappear.

BN: Then disappear again.

JHoye: Disappear, go home, yeah.

BN: How'd you first become an umpire?

JHoye: I just did it part-time right out of high school. Basically, like him, hang around and umpire little kids. I went to Ohio State and there was a guy at Ohio State named Tim Timmons who was also in the big leagues. He did a little clinic and I attended it and he asked, "Did you ever think about umpire school?" I said, "No, I don't even know what that is." So when I graduated from Ohio State in December, I went right to umpire school in January, and here I am.

BN: What school did you go to?

JHoye: Brinkman/Froemming. Brinkman sold the school to Jimmy Evans.

BN: The schools kind of get passed along.

JHoye: Correct. Correct. There's two survivors now, Wendelstedt [umpire school] school and Jim Evans…I don't know if that school's around any more – and then there's the umpire school. Like you said, they change quite a bit.

BN: You worked the first World Baseball Classic?

JHoye: I did. I was in Puerto Rico. I did two rounds in Puerto Rico.

BN: I was there then, too. Hiram Bithorn Stadium.

JHoye: From spring training, which tends to be of a…get the guys working…more of a relaxed atmosphere, to come and work those games – the country rivals – it was a big deal. And then I went right back to spring training and it was like ahhhh [exhale] because it had been so intense. They had the Puerto Rico/Cuba game, whoever won that game, they went on to the finals in San Diego. It was a big deal.

There's talk about having Opening Day there, in Cuba, during spring training. We just worked with Laz Diaz, who is Cuban, and we had talked about that. Obviously he would like to go there if that would happen. He wasn't sure when but he was hoping to be on the list to go. He filled in for us because Billy was gone for a week so Laz worked with us for a week. That was nice. It was nice to see him. I hadn't seen him for a while.

Postscript

On July 1, 2016, John Tumpane was made a member of the major league staff. By coincidence, the day he got the call he was working at Fenway Park and I was able to talk with him late that afternoon, within a few hours of him learning of his promotion.

BN: When did you get the call?

JT: This afternoon.

BN: Not last night or anything?

JT: No, this afternoon, from Joe Torre and Randy Marsh. They called me this afternoon and informed me that they've added me full-time to the major league staff, effective July 1. It's just an honor to get a call from them and it's just a dream come true. To put in all this time and just to see it all come together for myself and my family.

BN: You'd worked some 431 games as of last year.

JT: Yes, I'd just worked my 500th game last Monday night. This is my 15th season in professional baseball and I'm just happy that it all came together.

BN: You're one of the younger guys, because you started so early.

JT: Yeah, I started right out of high school. It's been a progression and I'm just glad it all came together.

BN: So you just got the call this same afternoon. How'd I find out about it so quickly?

JT: It's the age of the Internet.

BN: Yeah, I guess. Something like that. Where were you yesterday?

JT: We were at the New York Yankees. We flew in yesterday, and I got the news this afternoon.

BN: As far as you knew, today started off as just a day like any other day.

JT: Yeah. Just another day, working in the major leagues [as a call-up umpire], but today is different. Same game, different title.

BN: Well, congratulations.

JT: Thank you.

–end

11

Jeff Kellogg

It was almost a full year before I met up with Jeff Kellogg, but with his family ties to the Welkes, it made sense to connect with Jeff at this point in the narrative.

Interview with Jeff Kellogg on September 21, 2016

BN: Your father Wayne worked as an athletic director?

Jeff Kellogg: Yeah, he did. He coached for many years, and then for the last 20 years or so, he was the athletic director at Coldwater High School.

BN: How big is Coldwater, in terms of population?

JK: It varies, because we have lakes around us. I don't really know how big it is now, but at the time I'm guessing it was around 20-30,000.

BN: You still live near one of the Welkes?

JK: Tim lives about 10 minutes from me, and Bill's about 40 minutes away.

BN: So you could get together from time to time.

JK: We do over the holidays, yeah. He's married to my sister, Teri. Short for Teresa. She's a younger sister. I live about an hour from Coldwater now, so we all get together over the holidays.

BN: You knew each other growing up.

JK: Yes. I actually graduated with one of the Welke sisters and then I wrestled with one of the other brothers.

BN: I guess from talking with Tim, you worked together in the postseason a couple of times but you never worked…

JK: Not on the same crew during the season. Bill, I've worked a few series with Bill during the season, but I don't believe I've ever worked the postseason with Bill.

BN: When you get together, do you talk shop, so to speak, or trade war stories or that kind of stuff? You don't see each other that much during the year, because you're each going to different cities all the time.

JK: Right. Occasionally we'll see each other at the airport. We usually all fly out of the Kalamazoo airport, for the most part. Over the holidays, we might talk a little shop, but otherwise we're talking about anything but baseball. Especially football season. We all enjoy football so we'll talk football. It depends on the time of year.

BN: You were a National League umpire at first.

JK: Yeah, I got hired in '93 and then we combined in 2000.

BN: Did you play baseball in high school?

JK: Yes, I did.

BN: What position?

JK: Well, I pitched a little bit, and then I played left field.

BN: What got you interested in umpiring itself?

JK: When I started college, up in Central Michigan, I officiated intermural sports just to have some spending money. I enjoyed it, first off, and I thought I was pretty good at it – whether it was softball or football or basketball. I had actually considered going to umpire school. I knew Tim was umpiring. I didn't really have any conversations with Tim. I didn't know Tim that well. He's about five years older than me. I knew him, but I didn't know him. But I knew he was umpiring. At some point during those years of officiating intermural, I said, "Maybe I could go to umpire school after I graduate. We'll just play it by ear."

At this point, I transferred to Ferris State when I decided to go into Criminal Justice. After my second year at Central – I was in business school there – I decided I wanted to go into Criminal Justice and they did not have a Criminal Justice program. So I transferred to Ferris State.

I was watching the *Saturday Game of the Week* and the home plate umpire walked out to the mound to break up a conversation, and it was Tim. I was like, "Holy cow! He's in the big leagues."

BN: And he's on TV.

JK: And he's on TV, yeah. I finished up that year and graduated and I worked for about a year at the Sheriff's Department in Coldwater. At some point in there, I decided I wanted to go to umpire school and I contacted Tim to try and learn how you go about it, a good place to go, and that type of stuff.

BN: What school did you go to?

JK: I went to Harry Wendelstedt School.

BN: When you were with the Sheriff's Department, were you a police officer or were you doing other kind of work?

JK: I worked part-time on the road, and I worked part-time in Corrections. In the jail.

For umpire school, you usually head down January 1 and the school starts on the second. As of January 1, I was supposed to go full-time on the road. But I decided to go to umpire school, so that did not happen.

BN: Do you see certain similarities between that profession and umpiring?

JK: Really, I think just dealing with people. I guess we consider ourselves kind of like the police on the field. There are similarities and there are a lot of differences as well.

BN: The similarities are somewhat obvious. You want to make sure the game stays under control.

JK: Correct.

BN: I heard of one incident in 2012 at Camden Yards where you had to tackle a guy who was running around on the field there awhile.

JK: (laughs) Yeah, that wasn't my best move.

BN: I haven't seen it. Maybe it's on a YouTube video or something.

JK: I think you can still find it somewhere, because I know that some of the guys who I work with pull it up just to have fun with me.

https://www.youtube.com/watch?v=5Tg1MG_493E

BN: Well, you caught him and nobody else did, right?

JK: Well, yeah, I did.

BN: I heard that security was after him for a couple of minutes.

JK: At the time, the way they handled anybody who ran on the field was that they would not run after them. That was kind of their policy. He was on the field for quite some time. But when he ran toward home plate, I could see the catcher – who was taking warmup pitches at the time – kind of stand up and get ready in case he needed to react to anything. When he did that, I kind of leaned and maybe took a step toward home plate just in case anything happened and I might need to get in there. I guess it was at that point that he slid and then popped up and was getting ready to take off again. I looked up to see where the police were – where security was – and I said, "Nobody's going to get to him" – this happened in a split second – so I decided if I could catch him, I'd tackle him.

BN: I'm not sure if this is a related question, but do you remember your first ejection? In the big leagues.

JK: Yeah…I think it was either…it was either Barry Bonds or Jim Leyland. One or the other. I got one of them and shortly thereafter I got the other one.

[In the fifth inning of the August 15, 1992 game in Pittsburgh, home-plate umpire Kellogg ejected the Pirates manager Leyland while arguing a fan interference call made by 3B umpire Bruce Froemming. In the seventh, he ejected Barry Bonds for too strenuously arguing a called third strike.]

BN: You're the second umpire I asked that question of. I just wondered if it was the sort of thing that gets emblazoned in your mind forever. He didn't remember exactly, either. He kind of had it, but it wasn't like, "Yeah, I know *exactly* what happened."

JK: These years go by and they all kind of run together, but I just couldn't remember if I got Leyland first or I got Bonds first.

BN: You've been behind the plate for two no-hitters, I guess.

JK: Yes.

BN: [Anibal] Sanchez and [Ubaldo] Jimenez. I guess both times Miguel Olivo was the catcher.

JK: Correct. Yeah. Which I did not realize until after the second one. I went out to the plate the next day and he said something to me. I said, "Were you behind the plate in the first one? I guess I didn't realize that."

BN: Well, maybe he helped with one or two pitches, the way he framed the pitches there.

JK: (laughs) You never know.

BN: You've been a crew chief since 2010.

JK: Yes.

BN: Obviously, you get paid a little better and you have some extra responsibility, and it's an honor. All three of those things. Is it a lot of extra work and responsibility?

JK: No, no. Typically, the younger you are, the more work you do for the crew. You set up the hotels. Somebody's setting up the rental cars. We all kind of get involved in the flights, because when we go home, we take care of our flights going home and coming back.

BN: Then you're all going to different places.

JK: Yeah, yeah, but for the most part as a crew chief you are there just to mentor, and when things happen on the field, hopefully we've been around for a while – which is why we're the chiefs – and you should be able to step in and hopefully handle things in a way that they should be handled.

BN: I notice that you were the crew chief for the 2014 World Series.

JK: Yes.

BN: That must be one of the greatest honors you can have. I'm not asking you to toot your own horn, but that's my observation.

JK: Well, you feel good about the fact that Baseball appreciates your work. When I look out and see the umpires that are on the staff, there are so many good umpires and good people. When you get something like that, it's nice. There's no question about it. And you appreciate the fact that Baseball appreciates your work.

BN: I guess Dana DeMuth is one game ahead of you in working World Series games. He's got 29 and you've got 28.

JK: I did not know that. You must be talking active umpires. I'm just thinking about how many World Series guys on the staff have had.

BN: Yes, for sure. Not going way back when. Of course, you get in a World Series and you don't know if it's going to run four, five, six, or seven games.

JK: Right. Exactly.

BN: I'm hopping all over the place with my questions. Let me ask you: is there a reason you have #8?

JK: That was the number that they gave to me when I was hired. I was hired in '93. After the '92 season, Kibler and Doug Harvey retired. Harvey's number was 8. At that time, Eddie Vargo was the head supervisor on the National League and he gave me the number 8. I don't really know how I got it, but that's the number he gave to me.

BN: Do you remember any feelings of rivalry between the two leagues back then?

JK: There were perceptions that were different, but we all came from the same minor leagues. Some of the guys who were my best friends in the minor leagues went to the American League. At that time, when supervisors came around to watch you, if the American League saw you and liked you, they'd say, "We're taking his option" – which means the National League had to stay away. And vice versa.

We had some differences of opinion on things, but I never considered anything to be…we were happy with our staff. I was proud to be a National League umpire and I would have been proud to be an American League umpire, if they would have taken me.

BN: You were in a movie, around 2001? *Summer Catch.*

JK: Oh, yeah. Yes.

BN: How did that come about, that you were selected to be in that movie?

JK: They were filming a couple of the scenes in Cincinnati, and our crew was in Cincinnati. Somebody from Baseball called me up and asked me to be the one to go there and be the umpire. I told them I would. I went and sat in the dugout and they were filming these scenes over and over and over again. I think Griffey was playing there at the time, so he was there. When it was my turn to go out and shoot my scene, I went out and shot the scene and that was it. About an hour later, I went back and worked the plate that night.

BN: You make it sound like you did yours in one take.

JK: There wasn't a whole lot I had to do. I got behind the plate for a couple of pitches and they can cut and splice and do things however they do it. It was pretty quick and I was really out there for probably 10 or 15 minutes.

BN: Henry Aaron was there, too?

JK: Yes, he was.

BN: So was that about how long you were on the screen, for a few seconds?

JK: Oh, at the very end of the movie, it's just a couple of seconds. It's a shot of Griffey hitting. He actually didn't hit home runs, but he had swung the bat so many times, they said, "We've got one we can use" and that's what they went with. It's just a split second at the very end of the movie.

BN: I was in a movie once for just about that long.

JK: Do you get your residual checks for about 13 cents?

BN: It was in Kenya, in the 80's. I got paid something like 10 bucks for half a day's work. There weren't any residuals.

JK: I get checks every year from the Screen Actors Guild. Some are a dollar, some are two dollars, some are 15. It's just ridiculous.

BN: That they would spend the money on postage, yeah.

JK: Yes, exactly.

BN: Doesn't it just seem remarkable that of all the 76 major league umpires now, three of you are from Coldwater, Michigan?

JK: I think we're a little proud of that fact. And Scott Barry is from Quincy, which is right next door. It's right off Route 12, which runs right through Coldwater. It's 5-10 minutes away. It's right up the road. But, yeah, we're proud of the fact. There were a couple of umpires...I know of at least one who went through umpire school and umpired all the way through either Double or Triple A, as Tim was going through the minor leagues as well. Tim followed him. He did not make it, but obviously Tim did, and myself and Bill.

BN: A lot of people don't realize the many, many years you all have to put in to have the chance to make it to the major leagues, and I think that some people don't realize that some of you hardly ever get home during the season – though now you're allowed to have vacations during the season. The amount of travel, and never-at-home travel, there's something you sacrifice there, too. Is there anything you think that people may not fully appreciate about – not necessarily the difficulties, but about the responsibilities of the job?

JK: You've touched on a lot of things, but there's no question that the hardest part of the job is how much time we are away from our families. My neighbors have learned about me from how much I'm gone and how long I'm gone. To a person, they say, "I had no idea that was the life of an umpire." It looks one way for the fans, but it's a very different way. It's a stressful job. You're away from home, but there's a lot of good. You work seven, eight months out of the year. We do get four weeks off during the season now. Actually, I'm home right now. I'm off this week and then I go back and finish up in New York and D.C. next week. My family has been able to travel to different cities for the World Series and different things I was never able to do as a young boy or a young man. There's things like that that I think you appreciate. When I was young, I grew up in Michigan and I got to go to maybe one Tigers game a summer and that with your Little League function or what have you. My youngest son now, he goes to a Tigers game and he sits 10 rows behind home plate. I was always out in left field. They don't know any different, but I do, and I think all the umpires… there's things we can allow our kids to do, and our families to do, that we weren't able to do when we were young. That part of it is kind of neat.

BN: How many tickets are you allotted per game?

JK: We get six tickets. Each umpire gets six. As a crew, there's 24 available to people.

BN: Maybe you'd use those for the World Series, but for a regular game, that's quite a few. Maybe you don't get that many for the World Series.

JK: For the World Series, anything over four, you've got to pay for. It's different there.

BN: Six tickets, though. That's really generous of them, it seems to me.

JK: Yeah, it really is. That's negotiated, and that's been the way it's been ever since I've been in the big leagues. The way you do it now is a little different. Everything has to go through the computer and the league sees what you're leaving, but the actual number is the same.

When this year's all done, I'll have 24 ½ years in.

BN: How long do you think you'll keep doing it?

JK: I don't know. I really don't. I know the end is much closer than the beginning now. I don't really anticipate doing this into my 60s. I'm guessing three to four more years and that'll be it.

I will find something to do but it won't be...more and more, I think we realize it's a young man's game. It's a pretty physically demanding job as well as the mental part of things.

BN: That has impressed me from the very first interview I did with an umpire – the mental...stress, if you want to call it that, that you put on yourselves because of pride in doing the job right.

JK: Yes.

BN: More than one person has told me – especially before replay, which allows the possibility to correct plays now – even if their call was upheld, they might realize they could have been in a better position and still beat themselves up a little bit for that.

JK: Right. There's no question. Some games are bigger than others, but when you have a call that you have missed...first of all, you feel terrible about it, and secondly, it's on ESPN that night, all night and then through the morning, so instead of missing one call it seems like you missed 20 calls.

With replay, it's just a different element. There's no question you feel better knowing that, if there is a call missed, you were able to get it corrected, but it's difficult to work on the field sometimes after a missed call. You're thinking about, "What did I do? Was I too quick? Did I not get in the correct position to see it right?"

BN: That's interesting. I hadn't thought about that as much. Occasionally, before replay, you may have realized you made the wrong call, but you're not going to reverse yourself. Leaving that aside, typically you would assume you made the right call. But with replay you do, in some cases, get overruled, and then it has to weigh on your mind.

JK: It doesn't happen all the time, but occasionally when you go and put the headset on, you'll look up at the big screen and you'll watch it [while the umpires in New York are making the actual determination], and in some cases you can tell almost immediately, "I missed that one, and I can see why. I was blocked here..." Whatever the reason might be. There's other ones where you're watching on the big screen and you still can't tell, and it's overturned.

But we know in replay – when you're in that room – they can pull things up and you can tell if a guy's a quarter of an inch off the base, instead of being on the base, and so he's not safe now. He's out. As umpires on the field, we realize what's going on in that room because all of us spend time in that room.

Those are the calls that, when I was a young umpire, nobody blinked. Now you can see that quarter of an inch or half an inch. That's what the game is now. It's moved into that direction, and it's only going to continue to move further.

BN: I guess it was Bill Klem who said, in his heart he never made a bad call.

JK: (laughs) I think one thing we've learned over time, with those high-def cameras, is that there are times we thought we were right, but we were wrong, and we never actually knew it.

BN: But there are still plenty of times the cameras can't tell and it truly is inconclusive, so you're got to go with the call on the field because there's no evidence to overturn it.

[concluding remarks followed]

–end

12

Brian O'Nora

In a late-season burst over the final six weeks of the 2015 season, I was able to catch up with several other umpires, as their respective schedules brought them through Fenway Park.

Interview with Brian O'Nora on August 15, 2015

BN: You started working in the majors in 1992. Was it in 1996 that you first got hired? You worked a lot of games that year.

BO: '99. I was in the American League. There were no openings. All the openings were in the National League. I had 786 games, or something like that [before being hired.]

BN: How'd you first get interested in becoming an umpire?

BO: I read an article in *Sports Illustrated*. They had an article about umpiring schools. So I ended up in '85 going to Joe Brinkman's Umpire School. I was about 20, 21 when I read the article. I was working for an electrician and I was going to go into that field, but I ended up going to umpire school and – knock on wood – I've got a job today.

BN: So you went to umpire school and then the long process began.

BO: Yes, sir.

BN: When I was talking with Steve Palermo the other day, he said that even though the process was really long, most umpires have fond memories of the minor leagues.

BO: Oh, great memories! Absolutely. I had a lot of good memories of the minor leagues. We didn't make money. Jeff Kellogg, we were good friends

– we were in each other's weddings – when we got hired, we went to the extended spring program together and we made $19 a day. You had to pay your rent, your gas, so there wasn't much money left but it was a lot of fun. And actually we worked together our first year.

Bill's married to Jeff's sister. [Bill Welke]

We drove down to Florida together. Spring training. Extended spring, and then we drove back home. We worked the Appalachian League together and we were kind of partners. We became pretty close. He was taken by the National League and I was taken by the American League.

BN: Between the guys in the National League and the American League, did you feel a friendly rivalry back then?

BO: No, we were all just umpires. Calling games. That's it.

BN: Did you ever play baseball as a kid?

BO: I did, in high school. I caught and I played the outfield.

BN: So you got some time behind the plate back then.

BO: Yeah, a little bit. Actually, I never did any umpiring until I went to umpire school. That probably helped me because I didn't have any bad habits. So when they taught me…

BN: Last year, the first year of replay, there were two people that you ejected for something due to replay – Joe Maddon and Bud Black. What was that about?

BO: Once you go to Replay and Replay decides what it is, you can't argue any more. They came out and they were arguing. That's what it was about.

BN: There's nothing to argue about at that point. They could argue with whoever it was back in New York, but they don't even know who that was. Maybe they just had to make a show of it.

BO: I don't know.

BN: You have relatively few people that you've ejected over the years. I guess no one really likes to eject people.

BO: If they've got to go, they've got to go. If they just keeping pushing the envelope, once they get personal, it's easiest to get rid of them. That's all.

BN: I'm not talking about replay in particular, but when you make a call that – later, watching it on video or whatever – if you make a call that you realize was not the right call...

BO: That happens sometimes.

BN: Do you lose sleep over that sometimes?

BO: Oh, it tears you up, yeah. You want to find out why you missed the call. You look on the video and maybe your timing was too quick, maybe your angle wasn't good. You try to troubleshoot why you missed it so hopefully it doesn't happen again.

BN: I've had a couple of people tell me they've lost a lot of sleep over it sometimes.

BO: Back in the day you did. It used to tear you up if you missed something. Now that you have Replay, you can correct your errors.

BN: If it's challenged.

BO: They'll challenge anything.

BN: You don't want to give a challenge away too quick. But yesterday, the first play challenged was in the bottom of the first inning.

BO: It doesn't matter. They want perfection.

BN: And you do, too.

BO: Well, yeah, but no one's perfect.

—**end**

13

Mike Winters, Mike Muchlinski, Mark Wegner, and Marty Foster

Interview with Mike Winters and crew, August 17, 2015

In sequence, I talked with Mike Winters, Mike Muchlinski, Mark Wegner, and Marty Foster.

BN: The first games you umpired in the majors, were in 1988.

Mike Winters: Correct. I was hired by the National League in 1990.

BN: Tell me how you first got started in umpiring.

MW: I started umpiring Little League, at the Little League I played in, when I was 14. San Diego, California. The Clairemont Hilltoppers Little League. I fell in love with it. I found out right away that I was a far better umpire than I was a player, which isn't saying a whole lot (laughs), but I had fun doing it and kept wanting to learn more and to try to do it for a living.

When I went, it was called Bill Kinnamon's Umpire School, and that become Brinkman's.

BN: I think it was Steve Palermo who suggested a couple of days ago that a lot of umpires have really fond memories of the tough days when they were in the minor leagues.

MW: Oh yeah. We didn't have any money. We weren't staying in nice places. But we always seemed to be having a good time. It wasn't that the games didn't count, but they weren't under the scrutiny that you have in the major leagues.

BN: Most of the games wouldn't have even been on TV.

MW: It was very rare that there was a game on TV. I worked in the minor leagues from '82 through '89 and once in a blue moon you'd get a TV game. It was really rare.

BN: One of the thing I'd like to ask is when you make a call, if you later realize was the wrong call, does it really bother you a whole lot?

MW: Oh yeah. Yeah.

BN: It's not something you can shrug off as easily as it sometimes seems players do.

MW: I think it probably bothers them, too. When your whole job is based on your ability to get things right, when you get one really wrong, yeah, it bothers you. Nobody who's ever done this job has ever…not made a mistake. It's a particularly difficult job, even if you're good at it. It's true in every profession, but this job is tough and when you do make a mistake, it eats away at you.

BN: Have you got any relatives connected with baseball?

MW: No. I'm an only child and there's nobody before me or after me. My son has no interest in this.

[Some conversation followed about his equipment trunk, with all the family photos.]

BN: I'm interested in this. Some people don't realize that…it sounds funny to say this…but that umpires are people, too.

MW: That should be a bumper sticker.

BN: With replay now, do you find that…the call is reaffirmed most of the time. Do you find that something of a relief? You hate to have one go the wrong way.

MW: The calls have to be right. There's too much riding on the game and there's too much technology that can prove you right or wrong. Why not utilize it? Let's take advantage of the technology.

BN: Well, there was never a time you didn't want the calls to be right to begin with.

MW: Right. I've got no problem with it. If I've made a mistake, then let's fix it.

BN: In the end, after the replay, the final call is probably right. At that point, you don't have to worry that a bad call stood.

MW: Correct.

BN: I would think that might make you feel a little better.

MW: Just the fact that we're going to get it correct is…I'm finding that replay is another tool in our bag to help us get stuff right. We were getting like 96.9% correct, which is just amazing, but the ones we were wrong on…let's get those.

BN: You won't have to worry so much about ESPN running a reel, saying, "These are the ones that were right."

MW: They're still going to do that. When they're zooming in on an umpire, they're never going to say, "That was a great job."

BN: "Great positioning. Boy, did he hustle to get there…"

Mike Muchlinski: I grew up in central Washington state, about two hours east of Seattle. I played baseball growing up, up until I graduated from high school. I was a pitcher and outfielder and had never thought about umpiring. Over the summer I was trying out for a summer college baseball team and it just didn't work out. The head of umpires back at out little association there said, "Why don't you come do this with me?" I was like, all right. So I started doing it as a summer job, and then I went to school at the University of Washington in Seattle, and I was doing the same thing. I was going to classes in the morning and umpiring in the afternoon during the spring and summer. And I just fell in love with it. Met a couple of guys who were in the minor leagues and…

BN: Being around the game was one thing, but what did you like about umpiring in particular?

MM: I liked being around the game. At first, I just liked…it kind of completed the circle of what I thought to be a beautiful game, but didn't understand that side of it. It just completed my idea of how truly awesome the game is. Then, when I really got involved – when I went to umpire school and when I got to the minor leagues, I was like, "OK, there are guys who really, truly care about this profession" – and that it's a great profession. It's not just a bunch of amateurs doing this just for a couple of hours a day and collecting a check and moving on.

BN: You mean like football? I said that, you didn't!

MM: I really appreciated the amount of time and effort that guys put into this game. Being a young guy in the minor leagues and seeing what it took to succeed at the big-league level and trying to get there one day, yeah.

BN: One thing I've noticed is that a lot of the observers and supervisors – it's their job, but they put in a lot of time, from what I can tell, trying to help people coming up.

MM: A lot of time. There's more time put into it for us than just showing up at the ballpark, working a game, and going home. You know, you're not supposed to take it home at night – but you do take it home at night. The game. The mental aspect. You replay the game over and over in your head. You travel, you're away from your family at home. It's not just a simple three-hour night.

BN: You get video of each game that you can look at?

MM: Absolutely. The next day. I have access and I can analyze every single play that I have on the bases, or if I'm working the plate, and I also have video of plate work as well. Yeah, technology has helped us out as well. It's improved our profession and it's been great.

BN: Are you a major league umpire right now?

MM: Yes, I was hired in January of 2014. This is my second full season. I've worked with Mike [Winters] two years in a row. I worked with Mike a lot going up and down [when he was working in the majors as a minor league umpire] so I've spent the majority of the last five years with him. It was a nice transition to be able to go right to a crew where I understood the dynamic and knew the crew chief. That was helpful.

BN: Do crews switch up much from year to year?

MM: You will, but Mike, Mark [Wegner], and I all worked together last year. Marty's new, though we knew Marty. Next year, who knows? Mike and Mark have worked together a long time – six or seven years.

BN: I didn't know if they deliberately switched people up...just to do it.

MM: I think sometimes guys maybe need a shakeup. Maybe it's better for some guys to be somewhere else. I don't know.

BN: It can maybe even be a good thing to do for professional development, to become better at the job.

MM: Absolutely. Get a fresh take, from a different point of view's always nice.

BN: Have either of you got a little time?

Mark Wegner: If you can talk while we're playing cards, if that's all right. This is all part of preparing for the game.

BN: So let me ask you, Mark, how you got started. What interested you about umpiring in the first place?

Mark Wegner: I actually had zero interest in being an umpire. I played baseball all the way through high school. I had zero interest to do it but I was going to college, trying to make money, and my high school baseball coach talked me into giving it a try – just Little League stuff – and the first time I stepped on the field, I absolutely loved doing it. Little League through maybe 16-year-olds. For that summer, I did that, and then I decided I wanted to go to umpire school and hopefully learn more about it, hopefully come back and maybe do high school things or college. I ended up getting an opportunity in the minor leagues. I was only 19 years old at the time, and decided to give that a try and luckily it all worked out.

BN: What school did you go to?

Mark Wegner: The school at the time was called Brinkman-Froemming. Was there always a couple of schools to choose from? They changed names because they changed ownership.

Mike Winters: There were two schools when I went, and now I guess there's three.

BN: [speaking to Mike Winters] You've umpired about 3,300 major league games at this point, so you've only got about 2,000 more to catch up with Bruce Froemming.

MW: It's not going to happen. (laughs)

Mark Wegner: This is my 17th year. Ten years in the big leagues, and I spent seven years in the minor leagues before that. I was 19 when I went to umpire school. I was 26 when I was in the big leagues, and I'm 43.

Fenway Park umpires room card table, May 17, 2018. Photos of Hall of Fame umpires hang from the wall.

Marty Foster: I got into it like everybody did. I was in college and in summers I would go home and umpire Little League games. When it was apparent I wasn't going to play football anymore in college, I decided to pursue the umpiring route, just to get better games back home in Denver. Not to…I didn't even know about becoming a major league umpire.

So I went to Joe Brinkman Umpire School in 1987 and they selected me to go to the minor leagues from there and I thought, "I'm young enough" – I was 22 – "I'll hang out and see what minor league umpiring is all about." I got promoted regularly and I didn't spend too much time in any league. I was in Triple A before I knew it and in my third year, the American League started calling me up and down and then I got hired in '98. I've been working here 17 years now.

BN: Well, you've got some business to attend to here [playing cards, to get in some relaxation as a group before the game]. Thank you for taking the time.

–end

14

Dale Scott, Dan Iassogna, C. B. Bucknor, and Lance Barrett

[On the way in to the park, before entering the umpires room, Dale Scott went into Head Groundskeeper Dave Mellor's office to say hello for three or four minutes.]

Interview with Dale Scott and crew, Fenway Park, September 4, 2015

BN: I noticed that you have a degree in broadcasting.

DS: I've got an Associate of Science degree in Television Broadcasting.

BN: Does that mean you wanted to join the media?

DS: Well, you know what? I was working radio at the time – I was a disc jockey, started when I was 16, actually – and that seemed like the next progression, to go into television. I took a two-year degree at Lane Community College in Eugene, Oregon, where I grew up. Where I lived. I was also still working radio. It was a lot of fun. You learned all the aspects of it, from talent to floor director to cameras to lighting to technical director to audio, but I kind of got to the conclusion after I was done with that, that I didn't really want to go into television. (laughs) I really enjoyed radio then, and then I went to umpire school and all that stuff. It was a Top 40 station in Eugene – KBDF – from 1976 to '81.

BN: Do you keep an active interest in music at all?

DS: Not nearly as much as I used to. It's funny, we'll drive around [the crew] and we'll have Seventies on Seven, on Sirius, and I can tell you every year [of every track that comes on] or I'm pretty close. A lot of the music, though, I'm not…

BN: How'd you get into umpiring? You started at age 15?

DS: Yeah. Because I couldn't run, field, hit, or throw. I just loved baseball growing up and when my "playing days" were over, because I just didn't have the talent, a friend of mine had umpired the summer before – he was about a year older than me – he said it was a great summer job, you could stay involved in the game. That's how I got started. I really enjoyed it.

BN: Some Little League umpiring at first?

DS: Yeah. Just continued to do it. Moved up to doing high school and stuff, and then I also started doing football and basketball. At 21, I went to umpire school, and the rest is history.

BN: You officiated in some of the other sports for years.

DS: Oh, yeah, for about 18 years. I think '96 was about the last year. It overlapped a good 10 years with my work in the big leagues. Football overlapped a lot. I wouldn't get home until October and half the season's over in football, but I'd still do it. And of course I had all winter for basketball.

BN: One of your interests is politics.

CB Bucknor: He's running for President!

DS: You know, I've always been interested. When I was a kid, the conventions fascinated me.

CB: He's a Democrat, not a Republican like Michael J. Fox.

DS: I remember in 1968, my teacher took me to see Eugene McCarthy talk at the University of Oregon. Now, I was a little bored, to be honest with you. It seemed like it took forever. But it was an event.

BN: He spoke at Fenway Park that same year. I saw him here. He filled the park.

DS: I've always followed it from afar. I didn't really want to get into it. I've got a couple of friends at home who are a lot more involved in politics, so I pick their brains a little bit about stuff.

BN: You've been crew chief for how long?

DS: September of 2001 was my first month. The first full year was 2002.

BN: You get the assignments for the whole year before the season begins?

DS: We bid on schedules. There's 19 crews, so there's 19 schedules. You bid by crew chief seniority. Right now, I'm the fifth pick. You get the entire schedule for the year, including your off-weeks, your weeks of replay, and whatever. We do that usually in March sometime. That's how we get our schedule. So we've known we were coming here since March.

BN: You obviously don't have any minor-league umpires here now.

DS: Not now, but we've had them.

BN: What about for spring training?

DS: We get that in January. I'm in Phoenix every year.

BN: Is there one central person in MLB that you submit stuff to?

DS: Well, we have several supervisors. Randy Marsh is the head. Rich Rieker…We just saw Larry [Young] in Minnesota yesterday. Each supervisor has four or five crews, and Larry's been ours the last few years. We used to have Ed Montague.

BN: I was talking to Larry about the international side.

DS: Right, he's logged a few miles. I went to Australia last year when they opened there.

BN: Sydney. What was that like?

DS: It was a blast. We had a blast. I'd been to Sydney a couple of times before just for fun, but it was a fun, fun trip. We had a great time. We went wine tasting one day. We climbed the Sydney Harbour Bridge. Had a Sydney Harbour tour, a boat tour. It was fun. It was good.

BN: [to Dan Iassogna] One thing I read about you, you play the Scottish bagpipes?

Dan Iassogna: I do.

BN: That's a real Italian thing?

DI: (laughs) They actually started in Italy. It was a Roman thing, called the zampogna. It's a tuba with a bag, basically, but nobody pays it anymore. My daughters are Irish dancers. My mother's side of the family is Irish and English and Scottish. They started Irish dancing when they were really little, 5 years old. There was a guy who played the pipes that was in the school we went to. I had never played an instrument in my life and I asked him, "Did you play growing up?" And he said, "No, I picked it up when I was 40 years old. I had a good teacher..." I went, "Wow, I can do that." So, I started...I'm not very good at it. I'm better at the funeral stuff than the dance stuff.

BN: It's a little slower, right?

DI: I play the slow stuff better. I can play a couple of reels, a couple of hornpipes, and a couple jigs, and then I'm maxed out. A 6/8 march is about the fastest thing I can do, but I like playing.

BN: How did you get into umpiring to begin with?

DI: My dad was a high school football official. He retired as a school superintendent. I'm from Connecticut originally. That was his job in the summer, when he was off from teaching. When I went to college, he said, "Hey, a great way to make money is to start umpiring baseball games." So I used to umpire baseball. I went to UConn and in the summers I'd come home and work as much as I could during the week on a side job. It was my junior year of college. I wanted to be a fireman; that was my original goal. When I got out of college to become a fireman. Well, you know, 24 on, 48 off, and the 48 off I'll try to get on the college course.

My dad said, "I know an umpire. I student-taught with a guy named John Hirschbeck." He actually lived in the same hometown as my wife. He said, "I'll introduce you to him." So I met John, and then I was hooked. I want to see if I could make it or not. So I went to umpire school and got lucky.

I went to Jim Evans, when he was out in Phoenix. I graduated in '91 and went to Evans in '92. I started working in the big leagues in '98 as an up-and-down guy. Then I got hired in 2004. Steve Rippley retired and I got his job.

BN: It can take a while.

DI: It took me 12. It took me 12. I'm not a phenom, like Lance.

BN: I noticed Lance came up fast.

DI: Yeah, he didn't take very long.

BN: Maybe you've gotta have the right pull or something.

Lance Barrett: Or Replay come in.

DI: Or Replay.

BN: Yeah, six new people got hired the first year. That helps, right?

LB: That helps.

BN: And you worked in Japan at one point.

DI: It was a tour. They did that barnstorming tour at the end of the year [the 2006 Japan All-Star Series]. That was fantastic. I didn't realize that went all the way back to Lou Gehrig and Babe Ruth. I didn't know they started all that. I had no idea. It was a two-week trip. You were on the bullet trains and it was really a first-class experience.

BN: So, C. B. Bucknor.

CB: That would be me. The place to be, the C to the B.

BN: I actually sat next to your wife at Yankee Stadium about a dozen years ago.

CB: It had to be [a long time ago]. She doesn't come out to games much anymore. When the kids were younger, yeah. Three kids. Old Yankee Stadium? Yeah, she doesn't come out much anymore. She already put in her dues.

BN: What area of Jamaica are you from?

CB: I'm from the town of Savanna-la-Mar, on the west coast there, not too far from Negril.

BN: Most of my time in the music business was in Kingston.

CB: I've probably only been to Kingston five times in my entire life.

BN: I've been there more than you, then.

You came to this country in '73? How old were you then?

CB: Yeah, '73. I was 10 years old. My dad stayed back in Jamaica. My mom came first. Just relocated to get a better opportunity. Her brother sponsored her and got her to Connecticut. So Hartford, Connecticut was her first stop, and then from there she went to New York. She was in the health field.

BN: A growing field, still. What got you interested in umpiring? Up to age 10, were you even aware of baseball much?

CB: I got acclimated to it when I came to the country [USA]. It was close to cricket.

BN: It would be cricket or soccer there.

CB: Cricket or soccer, yeah, but I was drawn to it [baseball] because it was the closest thing to a sport that I was familiar with, which was cricket. I loved it from the very start.

BN: Did you play cricket as a kid?

CB: Well, you know, just playing in the yard. If I'm not mistaken, baseball is derived from cricket.

BN: So what got you into baseball, and umpiring in particular?

CB: Well, I played in high school. I played in college. I went to SUNY Cortland.

BN: What position?

CB: Center field. After I graduated...I had aspiration of getting signed but that didn't happen. I worked at New York Hospital Cornell Medical Center as a recreational therapist. I got five weeks' vacation after being on the job for five years so I used my vacation time to go to umpire school.

BN: That was your degree, in recreational therapy.

CB: Therapeutic Recreation, yeah. I wanted to become a better umpire. Some of the guys that I umpired with had gone to the school. Joe Brinkman's Umpire School in 1990. Just one thing led to the next. I moved on to the Umpire Development Program, started in the Penn League, and then just worked my way up. I was just fortunate – of course, there's some luck in there, too.

BN: I guess there always is, right?

CB: Yeah, anyone who says that there isn't, they're mistaken.

BN: Now you go back to Jamaica on a regular basis?

CB: Yeah, I have a program, a foundation. This is our 20th year. I started in 1995 with about 25 kids. Whenever you do anything for the kids there, they call it a "treat." When we started, we just called it the Treat. Then when I got my job [as a major league umpire, assigned #54] in '99, and I got a number, I added the number 54 to it and it's called Treat 54. In 2013, we got recognized by the Jamaica government as a charitable organization. Our official name is the Westmoreland Treat 54 Foundation.

We have the big party for the kids. Usually, it's the first Sunday in December. We started with 25 kids; last year we had over 800. Each kid gets a goodie bag with chocolate, peanuts, juice, and then we serve ice cream and popcorn, and then whatever their man gift is, whether it be a soccer ball, a hat, t-shirt...

BN: Are you dual citizen?

CB: Well, yes...

BN: Maybe you'll get a knighthood or something.

CB: (laughs) That's not important. We've expanded our program to seniors, where we help out a senior a year. We might re-do their floor and their sideboard, change out their windows. We also have a merit scholarship program for two of the primary schools. We've awarded over 21 merit scholarships for kids graduating from the sixth grade, going on to secondary school.

BN: It's good work.

CB: Well, you know, I figure I'm blessed. It's a blessing what I am doing and I'm just giving back to the community. I love that. That's like my *passion*.

BN: I can tell! Thank you very much.

CB: You're welcome. My pleasure

BN: Lance, can I ask you a few questions?

Lance Barrett: Absolutely.

CB: Ask him how he's going to get traded next year.

BN: Who are you going to get traded to?

LB: I've got C.B. on the trading block...

DS: They're jockeying for position to get back on this crew.

LB: For another umpire to be named later, and cash options, so we'll see...

BN: Were you all on the same crew last year?

DI: We were. Us three. [Dale, Dan, CB] He's new.

BN: Last year was your first year.

LB: Right. Full-time. Yes, sir.

DS: [Indicating Dan] He and I worked yesterday for our 1,000th game together. Which is a lot.

BN: How many games have you got overall?

DS: At the end of the season, I'll be about 20 short of 3,800.

BN: So you've still got about another 1,300 or 1,500 to go to catch up with Bruce Froemming, right?

DS: (wounded sound) Oooh.

BN: So how'd you get interested in becoming an umpire in the first place?

LB: My parents separated when I was young. My next-door neighbor umpired Little League games and I ran around with his son. We were 14. He said, "Hey, you want some spending money to put in your pocket, why don't you come umpire Little League games?" It ranged anywhere from $15 to $30 a game.

The funny thing is, I reached out to Dale and he responded to me and that's how he…

DS: It's my fault.

LB: It's his fault.

DI: And now they're working together.

LB: Found out about the umpire schools and which one to go to.

BN: How'd you know to reach out to him?

LB: A long story short, actually he ran Jimy Williams.

DS: Jimy Williams, right here in the '99 LCS. [October 17, 1999]

LB: I watched it, and we had just had a training seminar on handling situations so I reached out to him like, "Oh, man, that was awesome! I want to be an umpire." He actually wrote back and we met up when he came to Texas.

BN: You're from Fort Worth.

LB: Yes, sir. I am.

BN: It did interest me how quickly you did come up. You only worked 237 games. Some guys worked hundreds and hundreds.

LB: Right. Danny, unfortunately, he was going basically up the entire time in Triple A but there was just no jobs.

BN: Chris Guccione...

DS: Gooch the same way.

DI: He had twice as many as I had, and I had 600-plus. No jobs.

BN: So you were fortunate.

LB: Yes, sir. Very lucky. Very, very lucky.

BN: That brings up a question I had. When you finally get established as a major league umpire, do you get retroactive credit for all the major league games you worked as a fill-in, an up-and-down guy?

DI: The credit has a limit. It's not like a player. If the player does one game, they get one game credit. We do...is it a hundred games? If you have 100 games, you're hired as a second-year umpire. If you do 240 games, you're hired as a third-year umpire. The most you can start with is a third-year umpire.

LB: The way it works for us with our CBA...how we get paid is on your years of service. So like on the books, I have 3 ½ years because they credit some of that time for when you go up and down toward that. That's why for Danny it stinks, since he worked since '99 but the most you can get credited for is two years.

BN: He's been working since the last century.

You worked in the Venezuela Winter League. Was that any different in some ways? The fans...

LB: Yeah, it's nuts down there. I was telling these guys. Very passionate fans, and you see stuff down there you would never see here. In the playoffs, they have police in full riot gear with German shepherds along the warning track, just in case they start rioting over something. It's crazy.

BN: Pre-emptive.

LB: Yeah. I worked in the Dominican League, too. We had to forfeit a game one night because the fans were throwing stuff on the field – rocks, beer bottles...It's a little bit different down there, that's for sure. I remember laughing when we were going over the ground rules before the game and they said, "Oh, when the German shepherds..." I thought, "OK, they're busting my chops" but sure enough, seventh inning, you look down there and there's the German shepherds.

–end

The crew said they were heading on to replay after the Red Sox-Phillies series. Dan said of working replay: "It's a knee-saver."

15

Fieldin Culbreth, Jim Reynolds, and Paul Schrieber

Interview with Fieldin Culbreth and crew at Fenway Park on September 9, 2015

Jim Reynolds and Paul Schrieber also took part in the conversation. Manny Gonzalez declined on this occasion. I spoke with him at a later time, in April 2017.

BN: You used to play baseball growing up.

Fieldin Culbreth: I did. I played up into college, and then my senior year I had an arm injury – rotator injury – that today would be laughed at as far as injuries go, but in 1986 was a death sentence. Different times, different day.

BN: You can still throw a strike call, though, right?

FC: (chuckle) Right. But that ended the playing.

BN: And then how did you into umpiring? Had you done some beforehand?

FC: No, I had never umpired at all. It just so happened that my college baseball coach had been in professional baseball as an umpire. He talked about it from time to time, and some of the guys who were in the minor leagues with him would come over to the university from time to time and see him. Practice would stop and so we knew of his background. That kind of piqued my interest, especially when the baseball was over. Being young and have it end so abruptly, I didn't know what I wanted to do. I talked to him for a while and decided I wanted to go to umpire school.

Exchange of lineup cards before game between Yankees and Red Sox, July 26, 2019. Home plate umpire – Paul Nauert; Nick Mahrley, 1B; Fieldin Culbreth, 2B: D. J. Reyburn, 3B.

Jim Reynolds: Not much you can do with a UNC-Charlotte degree anyhow.

BN: What school did you go to?

FC: Joe Brinkman. There was two at the time. There was the Brinkman and the Wendelstedt.

BN: You were on a baseball scholarship? Did that end because of the injury?

FC: Well, that was my senior year. No matter what, that would have been the end of it.

BN: This is one of the older crews, if I can use the word "older" in quotation marks. A lot of crews have people of different tenures. Three of you guys all started in the twentieth century as major league umpires.

FC: You know, I haven't looked to see but I would be willing to bet that if I went and did the math on it, we would probably be at best middle of the road.

BN: I was just seeing that you had 18 years' service time, Paul is listed as 17, and Jim 15 ½, before this season began. Usually, you see one person might have 22 years, but another eight years, and the other two guys even less.

FC: We certainly have a good average, there's no doubt, but you might have a crew that's got a guy that's got 35 years and another guy that's got 19. Right off the bat, you've got more than 50 years right there.

BN: You're all pretty similar. You all either came in, in '98 or '99.

FC: That is correct.

BN: You all started before everyone was a Major League umpire.

FC: Yes, I originally worked in the American League. When I was coming up, I was just happy to be up and I certainly didn't have any time to realize any rivalry between the leagues.

JR: We had our hands full.

BN: One of the first things I noticed when I started interviewing people is that you all have these equipment trunks. Does it seem like they're the same kind of trunks you've had the whole time you can remember?

FC: Yeah, more or less. Yeah.

JR: I think they're a little lighter-weight now.

FC: Technology's taken some weight off here.

BN: How do you like Replay?

FC: It's here. It's baseball. It's the future of baseball, so I'm all in.

BN: Now you both are active in Umps Care. Maybe everybody is, to one extent or another. You're the Treasurer/Secretary [Jim Reynolds]. Tell me a little bit about it.

JR: Of the 76 guys, I'd like to say all of them are involved. We host 750 kids a year to the ballpark – kids awaiting adoption. I grew up in this area [Massachusetts]. I remember coming to Fenway. My father, my uncles, my grandfather would take me to ballgames. These kids don't have anybody to take them to a ballgame. It was such a formative part of my life, being in New England. That's the impetus behind the program. We bring them out. We show them the locker rooms. We take them on the field. We provide a goodie bag with Big League Chew, Cracker Jack, those kind of things. And we give them 20 dollars so they can act like a…I don't know the appropriate term here, but I use the term "normal kid" for a day. These kids won't have 10 dollars to buy a slice of pizza and a Coke. We try to do our best to provide them a normal day at the ballpark.

BN: I'll study the website to get some more details, but what should I know that I wouldn't pick up off the website?

JR: Well, just the amount of impact that we have, and the kids that we're dealing with. The hospital visits are extremely impactful. Two years ago, I was doing a hospital visit in Arizona at the end of August. I had a great visit. A lot of the parents were there, of course, because their kids were pretty sick. You go through these floors and you meet these kids, and they've all got smiles on their faces and they're all glad you came, thanking you.

BN: Did you wear something, like MLB shirts?

JR: Yeah. They know who we are.

That was the end of August. The first week of October, one of the mothers contacted us and said, "Hey, do you have any pictures from the visit?" Our executive director sent her some pictures. Her e-mail back was, "Thank you. I really appreciate this. Half the kids in these pictures are no longer with us."

It never comes across that way during the visit. They're so happy. Those are the kind of things, the kind of impacts that we're having.

BN: Coming from this area, you naturally know about the Jimmy Fund.

JR: Oh, of course.

BN: You talk about your operation there. I lost my mom to breast cancer when she was 49 years old. That's probably something that would have easily been addressed today.

FC: If it's caught early enough.

JR: All the umpires are involved. Umps Care is the organization it is now because our guys realize that we're blessed to be doing what we do and we finally got organized about giving back. We're all moving in the same direction.

BN: How old is it?

FC: In this...about 10 years old.

JR: We've all been pushing in the direction but we're really organized now – website, an executive director, those kind of things, after starting with a bunch of guys sitting around a table wondering how we can be the most impactful.

BN: How did you first become an umpire?

JR: A friend of mine got me involved at the University of Connecticut. Andy Baylock had a one-credit class up there and it was his way of getting free umpiring. Most programs don't have a JV program, but UConn had kind of a unique aspect. We would do the varsity fall games, which were just exhibition and then the JV regular season. That's how I got started. I put it off and put it off. He knew he always wanted to be an umpire. He knew John Hirschbeck. His father and John grew up in the same area, and so he knew that class was going on and he got involved right away. It took me a couple of years to get going, but that's how I got started.

Really, for me, I looked at it as a good way to earn some extra money on the weekends and at night, other than my summer job.

BN: There is a cluster of umpires that came from Connecticut, or came through Connecticut. I just met a guy upstairs last night who umpired 28 games – I looked it up – seven at each position. Matt Winans. I don't know if you ever ran across him.

JR: Matt was in the same program I was in at the University of Connecticut. He was the first one.

BN: He was just visiting. And then Dan Iassogna…

JR: He was the kid who got me involved. Danny's my best friend in the whole world; he was my college roommate and all that other stuff. That's how I got started.

BN: About three weeks ago at a charity baseball game, I ran into an old friend, Tim Samway. I told him I was working on a book about umpires and he said, "If you ever run into Dan Iassogna, tell him you met his babysitter." So I did, when I saw Dan last week. This guy was his babysitter when Dan was very young. Dan remembered him.

JR: The Hirschbeck brothers – Mark and John – I had the opportunity to work with both of those guys.

Umps Care group welcomed pre-game by Paul Nauert (L) and D. J. Reyburn (R), Fenway Park, July 27, 2019.

FC: Manny's going to decline. [Manny Gonzalez preferred not to be interviewed.]

BN: I was in Caracas a few years ago.

Manny Gonzalez: You survived?

BN: Yeah, I survived. I wanted to go to Salto Angel [Angel Falls] but I planned my trip so I was there during the season, so I could see a couple of baseball games.

MG: You went to some of the games?

BN: A couple of games. I've been to Cuba, too, and there were some similarities. Both places I saw a couple of players come right outside of the park, in full uniform, and start talking to people.

MG: Oh yeah.

BN: You wouldn't see that here!
   [to Paul Schrieber] First thing I wanted to ask you – your dad was a Triple-A umpire?

Paul Schrieber: Yeah. Harry Schrieber.

BN: That might have had something to do with how you got interested. How long did he do that for?

PS: He did it about seven or eight years. Northwest League and Pacific Coast League. His last year was '72 so I would have been 6 years old. Then he was a supervisor for a while and he would actually work with some of the Triple-A guys in Portland. I probably saw him umpire until I was maybe 9 or 10 years old.

BN: Fairly formative years.

PS: Yeah, though, to be honest, I didn't grow up wanting to be an umpire. I played. Played in college, just like Cubby [Culbreth], and it wasn't until college was over that my dad said, "I think you should think about being an umpire."

BN: What position did you play?

PS: Catcher.

BN: Behind the plate.

PS: Yeah. I took a few steps back. (chuckles) He had a few friends who made it to the big leagues and I gave them a call and said, "What do you think? Do you recommend it? Do you regret it?" They all said, "Go for it." They said, "You'll get to see the country. It takes a man to go on the field." They highly recommended it, so off I went.

BN: And then you had to put in 10 or 12 years…

PS: Yeah, they didn't tell me that too much! (laughter) I set off on the journey and eight years later I made it. That was nice.

BN: Is your dad still alive?

PS: Yes. He's 75 and his health has kind of taken a turn for the worse. The last five years, he's been batting Alzheimer's. [Some more personal discussion about families and health issues follows.] My mom passed away at 50; I heard what you said. Breast cancer. She had the real aggressive kind.

BN: I read that you left a ticket for her at your first game. [after she had died]

PS: It was very difficult. I told the league president at Double A, at some point I'm going to have to go home during the season – because she was terminal. I went home in May. My dad said it was time to come home. It was Mother's Day. I wanted to stay, but my dad said it could be two or three months. You've got to go back and work. I went back. It was the hardest thing I ever did, was to leave my mom. She died three weeks later.

BN: It's good you were able to see her again near the end and spend some more time together.

PS: Yeah, we did. We were really close.

BN: One of your hobbies is travel. Don't you get enough travel during the baseball season?

PS: It's a big world out there. I love going to Europe and just seeing buildings that are hundreds of years old. I don't travel as much, but I do like to. My mom kind of got cheated. She didn't get to travel. I just kind of said, "You know what? I'm going to have a balance. I'm going to save my money and go some places and see what's out there." My brother, he's just fine and content at home. He's in the car business. Actually, now he's in the motor home business. He's a finance manager. He's got a good job up in Oregon. He wasn't an athlete, but he's a good businessman.

BN: Where do you get let off here? I never thought to ask.

PS: Right where they park all the cars. [Outside Gate D]

BN: One thing you don't have to worry about too much is getting recognized.

PS: No. But the car kind of gives us away. It's a big Escalade.

BN: When it arrives, all the people around probably wonder who's in there, and then you guys come out and they probably think, "Who the heck are they?"

PS: (laughs) It's good to be incognito.

BN: If you were David Ortiz stepping out, you'd get swamped.

PS: When I was younger, I used to come out of the ballpark and they'd say, maybe thinking I was a ballplayer, "Sign that" – but now I don't get that anymore. I'm getting older. But it's a good job, especially a couple of months from now when the check keeps coming and there aren't any games. I've got two boys.

BN: Do you get it spread out over 12 months?

PS: Yeah. I just miss my boys. There's a lot of goodbyes. They're 10 and 12. It's all they know. And they're good with it. When I'm home all winter, I tell them, "I gotta go eventually." I'm coaching and driving them to school.

BN: You live in the Phoenix area?

PS: Scottsdale.

BN: So once in a while, you get assigned to work there.

PS: Yeah, I worked there twice this year. That's always fun. I'll bring them around the locker room. They made a couple of trips. They came to the Bay Area; we were there a week. We went to Alcatraz and stuff like that. And I worked the All-Star Game this year. That was kind of a last-minute deal. I brought them to the All-Star Game. They had a blast. My oldest one, he's really a jock. My younger one could kind of care less, but I still want to bring him for the experience.

BN: You never know when kids might change.

PS: It was a pretty big honor working the All-Star Game.

BN: I'm going to a board meeting of SABR in Phoenix near the end of October and one of the people I'll hope to visit at the time is Mark Letendre, because he's right there in Scottsdale.

PS: He's an amazing resource for us. Anything you call him about – anything – he's on top of it. "My knee hurts." "OK, you've got to do this, this, this, this. I'm going to set you up with this doctor…" "My filling fell out of my teeth." "OK, I've got the team dentist. You're going to meet at this time. Here are the directions. Give him a ring." He's really a great resource. I live in Phoenix, and he's got a rehab place. He sets you up. He's amazing. He will give you a really good perspective on how we look now as opposed to 20 years ago. You'll have a good talk with Mark. He's great.

–end

PART II

Being an Umpire

We've heard from a good number of today's umpiring corps, talking about themselves and their profession, often in depth. At this point in this book we're going to switch gears a little and hear from a number of other umpires on various subjects that have been introduced to get a more complete picture of their lives and work.

1

The Varied Backgrounds of Some of Today's Big-League Umpires

We've heard where a couple of dozen of today's umpires come from. Phil Cuzzi's father was a sheet-metal worker; Ed Hickox's was a factory worker, as was Tim Timmons'. Both of Jim Joyce's parents worked at Jeep Chrysler. John Tumpane's father was a salesman and his mother a nurse. Ted Barrett's mother was a nurse, too; his father was in the Navy, a radioman and then a recruiter. Laz Diaz's parents immigrated from Cuba shortly after the revolution there; his father had cut sugar cane. Ron Kulpa's father drove a forklift for 35 years, a teamster who worked for the Midwestern grocery chain Schnucks. Gary Cederstrom's father was a teamster, too, a truck driver. Carlos Torres's dad was a truck driver in Venezuela, often working away from home. Jerry Meals's father was a laborer for GM in Lordstown, Ohio. Jeff Nelson's parents were both elementary school educators; his father was an elementary school principal. So was Steve Palermo's father. Rich Rieker's father was a letter carrier. Paul Emmel's father was a chemist at Dow Chemical for 35 years. Andy Fletcher's father officiated high school football also for something like 35 years. Paul Nauert's father worked in a brewery and then, after it closed down, became a maintenance man for DuPont. Scott Barry's father works at an insulation factory. Gabe Morales's father worked for the San Jose Police Department; his mother was a high school guidance counselor. Manny Gonzalez's father was from Spain, his mother from Venezuela, where Manny was born and raised. His father sold automobiles for a car dealership in Caracas and later became manager in a Home Depot-like store.

They became involved in umpiring in any number of ways. Some had started other careers first – Dale Scott as a radio DJ and Phil Cuzzi as a junior high school graphics arts teacher.

Mark Wegner was playing baseball and said he had zero interest in umpiring – until he started doing it as a way to make some extra cash while in college, and fell in love with it. It's interesting how many had become "professionals" as young teenagers, picking up a few dollars working Little League or school games. Brian O'Nora read about umpire school in a *Sports Illustrated* article. In Lance Barrett's case, a next-door neighbor got him involved. James Hoye went to a clinic that Tim Timmons led.

Some had relatives who had officiated sports at one level or another. Angel Hernandez's dad started a program for umpires in the local Little League. Jeff Kellogg's father was the high school athletic director at Coldwater High School in Michigan. Fieldin Culbreth's father worked as a high school baseball coach but had umpired professional baseball.

The Connecticut connection brought in two college roommates: Dan Iassogna's father was a high school football official, and Jim Reynolds's father knew John Hirschbeck. Paul Schreiber's father Harry worked as a Triple-A umpire at one point. Clint Fagan's father was a high school umpire. John Tumpane's father refereed a lot of basketball. As we learned, Tim Timmons's father Jack Timmons not only worked in the fabric factory and selling concrete block, but is in the Ohio High School Athletic Association Hall of Fame for officiating.

How did Mike Estabrook get started?

Mike Estabrook: I just started kind of by accident. When I was 17, I was too old to play Little League any more but I still went out to the ballparks and one day the umpire didn't show up for a 10-year-old game. They were begging people to umpire and they asked me if I would. I said. "No." They told me they'd pay me like 20 bucks, so I said, "Sure."

That was the first game I ever did. They just bribed me with 20 bucks and I went out there and everybody started screaming at me and yelling, and I said, "Yeah, this is pretty cool." That gave me a lot of power in my right hand. I'll keep doing it.

Dan Bellino was working for a Federal judge before he ever umpired. He explained that his background was little different: "I wanted to go to law school since I was like 8."

BN: Whatever possessed you to even *know* about law school at the age of 8?

Dan Bellino: My mother was a court reporter in Federal court, and I loved the suits they wore. That's what really got me; I loved the suits they wore.

I didn't umpire my first baseball game until I was 23. I was a catcher in high school [Loyola Academy in Wilmette, Illinois.] But I was more of a basketball guy. I started refereeing basketball at 18. Umpiring was a complete afterthought. I never even considered it until about halfway through law school."

Dan is Dr. Bellino, with a J.D. degree – a law degree.

BN: Your area was always real estate law?

DB: Yeah. It's the only area that doesn't require me to be there.

BN: You and your father founded a real estate agency.

DB: Yeah, a RE/MAX. My father's been in real estate for 30 years. After her work as a court reporter, my mother became the comptroller for the Probation Department. She was in charge of the whole budget for the Federal probation. When I went to law school, that gave me a lot of contacts. And free parking at any Federal government building.

Dan Bellino's equipment trunk, August 2018, Fenway Park.

Dan's final law school research paper was about the mass resignation of major league umpires in 1999. His work for the Federal judge was with Judge Charles P. Kocoras.

DB: He's a Cubs fan. He just came to Wrigley when I was there a couple of weeks ago. He's a great man. I was with him when he became the chief judge. So, unknowingly, I got a huge promotion. It was just like dumb luck that he became the chief and I had the greatest internship/externship of anybody in law school – because he was the chief. I got very lucky there.

BN: Did he give you encouragement to go to umpire school?

DB: First he tried to talk me out of it. He asked, "How much money do they make?" He said, "You know, every lawyer who walks in there, that's the minimum of what they make." I said, "No, I understand." His season tickets were right behind home plate. He was great. The only thing he said to me is, "I can't guarantee there's a job for you if you come back in a year." I said, "I understand."

Adam Hamari's father owns a local paint store; his mother is retired from work as a receptionist at a hair salon. He started early. "I was self-driven. I cut lawns from when I was 11 years old up until I was 21 or so. I hated asking my parents for money. I never did, and I never liked when they gave it to me because I knew we didn't have a lot. I started when I was 12. They needed umpires in what was called the minor leagues – 9- and 10-year-olds. I wanted to make a little bit of money. If I can make $25 doing two games…I would do that.. And then I started assigning umpires for 12-year-olds when I was like 14. So I could assign myself games that worked around my dad's schedule, where they could drop me off. It worked out really well.

Then I went to school, finished my degree, and went to umpire school the next week. I was 22. I graduated with a bachelor's degree in math education. Northern Michigan. I went to umpire school the year the minor leagues were on strike. When we finished the evaluation course, they said, "Well, we can't promise you that you will have jobs." That was very unnerving because if the minor leagues didn't settle – which they actually didn't; it took two months and like two weeks. I went, "Shoot, what am I going to do now?" So I started going for my master's degree.

So I have a master's degree in Education Administration. I started that, and then I got hired. But in order to keep your teaching certificate active, you had to continue to take classes in the offseason to keep my certificate active. Once I got my master's, I thought, "Now what?" But things were starting to work out.

Vic Carapazza worked as an M.P. in the U.S. Air Force before becoming an umpire. "My mother worked in the restaurant business and my father worked with my uncle in the painting business. We didn't have a lot growing up, but we wouldn't have known any different."

After college, he went into the Air Force for a two-year stint and was stationed in Kuwait, but was sent home on a medical discharge. What was his specialization in the Air Force? "It's kind of like now. I was a cop. Military police."

After he returned, he worked with a friend doing some telemarketing but in 2003 went to umpire school. His first experience came thanks to Hank Webb, who had pitched for the New York Mets in the early to mid-1970s. "He takes credit for my career. It's sort of an ongoing joke with him. I used to play instructional ball at Joe DiMaggio Field across from the Phillies' spring training now. I was 16, something like that. He would go, "Hey, Vic. You want to make 20 bucks?" I'm like, "Sure, Mr. Webb." "Go put on that catcher's gear on." I would play a game at 6, and then I would put catcher's gear on and go behind my buddies and umpire a game. That's how I got started. Twenty bucks in high school at the time was huge.

"I think as a kid, you want to walk out here and play. At 16. I didn't want to walk out here and be an umpire, at the time. Then you get older and you realize you can't play anymore. And it's the only other job on the field."

Mark Carlson served in the Marine Corps. He'd been a catcher in high school and college ball, so he'd put in time behind the plate. "Yes, and then as a way to earn extra money instead of working at a fast food place or the mall or something like that, a friend of mine got me into umpiring. In college, and in high school as well, I started umpiring Little League and stuff. Yeah. It continued. I originally had the dream of making it as a player, but that didn't happen. Then I joined the Marine Corps after I was done with college. I got out of the Marine Corps and then a friend told me about umpire school. Pat McGuinness. He was a minor-league umpire at the time. He's the one who told me about umpire school.

"Even today, people still think that we're just local guys in the city who umpire the games. I had no idea about umpire school. He had gone to Brinkman/Froemming's two years prior. I didn't have anything going on at the time, so I said I'd give it a shot."

Several umpires had parents that did some officiating. Quinn Wolcott's parents were both elementary schoolteachers, his father teaching P.E. "My dad and uncle were local sports officials. They did football, basketball, baseball. My dad did softball. I started young. When I was 12, they said, 'OK, it's time to get a job. You want to mow lawns or paint fences?' I started umpiring tee ball when I was 12. When I was 13, I worked with 10-year-olds. When I was 14, I worked with 12-year-olds. Up through high school. It was $12 a tee ball game and $15 for a machine-pitch game."

Andy Fletcher said: "My dad officiated high school football for 35 years or so, maybe more. A little small college, but mainly high school. He also started a little league football league back in the middle Sixties. He coached originally but then for years he officiated every Saturday and Sunday afternoon. I would officiate with him. There were some really, really good high school and college officials that would work that league with him. They taught me a lot about officiating. Even though it's a different sport, they taught me the basics of officiating. So much of it is about handling situations. The same principles apply in handling situations.

In Todd Tichenor's case, it was his mother that got him started. His father had been head football coach in Holcomb, Kansas. "I was a young, young little boy. My dad passed away from cancer when I was 6. My mom, for a second job, she was supervisor of the ballfields. So I started ball-shagging. I started scorekeeping. Eventually, I realized that umpiring paid more than those. So I said, I'm going to start umpiring. So I applied. I'd go down to the ballfield and instead of ball-shagging I'd make a little extra movie money and it just grew into a passion for me.

I started ball-shagging when I was 8. Scorekeeping 'til I was 10. I did my first men's competitive fast-pitch softball game when I was 15. It's been a passion, and grew into a passion from there.

I played junior college baseball and basically this was a job for me. I couldn't ask my mom for movie money, you know. I had to make my own."

Doug Eddings's mother was also key. "I started umpiring when I was 12 or 13 years old. Growing up as a kid, I loved baseball. It was my favorite sport. I loved playing it. I loved everything about it. Being from Las Cruces, New Mexico, I never had a favorite team, but when I think I was about 12, they showed a lot of Cubs games on TV, a lot of Braves games, but I didn't really have a favorite team. I just loved the game, loved seeing the players, loved watching it, everything about it.

"I was playing one summer. My mom was kind of in charge, on the board of the Little League, and after I got done playing a game, she said, "We're short two umpires. They didn't show up. You're going to have to go umpire."

"Nobody wanted to be an umpire. I'm like, 'Mom, I'm not doing it.' 'Yes, you are, Mister. You're going to do it.' I had to work the bases, and I worked two or three games. It was kind of enjoyable, and after the two or three games, my mom gave me like 30 or 40 bucks. I said, 'What's this?' She said, 'Well, you're actually making money to do this. Little League pays.' Back then, it was like $10 a game or something like that.

Umpire assignments posted in Red Sox dugout, April 17, 2011: Doug Eddings, HP; Dana DeMuth, 1B; Kerwin Danley, 2B; Paul Nauert, 3B.

"My parents didn't have a lot of money. From then on, I've always loved it. I played all the time and then afterwards I would umpire. I played high school baseball, and always umpired on the side. One day in high school, when I was like 15, I read in *The Sporting News* about the whole process of going to umpire school, and I thought, 'That's what I want to do.' Ever since I was 15, I wanted to be a major league umpire."

Carlos Torres comes from Barquisimeto, in the state of Lara, Venezuela. "My dad was a truck driver. It was kind of hard – always away from home. I was studying at the university and in December, me and my brother… couldn't afford what we wanted. There was a clinic for umpires organized by the Criollitos organization in Venezuela. We did that to have money in December for new clothes and to help our mom and, of course, our dad.

"I fell in love with the job. I was making money. I was single. No kids, nothing. I was studying and making money, and I just fell in love with the job – and here I am.

"I met a big guy in my city, a professional umpire who was working in the Venezuelan Winter League. He saw me work a couple of games and he saw something. He invited me to a clinic, to see if I was going to be able to make it to the Winter League. It was in 2002. They gave me a chance to work in a parallel league for guys who do not get hired by the Winter League. I worked in that league for two years.

We worked in the Summer League. I was umpiring all year. I worked in the Winter League for four years before I came to the Major League Baseball umpires camp in LA in 2008. There was a minor-league supervisor – Jorge Bauza – who went to Venezuela. At that time, there was only one Venezuelan who was working in the United States – Manny Gonzalez. That supervisor asked me to come to the U.S. I said, 'Of course, that's my dream. But I don't have the money to pay for the school.' It was too much. He said, 'Okay, I'm going to bring you to the school. They give seven scholarships every year. You show them that you can do it, and that's what I can do for you.' That was great, but then I started thinking of the plane ticket. I didn't have the money to play for the roundtrip. The Winter League helped; they bought the ticket for me.

I came to umpires camp. I made it. They paid for the umpires school and my plane ticket, too. That was great. That's how I started."

David Rackley has been interested in baseball since he was an infant. "I played as a kid, since I was 3. My dad was an avid baseball fan and he played. I grew up in Houston, south of Houston. He grew up in Cincinnati and he tried out for the Cincinnati Reds, and he actually got invited back but he enlisted in the Marines – this was during Vietnam – and then he went to Vietnam for 13 months. When he came back, he didn't pursue any baseball career.

"So I played when I was a kid and then when I was 15...My dad had started umpiring. He had coached us when we were little, and then he started umpiring because he loved the game. I have two brothers, an older brother and a younger brother. He was coaching all of us. And then when I was about 13 he stopped coaching and he would umpire. Little League, Pony, and then some high school stuff. When I was 15, he was going to work a Little League game and the guy he was supposed to work with called him and told him he couldn't make it. He called a couple of other guys and couldn't find anybody. So he just gave me his uniform and I went and stood out there. I had never done it before but he said, 'You play the game. You know how it works.' It was little kids. I think it was either

T-ball or coach pitch, where basically they run around the bases and after five runs they switch sides. They don't even keep score, and everybody gets a sno-cone after the game. But they paid me $25."

He was a professional.

"When I realized that you could actually make money, as a 15-year-old, that was a lot of money. I started doing that. I wanted to work as many games as I could. I just fell in love with it. Then when I was 17, I hurt my shoulder playing football so that summer I couldn't play baseball on the varsity team so I just started umpiring – I could umpire varsity baseball that year because I wasn't playing. That's when I really felt it was something more than just doing it for extra side money. There was a passion there. I was with peers that I know and who knew me. To perform at a high level, at the varsity level, it was more than just getting a paycheck. I had a desire to perform [with excellence]. And then I went to a Gerry Davis clinic when I was 17. I didn't really know about umpire school until one of the minor-league umpires…he had a few minor-league umpires who were instructors, and one of them pulled me aside and asked if I had ever thought about going to umpire school. I said I didn't know there was such a thing. That's when I started looking into it. When I was 18, I went to the Harry Wendelstedt Umpire School and got placed."

Gabe Morales, who was raised in Santa Clara, California, couldn't get a "real job" – so he took up umpiring. His father worked for the San Jose Police Department. His mother was a high school guidance counselor. When he was a junior in high school and playing second base for the high school team, he wanted to earn a little spending money.

"I applied to some fast food and mall-type places, but my hours – I just practiced all the time and I had my schoolwork, so I didn't have enough time to get kind of a real job, but I knew the league I had grown up playing in – the youth league – they used teenage umpires. I got in contact with them and I started doing doubleheaders on Saturdays. Umpiring was good, because it was just weekends and in the season."

Coming from a family of educators, he didn't jump into umpiring full-time but instead graduated from Santa Clara University and then went taught for a while. "Teaching's always been in the background. After I graduated from college, I moved to Mexico for a little bit and I was teaching English down there for a little bit. I went to school in Guadalajara and I took a job in the state of Queretaro, which is right near Mexico City."

Jerry Meals was just trying to make this way in life, maybe umpire high school baseball.

JM: Where I grew up, there was a school behind my parents' property – 150 yards away. My mom was just a mom, and she worked at a grocery store as a clerk for a little bit. My dad worked building cars for General Motors in Lordstown, Ohio. Laborer.

But there were these two ballfields and there were a bunch of kids in the neighborhood so we played ball all the time. It was just what we did. When I wasn't playing, I just asked the local [Little League] commissioner if there was any chance I might be able umpire some of the games. I was 13. I started doing the 9-year-olds. I wasn't much older.

When I went to umpire school, it was just to…I'd never done anything else, other than Little League stuff – I was going to see if I could make a little extra money doing college and high school. Actually learn how to umpire.

BN: That's why you went to umpire school, not aspiring to work in professional baseball.

JM: I had no clue what professional baseball involved. No. I knew there were the major leagues, but I had no idea what the minor leagues were about.

BN: Or how long it could take to get from one to the other.

JM: No. No idea. I ended up getting into the game and I was just on the road, learning.

BN: You put in your years, like everybody has to. Was it just something that "got you" – you got the bug, so to speak? Or maybe it was just that once you started, it was easier to just keep going.

JM: You know what? It was just one of those things. It was not easy, by any means. I really didn't have a whole lot of other things to fall back on. I didn't go to college. If I weren't umpiring? I'd be a mechanic. Work on cars. That's what I did before I went to umpire school. At least, I'm guessing that's what I'd be doing. But I love baseball. I love the game.

BN: When you played, what did you play?

JM: Most of the time, second base. Being in it and then learning what it was like, and knowing now what the steps…how to get to the big leagues, I just thought, "You know what? I'll just keep going until they fire me or whatnot" and I just kept moving up. It took a long time, 15 years. It was just one of those things.

2

Relatives in the Game

As it happens, and perhaps not unexpectedly, there are several umpires who had relatives who preceded them. We've seen that Paul Schreiber's father worked as a Triple-A umpire, and several others had fathers or uncles who officiated in one sport or another. There are a few current umpires who had fathers, or others in the family (we have noted that Bill Welke followed in his older brother's Tim's footsteps, so to speak.) And that Jeff Kellogg is related to the Welkes through marriage. John Hirschbeck, who I interviewed in his final year of 2016, had worked in the majors for 32 years, 1983-2016. His younger brother Mark began major league umpiring in 1987 and worked until 2003. They were the first two brothers to umpire major league baseball at the same time. Hip replacement surgery forced Mark to leave the field.

Brian Gorman's father Tom Gorman pitched in a few games for the 1939 New York Giants. He returned to the minors, but then served in the Army during the Second World War, stationed for some time in North Africa. Indeed, in Tom Gorman's book, he talks about being in Libya and his Jeep running over a landmine that killed the driver.[7] During our conversation, Mark Carlson spoke up, asking Brian, "What did your dad do in the Army? Brian's response: "I think he was a sergeant at the end, but I don't know what his duties were. I asked if he brought anything back from the war, and he said, 'Yeah, myself.'"

Tom Gorman played baseball in the Mexican League after his return, later offered a job umpiring in the New England League – even though he had never umpired a game in his life. By 1951, he was working in the majors, a National League umpire, and worked until 1976, working in nine no-hitters and in five World Series. He later worked for a while as an umpire supervisor. Tom Gorman wrote the 1979 book with Jerome Holtzman, *Three and Two* (Scribner's). He notably said, "When I go, I want to be buried in my umpiring suit, holding my indicator."[8] And he was.

Brian Gorman holds a dual degree from the University of Delaware, in Marketing and Economics. "I started doing some high school and college ball when I went to college," he says. "I joined the local association and I was doing high school and small colleges around the Delaware area. Around sophomore or junior year, I went to my dad and talked about going to umpire school. His advice was to finish college first – good advice – and so after I finished the University of Delaware in 1981, in January of '82 I went to umpire school."

Gorman isn't as uncommon a name as, say, Wendelstedt, so a lot of people didn't realize the connection between father and son. Tom Gorman retired from the field when Brian was 18. He died while Brian was working in the Southern League, working his way up the ladder. But his father had exposed him to the game and served as a resource.

BG: He used to take me and my sister and two brothers out, one week at a time individually. Like a two-city trip. It was fun, yeah. As early as I can remember, from when we were little kids. You'd get to fly in planes and stay in nice hotels. That was cool.

BN: Did you take a lot of ribbing from other umpires as you were working your way through the minors?

BG: I think maybe a lot of people didn't even know. Obviously, my fellow partners knew and everything, but it was actually beneficial having a wealth of information at my fingertips. All I had to do was call him as I was trying to figure out things myself. He liked to come travel; he used to take a couple of days and I remember him coming when I was in the Florida State League and the Southern League, he came out for a week. In fact, the week before he died, he came out and saw the Southern League All-Star Game. That was the last game he saw me work.

As it happens, Tom Gorman worked home plate for the first game at Shea Stadium (April 17, 1964) and Brian Gorman worked first base at the last game at Shea (September 28, 2008). Was Brian aware of that connection? "Yeah. In fact, the Hall of Fame asked for my hat."

Jerry Crawford (4,371 games from 1976-2010) was the son of Shag Crawford (3.120 games, from 1956-75), a Crawford thus working games for more than 50 years, from 1956 through 2010.

And there were the Runges, a three-generation umpiring family who worked a total of 7,399 games: Ed (2,639 games, 1954-70), his son Paul (3,196 games, 1973-97), and Paul's son Brian (1,564 games, 1999-2012). As with the Crawfords, there was no overlap.

Hunter Wendelstedt and Mike DiMuro both had fathers who preceded them as major league umpires. Lou DiMuro, Mike's father, served as an American League umpire for 20 years, from 1963 through 1982. He worked 2,659 major league games. Mike's older brother Ray (born a year and a half before Mike) also umpired, working some 99 big-league games from 1996-1998. Mike himself broke into the majors in 1997, and through the 2018 season has worked 1,878 games.

BN: It may seem obvious, given your father, but how did you decide you wanted to go into umpiring?

Mike DiMuro: Pretty much just growing up around it, and my father doing it for so long, that was kind of the impetus for wanting to get into it. But he always wanted us to go to college. He said, "Whatever you guys want to do, get your education first and then go ahead." Fortunately, I was able to do that. I went to University of San Diego.

They used to call us twins in the minors because we look so much alike, but we're not really twins. He started two years before me.

BN: Ray worked several games in '96 and '97, but only 12 games in '98.

MD: I guess it was just that it wasn't looking like he was going to be in line to get a job. I think he was just kind of reading the tea leaves. He had his education and in the offseason he'd always been working in finance. That was kind of his other chosen career. It just didn't look like he was going to make it [in umpiring], so he decided to retire. He went to the University of San Diego. He owns a financial planning firm in Scottsdale, Arizona.

Their father Lou was killed while crossing the street after a game, struck by a car on a very dark street.

MD: Just didn't see him. No one's fault. Just an accident.

BN: I'm sure he would have been proud of you both, following in his footsteps.

MD: Yeah, I would think so.

BN: He didn't tell you, "Stay away from umpiring."

MD: No.

BN: Had you already started umpiring, maybe in Little League or something, while he was still alive?

MD: Yeah, I was doing Little League. After I finished playing, I would umpire. He saw me work one game, so that was nice.

BN: Let me ask you, what do you like most about umpiring?

MD: Gosh. It's just such a great profession. I think that always growing up in my family and being around it, I always knew since I was little that it was what I wanted to do. To be able to achieve your childhood dream and follow in your father's footsteps is the greatest.

Harry Wendelstedt worked 4,500 major league games as a National League umpire, over 33 seasons from 1966 through 1998. Son Hunter graduated from the Harry Wendelstedt Umpire School, worked his way up through the minor leagues, and finally began his own career in the National League in 1998. Hunter worked a few games with Mark Hirschbeck that year, and – later in the year – 19 games with his father.

Harry and Hunter both worked on the same crew in San Diego on August 10, Hunter at second base and Harry working the plate. They worked that four-game series, and then five games in Milwaukee later in the month and six games in St. Louis to close out August. They worked back-to-back doubleheaders in Miami ending the 1998 season on September 26 and 27.

Hunter Wendelstedt: I went to Loyola. My fraternity brothers were all pre-med and pre-law and I was a history major. I knew how terrible it was that teachers get such a low salary and I thought I had some higher goals. I went, "I can't be a doctor. I can't be a lawyer" as a history major. I loved to teach and I loved to teach people things, but umpiring was a direction in a sport that I loved and it helped me to do a little bit of both. I just left because I had no passion for what I was doing, and so I wanted to look at different avenues. That's why I decided to go to umpire school. I was granted a scholarship to the school, so it worked out good for me.

BN: When you were there as a student in the school, did you ever have the feeling that the instructors were a little tougher on you than on some of the others?

HW: Oh, absolutely. No doubt about it. From top to bottom. I stayed at the hotel. Had a roommate. We had our routines. We were very serious about it, because I knew that when I was done with that – if I didn't get to start doing what I wanted to do – then it was back to college for me and the life of a history teacher. That's kind of how it went down.

BN: You didn't seem to advance any faster than anyone through the minor leagues. You worked your way up through the Appalachian League, the South Atlantic League, the Florida State League, Eastern League, International League, Pacific Coast League, Arizona Fall League, and the Florida Instructional League.

HW: You've got to get experience. I'm starting to get that experience, but he [Dad] always said, "You've got to get tens of thousands of pitches, you've got to get tens of thousands of plays, with consistency, to not only get you there but to keep you there."

It's a labor of love with umpiring. It's an incredible profession. You can take your pick – "Baseball's been very, very good to me" – but it's one of those things. That's how it was. The only way you get better is seeing the tens of thousands of pitches and plays. That's what makes the difference between a big-league umpire and someone who only makes it to Triple A.

Umpire Bill Haller was an American League umpire who worked 3,069 games from 1961-82. His brother Tom played ball, usually as a catcher for the Giants, Dodgers, and Tigers, breaking into the majors (but in the National League) in the same year, 1961, and playing through 1972. Only in the last year were the two Hallers in the same league. As Alan Cohen has written, "On July 14, when the Tigers played the Kansas City Royals, the plate umpire was Tom's brother Bill. It marked the first time that brothers had appeared in the same game as catcher and plate umpire."[9] It was the only game in which the two Hallers both worked at their respective professions.

Another case of relatives in baseball involves the Wolfs. Umpire Jim Wolf worked his first major league game in 1999, and through the 2018 season has worked 2,313 games. His younger brother Randy Wolf started his major league career as a left-handed pitcher for the Philadelphia

Phillies in the same year, 1999. He pitched for 16 seasons, retiring after the 2015 season.

Jim is seven years older than Randy. He was a catcher in junior college and started umpiring, mostly for fun, during intrasquad games when he wasn't catching.

Jim Wolf: One day, I thought, "I wonder if I could put on the chest protector and put on the catcher's gear and just work behind the plate." I thought, "This is kind of fun. I wonder if I could make any money doing this." I inquired about umpiring where I played PONY ball at. I remember on the bases, I'd get 20 bucks and behind the plate you'd get 25.

A friend of mine who'd gone to umpire school was working with me there at West Hills. He said, "You know what? If your playing career doesn't work out, you should go to umpire school." I was still playing JC ball. I played JC in '90 and '91. When '92 rolled around, I didn't get drafted or anything like that, so my playing career was done but I continued umpiring. I became a personal trainer over at a gym, so I had two jobs. Finally, in '94, I said, "You know what, this personal training thing isn't working out. I'm not going to put out some DVD or anything like that. I've got nothing to lose. I think I'll go to umpire school." I loved it. It was fun.

BN: What school did you go to?

JW: Harry's. Harry Wendelstedt's. I was very fortunate in my year. At the time there were three schools. There was Jim Evans School and there was the Brinkman/Froemming School. Of all those guys that they selected 30 from – 10 from each school – and I was the only one…I'm not tooting my own horn, I'm just saying how lucky I was…I was the only one from that class to make it to the big leagues.

BN: One person from all three schools together, then.

JW: I was really lucky. I never take that for granted.

There were games that Jim worked when Randy was pitching. In fact, the very first game Jim worked was September 2, 1999 at Candlestick Point, and the Phillies were the visitors. It was not a game Randy pitched.

JW: My first game in the big leagues, he [Randy] happened to be in the third-base dugout and I worked third base. It was like from me to the corner over there, it was great.

BN: Did he ever give you a hard time?

JW: Yeah. In Spring training. He was pitching and I was working third base and there was a check swing, and I said, "No." Finally, the third out and he walks off the field and goes, "Come on [about the check swing]." And I go, "Quit begging."

BN: I had read that when you umpired games he was in, you weren't allowed to call balls and strikes but that was the only restriction.

JW: That's right. That was for the first half of the season. In the second half of the season, if the team was in contention, then they would just remove me. It was a relief for me, because nothing good could come out of it on my end. No matter how good a story, it could be spun.

BN: It's like umpiring in general, the only time you're likely to be in the news is if something…

JW: Something unfortunate, yeah. I could be correct, but controversy is controversy.

We'll close this section by noting another relationship by marriage. Vic Carapazza is married to former umpire Rich Garcia's daughter Stephanie.

And we will note that there could be another father-son team in the future. Ted Barrett's son Andrew made the move from nuclear weapons maintenance to umpiring.

Ted Barrett: He went to umpire school in January of '15. He worked the '15 season in the Arizona League. Arizona rookie league. Then he worked Instruction League in Florida. He worked minor-league spring training this year. He's in extended spring training now, waiting for the season to start. He'll probably be in the Northwest or Pioneer League.

I wouldn't let him go to umpire school out of high school. His buddy did, and his buddy is now in Triple A. But I told him he had to get a college degree or join the military. So he did four years in the Air Force. When he got out, that's when he went to umpire school.

I never encouraged it. I never discouraged it. He always followed in my footsteps a little bit, other than he didn't play football. He played one year but it wasn't his cup of tea. He played baseball. He boxed a little. He kind of grew up in the gym, so it was kind of natural. That I did try to discourage, but…

BN: What was his specialization in the Air Force?

TB: He was nuclear weapons maintenance. The sad thing is, he really wanted to travel. He joined the Air Force and he did four years in Albuquerque and North Dakota. Underground. I said, "Let me drive you to work so I can have your truck and I can run around." He said, "No, Dad, you can't get close." It was 45 minutes for him to go through security and then go underground. I said, "Man, it sounds awesome." He goes, "It sounds awesome, but it's not. It's pretty boring."

By spring 2019, Andrew had worked his way up to Double-A umpiring, but father and son enjoyed one special moment on February 23 in the Cactus League, working the same Brewers/Cubs spring training game in Mesa, Arizona, with Andrew working the plate.

3

What Else Might Some Umpires Have Done if They Hadn't Made It to the Majors?

Embarking on the road to become a major league umpire is a daunting proposition. As we have seen, people drop out along the way – for any number of legitimate reasons. We need not detail those here, but one of the questions posed to today's umpires in the interviews was: what do you think you would have done had you not become an umpire?

We've seen several people answer that question – when he lost his job at the time of the mass resignation, Ed Hickox became a policeman and still works for the department in the offseasons. Phil Cuzzi probably would have gone back to teaching. Let's look at what some other umpires had to say.

Bob Davidson and Tom Hallion were two others who – like Ed – left at the time of the mass resignations, but decided to work their way back. Bob had worked in radio during his time away. "Sports radio 850 KOA in Denver. I worked pretty much full-time. I did radio at KOA for three years. I had my own show and everything. But then our ratings were bad so I got fired, basically. I got fired from radio and that's when I decided, well, maybe I better try to go back into baseball." He'd heard that Ed Hickox had started on his way back in umpiring, and so both he and Tom Hallion decided to do so, too. But before he'd begun umpiring, what career path might he have pursued? "I probably would have been a police officer. I was going to school to become a…education, you know, a coach. Hockey coach. Baseball coach. Whatever. I went to umpire school and then I never went back to school."

Paul Emmel said, simply, "I have a finance degree. From Central Michigan. So I would have stayed somewhere in that arena."

Tom Hallion still works as an investment broker on the side. When he found himself unemployed after the 1999 resignation, he chose yet another path – neither umpiring nor taking advantage of his degree in Engineering. He became a broker with Paine Webber.

Tom Hallion: I came in just as a new broker and got my Series 7, 66, and 63…

BN: Those are levels of certification?

TH: Yeah, and depending on the amount of time you're there and depending on your production, you get different levels.

BN: You must have been pretty good at it.

TH: I was fortunate that I had good family and friends that helped me out and got me started, and I went from there.

Indeed, he is currently a vice president at Raymond James.
TH: I don't run any funds. I just do asset allocation, stocks, bonds, mutual funds, just that sort of stuff. I enjoy it and it's something I want to continue to do.

Scott Barry was pretty clear what he would have done, too. His father still works at an insulation factory. "He's been there for 30-some years. My mom used to work at the high school, when I was a kid. She was in the lunchroom. All through middle school and high school, she worked there." He majored in social sciences, but minored in health and physical ed. "I'd have been a high school athletic director. I would have gone on and done that, for sure."

Will Little umpired rather than go to medical school.
Will Little: I played baseball for four years, through college. Second base, shortstop most of my years through college. Really, I had full intentions and plans – took my MCATs – to go to medical school and follow that path, but as my senior year was winding down, I had no real desire to go straight into medical school and try to follow that field. I like the outdoors. Grew up on a farm. Long story short, an umpire around home who did some youth leagues invited me to come work some games for him over the weekends and through the weeks. I did that for about six weeks and I fell in love with umpiring from there on. I quickly jumped into doing

college with that league, within those six or seven weeks. That part of was more fun, to me, because it seemed to be more competitive – calling the strike zone, for example, whereas for little kids you're more or less managing them as little kids.

I got word that there was an umpire school that could get you into the minor leagues, and maybe make it to major league baseball. I didn't know much about it. That was in the winter of 2006. I looked it up on the internet. I decided I'd give it a shot and hold on my MCAT scores, and not yet apply for medical school. I went to umpire school. Went to Jim Evans. Got a job in the minor leagues, and from there fell in love with it and never looked back.

Dan Bellino probably would have continued to work in the court system, and/or be more active in the real estate firm he owns with his father. With his master's degree in Education Administration, Adam Hamari would likely have worked in education.

Tripp Gibson was an art major and probably going to become a teacher. "My area of study was Printmaking. It had evolved from my work at a screen-printing shop on campus (I worked there for five years) and my love of silkscreen printing. I would work in the studio during the day and print on paper and canvas and then print t-shirts later in the day at work."

Maybe Dana DeMuth would have worked at his mother's tool and die shop.

Ben May said he would have been "a cop, an umpire, or a train engineer…I've always loved trains."

Andy Fletcher figured he probably would have gone into law enforcement. He explained: "There are a *lot* of former minor-league umpires who go into law enforcement if they don't make it to the major leagues. One of my best friends is a guy named Mike Snader, who is a resident security agent in Phoenix for Major League Baseball. He's also a Scottsdale police officer. I did some ride-alongs with him when I was in the minor leagues. I worked with him in Double A and then in Triple A in the Pacific Coast League. I also have just a lot of other friends at home in Memphis who are police officers. It just seemed like something that would interest me."

Law enforcement – and then some – for Doug Eddings. In the *2018 Umpires Media Guide*, he let it be known that he "would want to be a Secret Service agent if he was not an umpire."

Back in 2001, there was a time that a member of the Secret Service actually dressed up as an umpire before a major league game, as part of his work to protect President George W. Bush. No one attending the game knew the faux umpire was armed. Umpiring may share certain similarities with law enforcement, but major league umpires do not pack a pistol. Interested readers are urged to read the story in *The SABR Book of Umpires and Umpiring*.[10]

Nick Mahrley might conceivably have stayed in the military. He served in the U.S. Air Force.

NM: I worked on survival equipment and emergency systems in F-16's. We packed parachutes and stuff into ejection seats, and worked on all the equipment that a pilot uses when he ejects from an aircraft in an emergency situation.

He'd umpired when he was in high school, but then gave it up. When he completed his service, though, baseball grabbed his attention once more. "I definitely thought about trying to go work on aircraft, commercially. My stepdad was a police office in the Chicago area for 30 years and that was something always interested me as well. Police work. I went on a few ride-alongs when I was younger and it was pretty neat.

"I didn't know exactly which direction I wanted to go. I went to spring training in Arizona with my family visiting some of the different camps. We visited some of the minor-league fields and we saw that the umpires were really young guys and I thought, 'Wow, I'd really like to do that. That would be awesome.'"

The ejection seats had only to do with aircraft and nothing to do with umpiring.

4

Umpire School

Umpire school is difficult – and highly selective. As Jim Wolf told us, the year he graduated, he was the only one from all three schools taken together who ultimately made it to the majors.

Phil Cuzzi went through school four times – to the Wendelstedt School twice, then to Joe Brinkman's school, and then back to Wendelstedt. It's not uncommon for determined candidates to go twice.

Paul Nauert, for instance. Paul had worked 2,296 major league games since 1995.

BN: How did you get into umpiring in the first place?

PN: On a dare. I was living at home. I couldn't figure out what I wanted to do with my life. I had never umpired at any level. A friend of mine — we were playing in a basement band – was umpiring, and he actually introduced me to the umpire school. He said, "Hey, I'm going to go to Florida, to this umpire school. Do you want to go? It was the Wendelstedt School. And I was like, "What are you talking about?"

So he told me, and I went, "Wow." I went and talked to my dad. My mother was a stay-at-home mom. Raised nine kids. My dad worked for a brewery, until they closed down. I don't know if you ever remember Falls City Beer. Then he took some odd jobs, until he took a job with E.I. DuPont. He basically was just a maintenance man then.

I think it was the first time my dad was actually happy to give me money, because he knew I was leaving home. I did not know what I was getting into. I just knew I had a chance to go to Florida, and a chance to get away.

Aspiring umpires working on mechanics at the Wendelstedt School in January 2017.

And then when I got there, after about two weeks at the school, something clicked. Something said, "Wow! This might be something to look at." But because I had never umpired before, when I went in for my evaluation, I did not get a job offer that first year. I was told that I needed experience.

BN: Had you played baseball?

PN: I played. I understood the game from that aspect. I took to heart everything they told me, and said, "Okay." I went home and worked and I said I'll give this one more shot. If it works, great, and if it doesn't, well…

I borrowed money and I went back again. And I was very fortunate when I went back that I was the top returning student. Then it all just made sense to me. After my first year in the game, I was invited back to teach at the Wendelstedt School, and I ended up teaching there 20 years. Like I said, umpiring…it all just started to make sense.

Dana DeMuth enjoyed his time at the Wendelstedt School so much that he's ended up teaching there twice as long – for 40 years.

Dana DeMuth: I was a student originally at the Al Somers School in 1976. It was Al Somers' last year of having it. '77 is when Harry took over. The school used to be out at the Speedway. That year – '76 – I did not make it. I was 18 years old at that time. I had to go back home and work, and practice. And then the next year I came back and Harry had bought the school. I came back as a second-year student, and that is when I got my job. I went from the school to the very first advanced course. That was held at that time in Bradenton. They would take the top 30 out of each umpire school.

My instructors that first year were Hall of Famer Al Barlick, Ken Kaiser, and Dan Morrison. We worked Pirates intrasquad games. It was really nice to be doing that kind of ball right out of umpire school. Then they placed us. Larry Poncino finished first in that class, Rocky Roe placed second, Tim Welke placed third, and I placed fourth. We all went up through the system and made it to the major leagues.

The next year, 1978, Harry asked me to come back and instruct. I've been with them ever since, missing only three years – because of winter ball – and another four years when my son was in high school.

If I didn't love...the loyalty I have to this school. To see all this school has done. Even if I retire in two or three years, Hunter has assured me that I can still come here and work, which I love. I'm very lucky.

Ron Kulpa left college with only one semester to go before graduation. He decided he wanted to go to umpire school instead. Ron attended the Harry Wendelstedt School for Umpires. He had not realized how selective the process was.

Ron Kulpa: When you get down there, it opens your eyes. I didn't realize that only 1% of the minor-league umpires made it. I had no idea. We're sitting in the same classroom and one of the instructors stood up and said, "Look around the classroom. Usually only one person per class makes it to be big leagues." There was 182 people. I looked around. Then we went around the room, we went in alphabetical order and we all stood up and said our name. Sure enough, we got to the W's and Hunter Wendelstedt stood up and announced himself, and I went, "Holy cow! I picked the wrong year to go to umpire school."

It turned out to be a good year. Hunter made it, as it happens. So did Ron. And so did Lance Barksdale.

Hunter Wendelstedt, of course, had grown up at the school.

HW: Ronnie Kulpa, he'll tell you that I went to umpire school 21 times before I graduated. Yeah, I was always around but it was always Saturday.

BN: When you were young, did you do jobs at the school, you know, helping clean up?

HW: Oh, Good Lord. My gosh. I would pass out the tests. Whether it was Gerry Davis or Bruce Froemming or guys like that, I would go take them a bottle of water out at the pitching machine. I would do all kinds of different odd jobs.

And then, after I had gone through school, my dad was great because you'd start at the bottom. He had a great process that we still use. When you first come to the school, you're doing equipment. You're going to oil the gloves. You're going to make sure that we have the gloves out at the stations where we're instructing things. You're going to make sure the catcher's equipment is out. Then the following year, you're going to take the lunch orders. The next year, you're going to pass out the rule books and you're going to sit in the classroom and make sure that every word of the rule book is covered. It's a very big learning process for instructors at the school also.

And, as he said earlier, as a student at the school, the instructors at the time were, if anything, probably a little stricter on him than on the average student. Harry Wendelstedt made him work his way up, the same as anyone else.

Before Brian O'Nora had gone to the Brinkman School, he had never umpired at any level – not amateur, not Little League. He went to Cocoa Beach and heard the introductory talk there, too: "Look around the room and only a very few of you are going to make it to the major leagues." Recalling his year, he said, "Well, it's kind of funny. Around the third week, I looked around the room and…'Yeah, I'm doing all right at this.' I ended up finishing second in my class and getting a job."

Joe West recalled how he got his start, and how he did at school.
Joe West: "This guy Malcolm Sykes was the supervisor of umpires in the Carolina League. He saw me work a high school game and he said, 'If you're going to do this, you ought to learn how to do it right.' He took me to some clinics. He taught me a few little things, like how to take your mask off without your hat coming off. He's the one who arranged for me to go to umpire school, because he thought I had a chance of making it. He said, 'You go down there and do what they teach you and you'll do just fine.' I was lucky enough I finished first in the class. With some good umpires. Steve Rippley, John Shulock."

Classroom work at the Wendelstedt School, January 2017.

Not everyone went to umpire school with the dream of making the majors. Rob Drake was at Cal State Northridge when he realized he needed a job. He'd umpired some Little League games when he was in high school. $25 a game, which could be $100 on a weekend. He called the Little League near the college and was connected to the woman in charge of the umpires (her son Eddie Zosky had once been a shortstop in the Blue Jays minor-league system). She was impressed with his work and asked where he'd gone to umpire school. Rob said he really didn't know what she was referring to. She brought him some brochures. He decided to give it a shot. "I had no idea where it would lead. I thought you'd go there and come back and you'd work college baseball. I didn't know there was another path out of it." Rob was majoring in elementary education at the time. His father was in real estate and his mother was the CEO of a doctors' malpractice insurance company.

Rob Drake: "When you go to umpire school, you sit alphabetically. We're about 2 ½ weeks into it and it starts to rain. We stayed in the classroom. And Mike DiMuro got up in front of the class. He was in the Texas League at the time. He starts telling stories about life on the road, traveling from El Paso to Midland. Working in a game, and then getting in a car and driving. And I sat there – you know, when there's something you don't understand and you're trying to comprehend it – I sat there for about a half an hour listening to everything he's saying and trying to… I'm thinking,

'I know he lives in Arizona, I think at the time. What's he doing in Texas? Why would he be there?' I finally turned to the guy next to me and asked, 'What's he talking about?' He goes, 'He's talking about the minor leagues.'

"I'm like, 'What's the minor leagues?' He looks at me like I had three heads, and he's like, 'What are you here for?' I said, 'I don't know. I'm here to learn to be a better umpire and go home and do college games.' He goes, 'No, this is how you get to the big leagues.'"

BN: So you were actually IN the school…

RD: Two and a half weeks before I realized. He said, 'Yeah, you have to go to one of these schools to get into the minor leagues and that's how you can get to the big leagues. Everyone in the big leagues went to one of these schools.' I went, 'No kidding?'

"I remember calling my dad on the pay phone and saying, 'Dad, you're not going to believe what I found out today.' He says, 'Well, how are you doing?' I said, 'I'm doing really good. Most of them aren't really that good.' At umpire school, the majority are really not that good. There's really only 15 or 20 that are really exceptional.

"I went on from there to the minor leagues and the rest is history."

Rob's story is an outlier. Most who go to umpire school with the dream of making the majors, and most either don't have all that it takes to rise to the top or can't stick with it, persevering for maybe 10 years or so to get the call.

Mike Estabrook wraps up this section.

Mike Estabrook: They tell you when you go to umpire school that less than one percent will get work in the big leagues. When you go to umpire school, you're rolling the dice right out of the gate. I went to the Wendelstedt, in 1999.

BN: Some of these guys have been instructors there for years [gesturing to Dana DeMuth, Ed Hickox, and Greg Gibson.]

ME: I'm in the game because of all of them.

BN: All three of them?

ME: They were all there when I was there. They were all instructors.

BN: And they gave you good grades.

ME: I guess! Gibby says he didn't, but…(laughs)

In umpire school, students are taught about the umpires who preceded them. On September 19, 2017, major-league umpires all added this memorial patch to their uniform. Honored were four recently-deceased umpires: Russ Goetz, Mark Johnson, Steve Palermo, and Ken Kaiser.

BN: Over a hundred people in the room, and they tell you only one is going to make it.

ME: And that's the way it was in my class. At the Wendelstedt in '99, I was the only one to get hired.

BN: And had it not been for Replay coming in, you might still be waiting.

ME: It's just being in the right place, right time. A lot of guys have got family, or another opportunity opens us where they can make more money at the time.

5

The Long and Difficult Road to the Majors

Are there many jobs that have this long an "apprenticeship?" After umpire school, it takes maybe 8-to-10 years to have a shot at making the majors. A large percentage of those who set out on the path don't make it the whole way. One might graduate first in the class, but that's just the beginning. You have to be prepared to spend those many years working for very little money, being evaluated and graded at every step along the way. Any number of things in life can interrupt the journey. Even when you get to Triple A, the last rung climbing the ladder, the pay isn't any higher, the challenges to one's personal life aren't any easier, and you're being scrutinized even more in evaluations – as well as waiting for a possible opening. Even after he got the call to start working as a "call-up," "fill-in," or "up-and-down" umpire, Chris Guccione still had to work an incredible 1,255 major league games before he got hired as a major league umpire.[11]

Everyone's got their own stories, and if they're major league umpires who have made it, they can look back and maybe share a few fond memories. Mark Carlson and Chris Guccione worked together for a month as a two-man crew in the Midwest League. Gooch called up one memory:

"Chevy Trailblazer (laughs)."

Mark Carlson: "And then I left and he had to rent a car."

CG: "Yeah, I had to rent a car and Brian Knight came in."

A light-hearted moment. But the reality of it is that life was very difficult, financially, and more so for anyone thinking of starting a family.

You could tell yourself that you were investing in your own future – but over the course of those eight to 10 or more years, one's resolve is tested. Quite a few simply have to leave at one point or another.

Kevin O'Connor grew up in the same Massachusetts town as Steve Palermo. He started early, making $2.50 a game while in Little League umpiring "minor league" games of 9-year-olds. He went to Joe Brinkman's school in 1983. Of the 450 students in the combined schools that year, 16 ultimately got spring training jobs.

Kevin O'Connor: "Tommy Hallion and Charlie Reliford, I was in their first spring training camp. I had some good teachers.

"That year, I worked in the New York/Penn League. I went to Instructional ball in Florida that fall. The next year, I was promoted to the Florida State League. I was there for two years. Then I went to the Eastern League – Double A — for three years. Then to Triple A, the International League, for four years."

Come 1992, though – now obviously 10 years in – he got the word from Marty Springstead: there just weren't any openings foreseen. He had been in industrial sales during the off-seasons, and his move was to go full-time while also working as a substitute teacher in Oxford, Massachusetts. In the late 1990s, he began to work in real estate and currently owns the RE/MAX franchise in Oxford. He'd invested a decade, but was now on the outside. Nine years after that, he got back in the game and since 2001 has worked as an Umpire Observer. He's one of those who evaluates both Triple-A and major league umpires. It's a part-time job, for which he is paid on a per-game basis. He keeps active in real estate but has been able to use his expertise to help provide better umpiring for baseball.

Recall above that even though Clint Fagan had worked six years as an up-and-down umpire, with over 500 games in the majors, he decided he had to make a move after the 2017 season and is now spending full time with his family, working in insurance and studying law.

Getting selected to work as a "fill-in" ump finally provides some good income, since when a Triple-A umpire gets the call to work his first big-league game, he knows that for each game he works, he's going to get paid major league scale. If he should work 40 games in his first year as a call-up, at least for those games, he's making 25% of a major league umpire's salary.

And some of them work a lot more than 40 games. In 2017, Stu Schuerwater worked 153 major league games, far more than the 118 he worked after being promoted and becoming a member of the major league staff. In 2009, Scott Barry worked 155 games in the majors. He notes, "Plus I had six in Triple A that year." That's a total of 161 games, just one less than the 162-game major league schedule. "I was getting experience, that's for sure." Indeed.

Sam Holbrook and D. J. Reyburn reflected on one of the big differences between players and umpires.

L to R: D. J. Reyburn, Sam Holbrook, and Bill Nowlin panel at a University of Massachusetts Lowell class held at Fenway Park on May 2, 2017.

Sam Holbrook reminds us of the big picture: "If you're a Bryce Harper or somebody like that, a good baseball player, you can go straight from high school to big leagues, but as an umpire, we have to hit every level. You have to spend at least one year at every level coming through. So you work your way up. Supervisors come around the minor leagues and evaluate your work; if they feel that you're ready to move on to the next level, when there's an opening they will promote you to the next level. Once you get to Triple A, the major league supervisor will come down and watch you work. If they like what they see, they will invite you to spring training. The minor-league umpires, there's usually around 20-25 of them that work on site with us during spring training, get their feet wet a little bit, let us get to know them, let them get to know us. They're evaluated during spring training as well and if they rank high enough within that pool of 20-25 then they will be assigned throughout the year to come and fill in for us if one of us gets injured or we have some time off or something along those lines. There are 76 major league umpires and in order to get one of those spots, one of us has to pass away or retire. This past year we had four retirements – which was quite a few – so four Triple A umpires had their dreams come true this spring."

D. J. Reyburn adds, "When you get up to Triple A because you've spent eight years or so getting there, and so you're 28 and your friends are making decent money and starting to get into that adulthood stuff with kids – and you're kind of on hold." Along the way, what was once pursuing a dream has become transformed into achieving a goal – to stick with it, and finally make it. "Officiating in baseball is quite a bit different than other sports because we have the minor leagues. Most sports get their officials from the college ranks."

A major league baseball team might draft a kid out of high school and sign him to a bonus of a million dollars or more. However talented he (or she) may be, there is very definitely no signing bonus for an aspiring umpire. D.J. adds, "A lot of guys, myself included, lived in my parents' basement in the offseasons."

Umpires will often work through the winters, too, when they can. Things can happen, though. In January 2010, D. J. was working first base during a game in Dominican baseball when Licey Tigres manager Jose Offerman escalated a verbal argument with the plate umpire into throwing a punch at Reyburn, knocking him to the ground. Offerman was arrested for assault and suspended for three years, but there were threats after the game and the American umpires were pulled out of the country as a precautionary measure. He left with regret. "I really enjoyed my time in the Dominican – just great people. You work with local umpires. Great guys. People really take care of you down there, and not to be able to see it through was the worst part of that."

Travel on the road involved spartan accommodations, with even Triple-A umpires grateful for a pre-game meal brought them by the umpire's room attendant in a styrofoam container. Things have improved over time. One time in Norfolk, back in 1995, Bill Miller got robbed in his hotel room. "It was a bad situation. It was one of those things I wasn't expecting. I was expecting my crew chief to come down and knock on the door. We were going to go out for a beer, which we hadn't done all season long. So I was looking forward to it, and these guys got in and tied me up and got a gun to the back of my head. It was a life-changing moment. It would have ended before I started. Sometimes you look at second lives, second chances. Things could have gone a different way."

In 2018, Triple-A umpire Alex Tosi talked with me before a game in Pawtucket.

AT: The money has gotten better, but as far as the standard of living – the hotels that are required. We used to have to drive our own cars. The gains that we've made over the last 15 years have been [very good]. Not too long ago guys in Double A were sharing hotel rooms. The chief would get his own room and the other two would share. Fully grown men sharing rooms for five or six years?

BN: I'd heard now that the hotels are supposed to have the doors open to an interior corridor, as opposed to out to a parking lot.

AT: Did Sean Barber ever mention anything to you about that? He got held up at gunpoint, which is why we have to have indoor rooms. You'd have to ask him about that. Somebody came up to his door from the outside and put a gun to his head.

Jeff Nelson was able to benefit from some of the improvements. He went to Brinkman, then to spring training with the Yankees, and worked in extended spring training in the Tampa/St. Petersburg area.

Jeff Nelson: In June, I worked the Pioneer League, and following the Pioneer League I worked the Arizona Instructional League. It was a busy first year, from January to Halloween. It's exciting when you first get in. You're finally a part of something and you enjoy it and all the experiences are new. It's kind of a cool thing.

BN: Then you worked the Florida State League. That was all two-man crew?

JN: All two-man crew. The first time I worked in a three-man crew was in Double A, in the Eastern League in 1992 and 1993.

BN: One of you had a car and you all drove around together?

JN: In the Florida State League, and the Pioneer League, the other guy had a car. In the Eastern League, they started providing vehicles. We were able to use a vehicle provided by Umpire Development at the time. That was good. That was the first time it had happened; I think it's because the Commissioner's office gave a subsidy to the minor leagues that allowed them to do some things like provide transportation for us.

It still wasn't easy being on tenterhooks, so to speak, the whole time. Jeff Nelson worked his first series at Dodger Stadium in May 1997. One thing about it that he recalls as nice: "I was able to have some of my college friends in the stands to watch that series. It was kind of fun to have someone else be there for my first series and kind of share the experience."

BN: They didn't try to razz you or anything – give you a hard time?

JN: No. No. They knew I didn't have a job. Most people know that when you're going up and down, you don't have a job. You're walking a tightrope, a high wire, and you don't have a lot of room for error. If you miss something when you're going up and down, that can affect your eventual disposition as far as eventual hiring so it's not a light-hearted thing. It's an audition.

For the most part, though, it's just the economics of it that makes life difficult – as D. J. Reyburn says, this is while your friends working in what someone might call the "real world" are beginning to pull in better pay. Recall Dana DeMuth working in his mother's tool-and-die shop in the offseason.

Vic Carapazza recalled:

VC: We made…yeah…not very much. Even in Triple A, I think I made like three grand a month. My wife told me I made 15 grand for the year, doing umpiring. So you have to work.

BN: At least one other job.

VC: At least one other. I did that, and I picked up any other work I could get. If buddies needed any help at work, I would do it. I worked in Lowe's. Home and garden. After the season. I enjoyed it. I didn't make much money, but when you've got a kid, you've got to work.

Very hard. My wife worked. I worked, like I said, at Lowe's, too. It's a grind, but I'm sure everyone you've talked to said the same thing. Your dream is to make it, and I was blessed enough to make it. In the end, it was well worth it.

BN: Not everybody sticks with it.

VC: No, it's a grind. I'm talking to a buddy now who – he would have made it, but he got out in Double A. Nick. The career of on the road got to him. You're away from family. It's not for everyone, that's for sure.

It's a grind, for sure. Call-up umpires don't get the negotiated four weeks of vacation during the regular season that major league umpires get. When we spoke in late July 2019, Nick Mahrley said he'd been married a year-and-a-half. "Seeing each other when we can. Going up and down, it's…going up and down is really tough. You're not home. You don't get vacation."

BN: You could work 140 games if you're lucky…

NM: Right. And you'll take very single one of them.

You never know. We went through a period when there were a couple of jobs here and there. It's definitely a gamble. To make it this far is awesome, but there's one final step and some of that is a little bit of luck. You can be an amazing umpire, worthy of becoming a major league umpire full-time, but if there's no openings, you're not going to become a major league umpire.

When he was a call-up umpire, Rob Drake worked more than 140 games for three years in a row. He joined the major league staff in 2010, after paying pretty heavy dues. As a call-up umpire in 2007, he worked 159 major league games. He already had eight years of call-up work behind him.

RD: I started going up and down in '99. I got to where I was pretty high on the list of up-and-down guys. Back then, yeah, we worked pretty hard.

BN: You got the work, for one thing. You got paid, which was good, and they wouldn't have kept calling you if they didn't like your work.

RD: You just try to stick it out until there's an opening.

BN: But 159 games, that's like three games off.

RD: Yeah, it's a lot.

BN: And then you worked 154 games the next year and then 153 games in 2009.

RD: I think I ended up with 1,200 before I got hired.

BN: By my count, you had 1,215 games and Chris Guccione had 1,255, very similar numbers.

RD: Me, him, and Lance Barksdale were all up there. Just dying to get hired.

Doug Eddings comes from Las Cruces, New Mexico. Unlike an umpire who might live in, say, San Jose, there's no assignment that's going to allow him to stay at home during a series the way an umpire who is working games in San Francisco or Oakland might. "Being an umpire, your personal life is kind of a mess. I was married once. Didn't have any kids." His father had worked 35 years as a lineman for Mountain Bell and his mother as a school nurse. "After I divorced, I bought a lot up in the hills about eight miles outside of town. My parents lived in the same house for 49 years. When I bought the lot, I said, 'I'm going to build this house and I'm going to build it big enough where you guys have one side and I'll have the other side. We'll share the kitchen. Whoever I end up with, they'll know my parents are with me. If they don't accept it, then they're not the person for me.'"

His life has changed, but with it the challenge of being on the road for so much of the year. "I'm married and have two kids," he said. "I have a 13-year-old stepdaughter and I have a 2-year-old daughter."

DE: You've got a lot of Facetime-ing and stuff like that. It's hard for her to understand. She loves Daddy being home, but then going away she kind of fights it. Yeah, it's tough.

BN: You were just home for the All-Star break?

DE: Yeah, for the All-Star break. It was kind of nice. As a major league full-time umpire, you get four separate weeks during the season. We were on a break right before the All-Star break, for a week, so it turned into 11 days. It was nice. A great time. And actually I go back on my block vacation next week so that will work out nice.

BN: She's going to get spoiled!

DE: Exactly. Yeah.

BN: Of course, that makes the winters all the better, too.

DE: Very much. I still pinch myself. Next week as I watch games going on…for 10 years in the minor leagues, that was the real grind. Making absolutely no money. The travel's terrible. The hotels were terrible. It was a grind, but now to be off while they're playing, it's nice. I still kind of pinch myself at how lucky I am.

Hunter Wendelstedt made is clear that umpires give up a lot. "We're sacrificing a normal life."

HW: At any level of umpiring – some people will not believe this and some people would maybe smirk, but at every level of umpiring, there is sacrifice. The Little League World Series? Those guys get their expenses paid, but they're volunteering their time. In a lot of Little Leagues, the umpires volunteer their time. When you move a little bit forward, you get to high school. Once again, they're changing in the car.

Sure, they're getting paid something for high school but they're taking time away from their family to volunteer that. In college, you're volunteering now – getting paid, but you're sacrificing something at each level of the game.

For us at the major league level, the main thing we're doing is we're sacrificing a normal life. People don't understand that. We love the game so much and we're blessed to be surrounded by our family, but we're all sacrificing a normal life. Even though we make good money, I'm still gone for Easter, I'm still gone for the Fourth of July. I think in my 21 years I've been off once on the Fourth of July. I'm gone for a performance if my daughter's in a play. Those are things that you miss out on.

The four weeks of vacation helps a huge amount – even though it's also a hike to make it home to, say, New Orleans (as in Hunter's case) after wrapping up a Sunday game in Seattle. He is very grateful to have made it, though, and to be able to provide for his family while working at a craft he loves: "The way that umpires look at it is, we're going to miss out on those things but the opportunity that we have to give to our loved ones supersedes that – plus, from the umpire's standpoint, our love for baseball."

6

Getting "The Call"

There are numerous phone calls along the way, but every umpire hopes to get two calls in particular as he works his way up through the minors. I say "he" because – to date – no woman has yet been promoted to Triple A, or the majors. The first call is the invitation to work a major league game, a reassuring sign that you're a solid candidate for a major league slot. If all goes well and you continue to make the grade. The second call is the one that informs you that you are being officially hired as a member of the major league staff. You have finally made it! (In fact, there still remains a two-year probation period but umpires have been vetted so thoroughly by this point that one would have to truly screw up big-time to fail to pass probation.)

Given the years and years of devotion, and evaluation, and sacrifice, both are life-changing events and understandably extremely emotional. Every umpire remembers the call.

Brian Knight was asked, "Do you still remember the call when you got hired?"

BK: Yeah. It was in 2001. It was May 6. I was in Des Moines, Iowa and my hotel phone rang. One of our supervisors at the time was Tom Leppard, and he lived in Des Moines. He'd always come watch us at the Des Moines Cubs games. So I pick up the phone and say "Hello" and he said, "It's Tom Leppard." I thought, well, he's just calling to say "Hi, I'm going to come out to the game tonight. How're you doing?" He said, "So, what time is your game tomorrow?" I said, "Well, I think it's at 7 o'clock." He said, "Nope. You've got a 1 o'clock game in Dallas [Texas Rangers]. They got rained out yesterday. They're not playing a doubleheader. They're doing a makeup game. So you need to be in Dallas." Wow, cool.

Approaching the plate, last game of the season, September 29, 2019, Fenway Park. Umpires L to R: Mark Ripperger, HP; James Hoye; 1B; Brian O'Nora, 3B; Shane Livensparger, 2B.

So I went to Dallas, and it just so happened that my grandmother was still living and she was visiting her sister in Arlington. They're playing the White Sox on May 7 and since they were playing a makeup game, there was only about 2,000 people at the game, in this massive stadium. [The listed attendance figure of over 30,000 counts tickets sold, not the actual attendance.] I worked third base and my grandma was sitting right there. It was a neat experience. Wally Bell had the plate and he walked all the way down to her and gave her a baseball.

BN: What about the next call, in 2011?

BK: That was the really good one. You know, I kind of knew it was coming. I had stuck around long enough that I was the next guy. It was in the offseason. It was right after New Year's. Mike Port, who you probably know, is the one who called me. He didn't really say, "Congratulations. You're on the staff" – I still had to pass my physical – "But we'd like to invite you to come down to our meetings next week and, pending your physical, we'd like to invite you to be on the major league staff." So the first thing I did was I drove – I live in the Sacramento area now – I drove across town to where my now-wife, then-girlfriend was working and I called her. I was standing in the parking lot. She came down, and said, "What?" I told her, and that was kind of special. It had been a long time – 10 years going up and down. Really, the first five, six of those first 10 years was really literally going up and down.

BN: 730 major league games.

BK: 730, over 10 years, yeah. But I didn't break 100 until maybe my sixth year. I think '06 was the last year I worked in Triple A.

Lance Barksdale worked 14 years before he got the final call. He had an extra reason that it was a good day he got the call.
LB: I was in the minor leagues from '92 to 2000. From 2000 to 2006, I had 850 games before I got a full-time job. There was no jobs. My last six years were pretty good, though. [He was making major league pay while working those 850 games.]

In '06, Terry Craft decided to retire midway through the year, and I'll always remember the day I got hired. I actually got hired on my daughter's birthday.

My daughter and my wife were eating lunch for her birthday and I called my wife and I told her, and she started screaming in the restaurant. My daughter said, "Mama, you're embarrassing me." She was screaming in the restaurant.

Will Little: Major Lotto.

BN: A big jump in pay and benefits.

LB: Just the benefits, even! When you've got two kids, just your benefits – your health insurance and everything, is huge.

Mark Ripperger was teaching at the Wendelstedt School when he got the call. It was by no means a total surprise, but the reality of it nonetheless had an impact on him that day.
Mark Ripperger: it was in January of 2015 and I was down at umpire school, teaching. At the Harry Wendelstedt School. I got a heads-up from one of the supervisors to be available for a phone call. I knew some jobs were coming out and that I was in the running.

BN: There were two new positions due to replay, and Tim McClelland had retired.

MR: I knew they were coming out soon. I didn't know that they were coming that day necessarily. I was just told to be available all week.

I was very nervous. It was quite the phone call. It was pretty special. Afterwards, I had to go away from everybody, and I was walking around by myself. I wasn't doing too much teaching. I was just walking around and watching the guys working and just thinking about it all. I had to get away from everybody because they were all teaching, so I went and sat in the car and took the phone call. Afterwards, I just felt numb. I started to cry a little bit myself, and then finally I got myself out of the car and started to call my family. Then I talked to some of my close friends who were there on the staff. I called Mike Winters to let him know because he was responsible for getting me in there.

I had to make a lot of phone calls after that, to thank a lot of people that helped me. Yeah, it was a great day.

BN: By pure coincidence, John Tumpane was here a few days ago and I talked to him within three hours of him getting the phone call.

MR: It's pretty exciting. I just saw him in New York last week. He and I taught down at school together. He was there when I got my phone call.

Dan Bellino chimed in: "I think everybody was ecstatic the day John got the call. His road was a very difficult road and he's such a great person. He deserved it more than just about anybody I know."

Chris Conroy recalled the context of his own call.

Chris Conroy: Some guys eventually, along the way, life gets in the way. More often than not, it's like you get married, you have kids. "OK, I need to make more than like $2,400 a month for six months."

BN: What do you think you might have done if you hadn't…?

CC: I don't know. I did a lot of substitute teaching and coaching in the offseasons. I always thought if it didn't work out, I would do like a teaching/coach kind of thing. I had done two or three years in Triple A and nothing was kind of happening, and I started thinking, "Well, all right" and started thinking about life after baseball. Then things, for whatever reason, just started to break my way a little bit.

He and Sean Barber talked about what it was like working as an "up-and-down" umpire.

BN: You know where you're going tonight, or tomorrow? [The conversation was on a Sunday, the last day of a series].

SB: I do. Usually I find out toward the middle or end of the week if you're going up next week. But then, if you're down, anytime somebody gets hurt, somebody gets sick, I get the call and I've got to go.

CC: You can't go anywhere without your phone if you're in the minor leagues. The only place I didn't take my phone was into the shower.

SB: And it's sitting in the bathroom.

CC: It's anytime, anywhere. If they need somebody and they can't get ahold of you, they just go on to the next guy, and you've missed out on a chance to get up here and make some more money and get the experience. That's the worst, when you call back and they say, "I'm sorry. I had to…"

SB: Had to use somebody else.

BN: So you could make almost as much here in half a week as you might make in a month.

SB: Everybody in Triple A is probably making roughly at least $3,200, I might say. So, yeah, within a week up here you've made your salary for a month and then some.

CC: If you put salary and per diem together up here, in a three- or four-game series, you're almost equaling your whole monthly salary in the minor leagues.

BN: Definitely gives a taste of why you'd want to stick with it.

SB: Yeah, once you finally get to the up-and-down, that's when it gets easier to hang around than working spring training and…this is what I put 10 years in for down there.

BN: Once you make it…

CC: Yeah. that's a phone call you dream about.

BN: One of the better phone calls of your life.

CC: Oh yeah. When you get the call that you're on the up-and-down list, that's kind of like the first hurdle, but then the next one when they tell you you're hired, that's…

BN: Where were you?

CC: It was during the season. I was home on an off day. I had my wife and kids with me. They were like right there to experience it. It was Monday, June the 10th, 2013. I was like "Wow" when they called. I was scheduled to go to New York the next three days. They said, "Go to New York. Work that series, and then when you're done Thursday, get on a plane and fly to Arizona. If you pass your physical, you're on staff."

I don't remember the conversation much after that. I think I managed to say "thank you" and stumbled through it. Then I got off the phone and I cried for 10 minutes. (laughs) My daughters are looking at me like, "Is he all right?" They kind of figured out it was all good, and then it was like… Group hug!!!! It was pretty cool.

It's not beyond the supervisory staff to have a little fun with The Call. Dan Bellino tells how his came.

DB: March 9. Spring training 2011. They called me and told me that my identity had been compromised and I had to get on a conference call with baseball security. I got on the conference call and it was all the supervisors and they said, "We have to make this decision and we have to make it now…and effective immediately, you're the newest addition to the major league umpire staff." It's a crippling phone call. Very humbling.

Manny Gonzalez grew up in Venezuela. His father worked at a car dealership and later became a manager in a store akin to Home Depot. Manny played baseball there and worked some games as a boy, went to college for three years, and was perhaps in the right place at the right time.

MG: Richie Garcia came down to Venezuela. They were looking to offer some scholarships to give to minorities to come to the U.S. as umpires. I was lucky enough to get one of them in 2002. I went to the Jim Evans Academy, and then the history started.

I never thought about making it to the big leagues, to be honest. To me, it was a year-by-year thing. I was learning the language. I was learning the culture. I was 21 years old. I was just moving forward and trying to understand everything here. I love it. I fell in love with the country, I fell in love with the people, I fell in love with the sport. I love it. I never complained about the travel or anything. To me, it was new. It was good. You know how it is in the minors, but it was all a learning experience for me. Learning about the culture, every state, every city, every small town. It was amazing.

BN: Well, you get a lot of travel as an umpire.

MG: Yes, we do. A lot of miles. I think this year, we'll do around 32,000 miles. It's a lot of travel. In the minors, as you know, it's a little bit tougher. We drive, or we take early cheap flights to the next city. It's tough, but for me it's a lot of fun. I love it. I've been blessed to be where I am right now. This is my fifth year full time.

BN: You've got to remember when you first got the first call to be hired as a major league umpire?

MG: My first game was in Miami. May 17, 2010. I worked with a great friend of mine, Laz Diaz, and Wally Bell – my mentor, who was a friend and almost a father to me. He was a great guy. And James Hoye, he was a good friend of mine, too. We worked the two-game series in Miami. I was in Indianapolis when Cris Jones called me. He said, "I need you in Miami. You will become the first Venezuelan umpire to work in major league baseball." I couldn't believe it. I didn't know what to do. I was with my crew in the locker room. I told my boys and they were so happy for me, and we all went out and had a good time to celebrate.

BN: That was in 2010. Three years later you got another call.

MG: I was in Caracas. I was working the winter league. Mr. Joe Torre called me on January 6.

BN: You just happen to remember the date.

MG (laughs): Yes, I do. I remember everything. And I remember that day because it was the last day I worked in Venezuela. He told me they were looking to hire me, and that was great. I was by myself in the hotel when he called. Then I just called my wife and my daughter, my family, everybody. I was so happy. It was a great experience.

BN: Did you get good publicity in Venezuela when you got the first call back in 2010? Was there a lot of publicity about you?

MG: Yes. It was crazy. I was on the front page of every newspaper in the country. I remember my dad – our dining table is about an eight-seat dining table at home – and my dad had it covered with the front page of every single newspaper in Venezuela that had my picture on it. It was just unbelievable.

BN: They'll have to put up a statue soon.

MG: They probably will (laughs).

Carlos Torres coincidentally got his call on the same date. He'd worked some major league games in 2015 and then a full 141 games in 2016. He got the call early in 2017.

Carlos Torres: January 6. I am never going to forget that date.

BN: Where were you?

CT: I was in my apartment. I was cooking with my wife. My kids were playing video games. The supervisor called me the day before and he told me, "We want to talk tomorrow, about spring training. Will you be available tomorrow?" I said, "OK, cool. I'll be here." He called me on the 6th, and once I heard him say, "Now you're with Major League Baseball. You are one of the 76 guys," I just cried and cried. I couldn't even talk, to be honest. I was hugging my wife and my kids and was crying and crying. The supervisor asked, "Are you okay?" I said, "Sorry, I can't talk. I'm sorry."

The first people I called was my mom and my dad. They were all crying, too.

BN: They had to be very proud of you.

CT: Oh yeah, they are. And so is my brother, and my sister and all of my family. Everyone is proud of me. This is huge for my family.

Getting "the call" can make it all worthwhile, though. There is more than one step along the way. Just as I felt fortunate (not as fortunate as he felt!), it was nice to see John Tumpane the day he got the call that he had been appointed to the major league staff. Brennan Miller worked as a call-up umpire in 2019. As a kid, he had umpired high school games working alongside his father. He thought he'd likely go into law enforcement, but so many people encouraged him to go into umpiring that he did, in 2013 at age 21. Working his way up, he was in his third year working in the International League. He became a crew chief. Working at Fenway Park on July 13, he noted, "My crew is actually in Pawtucket now. They're only an hour away." The day was one of note, however. He got one of those calls you hope to get along the way.

Brennan Miller: This whole year has been kind of a rush for me. I went to Fall League for my first time this last year. Got spring training. Got a number. Became a call-up. And as of today became a rover.

BN: As of today?

BM: As of today. I received an email with an updated call-up and rover roster and my name had been moved over to the rover list. It's all just a whole big whirlwind.

What does "rover status" mean? The rover is no longer on a crew. Brennan was a crew chief but being named a rover means that he is no longer on a crew. When he goes down from the big leagues, they'll tell him where to go, wherever he was needed. (He doesn't return to his crew, because he no longer is on a crew.) He'll be jumping around crew to crew. When a rover comes down, they'll work a four-man in Triple A until a callup is needed. It's lot of moving around. You don't get to see the friends on the crew you were with, day in and day out, but you get to meet a whole lot of other colleagues. And it's another mark of approbation, another milestone on the way toward getting the most sought-after phone call of all.

7

"Nobody Notices You Until They Notice You"

Having made the major leagues, now umpires are celebrities, right? Stars. Far from it. Instead, what they all seek is anonymity. Not to be noticed. That's a defining mark of a successful game – the umpire wasn't part of the story line. To come as close as they can to what Tony Randazzo called the umpire's perfect game.

Circumstances sometimes threaten to take away an umpire's edge. When I spoke with Jerry Meals in June 2016, he and his crew had had a difficult time getting to Boston in time for the evening's game.

Jerry Meals: We had a day game in Houston. We got to the airport fine. Weather was coming in. They pushed back our flight because it was late leaving Cancun. It landed. It got there. And then they kept pushing it back, pushing it back, saying that they had a flight attendant that wasn't going to show. They were waiting on another one, and finally they just canceled it. That was about 10 o'clock at night. We'd been there for five hours, after the day game. Now we had to scramble for a hotel.

Luckily, that morning I had texted our travel agent and said, "Listen, we've got some weather coming. Just in case, can you put us on something first thing in the morning?" If we hadn't done that, we wouldn't have gotten here. There was just nothing else going.

We were back at the airport at 5 in the morning, we fly here, got to the hotel here around 1 in the afternoon…and then you're expected to be perfect. (laughs)

Fortunately, umpires have been very adept at planning their travel, with good backup arrangements both for flights and accommodations. But it can take a lot of work making multiple reservations and then canceling the ones not used. The August 7, 2019 game in Boston against the visiting Kansas City Royals was tied 4-4 after nine innings, suspended due to rain just as the 10th inning began. The Angels were due in the next day, and the Royals had to be in Detroit. The game resumed on the afternoon of August 22, an off-day for both teams, and the Royals flew back to Boston. Needless to say, umpires were needed. The crew that had worked on the 20th and 21st against the visiting Phillies had a scheduled day off on the 22nd, so they were asked to change their flights and work the game, then head to their assignment in Chicago on the 23rd.

The weather was kind of iffy on the 21st. Had that game been suspended, too, there could have been a real situation. Fortunately, the weather changed. And, as it happened, the game on the 22nd only lasted 12 minutes. The Royals went down 1-2-3, and the Red Sox scored in the bottom of the 10th, needing only nine pitches and an intentional walk.

Dan Iassogna talked about the travel adjustments: "We've probably got seven to nine flights booked for today. Just depending, because you don't know – the game could go 15 minutes, or the game could go...longer."

BN: You always book refundable tickets and you often book an array of them, just to have more choices available to you, depending on the circumstances.

DI: Exactly. After a day game, you always have at least two flights – depending on if you're in a hub or not. You could have four or five flights but if you're coming out of a smaller airport like Kansas City or St. Louis – Pittsburgh, even – you've only got one shot, so if something happens, you stay the night.

BN: You've already checked out of the hotel today, though, because it's a day game and you know you've got so many options. Will you all four travel together probably?

DI: We're going to try. We're all on a bunch of different...I joined the crew late. These guys knew about this way before I did. I got on most of their flights, but there were some that were sold out so I'm on a couple of different flights just to make sure. We're on a couple of direct flights and then we have four or five connecting flights, on different airlines.

On August 6, I had talked with Tripp Gibson about their travel arrangements. As it happens, he had been on the crew which worked the game that was suspended.

Tripp Gibson: We are actually professional travelers. Beyond belief. I don't think people understand how difficult it is to work a game and then have to take a commercial flight. Tomorrow night, we have a night game. We're not flying out until the next day. We're actually going to New York, so we get to fly the next day. There are times when you may fly across the country. You may have a day off getting there but you have to fly across the country. The travel is one of the most difficult parts. Going in and out of airports. Taking taxicabs. With rideshares now – Uber and Lyft – that's gotten a little easier. Going in and out of hotels. You're booking all the reservations for your flights, all your reservations for your hotels, well in advance. It can be tedious. It can wear you out. It's tiresome. Besides the work on the field, that's actually one of the most difficult tasks that we have.

BN: Do you share – if you're with a given crew for a period of time – do you share the duties of booking?

TG: If I find a rate at a hotel that I think is really going to be good for us, I'll book enough rooms for the whole crew. And then make changes accordingly. The crew rotations change here and there depending on the travel, and different things. Injuries. So you try to book four hotels in every city. There may be other hotels in the same city that another guy booked. So you'll decide from there.

BN: So you'll book a lot of extra hotels, and just cancel some.

TG: Oh yeah, absolutely.

BN: Same thing with flights? If you've got a choice.

TG: Yes, if it's available, we will do that. Our job is to get to the next city as soon as possible. Sometimes you're taking a 6 AM flight, or the first flight out in the morning. You work a long game that's 3 ½ hours and you don't get to the hotel until 11:30 or midnight. Then you get up at 4, shower and go to the airport.

BN: And then you get to the hotel and they don't have a room ready yet, maybe a 3 o'clock check-in.

TG: That happens a lot.

Even with all the headaches of planning travel, with multiple flights and multiple hotel rooms, umpires still find rewards. A few months earlier, Ron Kulpa commented, "The toughest part of our job is the travel. Tomorrow I wake up at 4:00 AM. The teams are lucky. They get to fly out on a charter, but we're going tomorrow at the crack of dawn. That's probably the hardest part."

In the 2016 interview, he had said, "The travel beats you up a little bit, but I tell you what, walking on that field every day, it's a blessing. It really is. Like yesterday. Yesterday at Fenway, I looked around and I thought, 'Man, this place…this place is rocking.' When you come to Fenway, you go to Wrigley, you go, 'This is what it's all about.'

BN: You don't get asked for too many autographs, though.

RK: No.

BN: You guys can walk into a park and almost nobody knows who you are, and that's really the way you want it.

RK: Right. It's the old cliché – if no one notices you, you did a good job.

Mike Estabrook also mentioned feeding off the energy of a good crowd.

ME: I like working with the guys. I love traveling around. I love the challenge. It's probably one of the most challenging things you can do.

BN: The travel can get pretty hard.

ME: It's very hard, the travel – being away from your family – but I like the adrenaline. When you get to the locker room and you're working with the guys and you walk out there onto the field, it's a challenge. It's very difficult to do it. It's not easy.

BN: It's a big responsibility, too.

ME: Well, sure. They entrust the game to us. But I like it. To me, it's the best job in the world.

We've heard Phil Cuzzi and Laz Diaz both recount running into unknowing fans before or after games. Typically, though, umpires arrive at the park around the same time the gates are open to the public and they walk through the crowds completed unnoticed.

Occasionally, there's a fan like Paul Horton of Connecticut who will seek out autographs from umpires and there are a very few who know some details about the umpires' lives. A distant relative of Canadian hockey great Tim Horton, Paul goes to about a dozen games a year and always asks for the umpires to autograph something for him. In 2015, he said he has about 40 or 50 autographs of current umpires at this point. Some, of course, are friendlier than others. He will also ask for player autographs, too, when he can. Once in a while, he will see someone else ask the umpires to sign something, but very rarely. He values the umpires' work as an integral part of the game, and finds himself sometimes watching the umpires more than the game. He enjoys watching them work, the different ways that umpires make strike calls, for instance.

That brings to mind a tangent regarding Tom Hallion. He's earned a reputation for very demonstrative strike calls when working home plate. We talked on August 15, 2017, the day after the game ended with Andrew Benintendi striking out, thrown out at first base after the catcher dropped strike three and had to fire the ball to first base to secure the out and win the game. Asked about his strike calls – one can see some of them on YouTube – Tom gave the history.

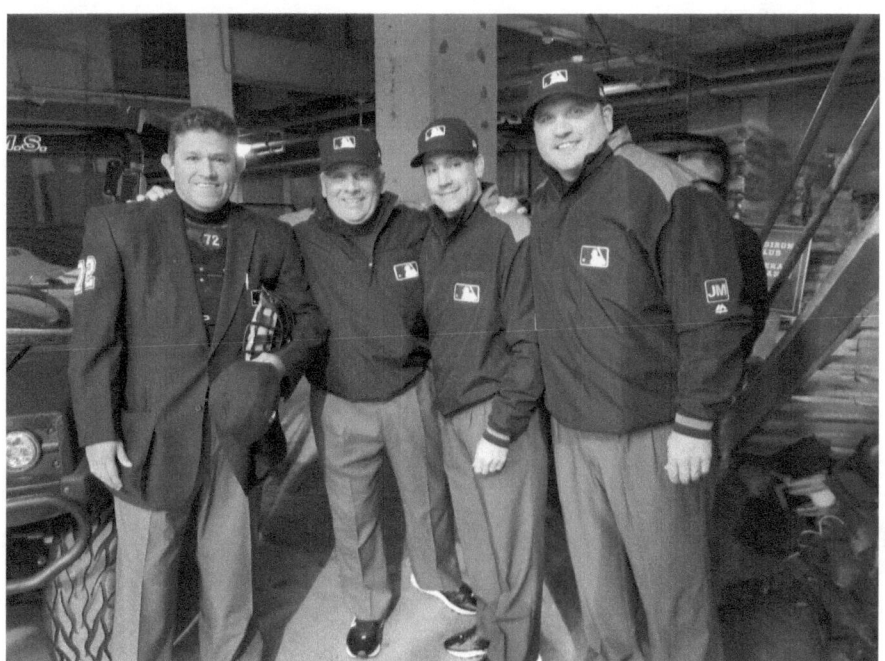

Under the stands just before emerging onto the field at Fenway Park, April 24, 2019. Umpires L to R: Alfonso Marquez, HP; Larry Vanover, 1B; David Rackley, 2B; Dan Bellino, 3B.

Tom Hallion: I'll tell you how that all came about. When I lost my job [during the mass resignation in 1999] and I had to go back to the minor leagues, that was a real mental challenge for me. I spent 14 years in the National League, and then I'm going back down to A ball. That was a challenge. So I wanted to have something that I could kind of focus on, concentrate on, that would help me get through the process. What I decided was that I wanted to come up with a "strike three" call that was different. Nobody else had anything like it. It was going to be different. It was going to be "Tom Hallion's strike-three call."

Really, that was kind of it. I kept working on it in the minor leagues for the two years, and then when I came up to the big leagues, I started it, and it has since become its own little thing. It's not a big deal but it's a...

BN: A signature.

TH: A signature. Strike three. I would say most players like seeing it. They might not like it happening when I do it to them, but I think they...they know it's me...I call my baseball game. I'm a fair official, and if I call you out on strikes, it's because I thought it was a strike. That's the only reason. And that's my call.

BN: I was wondering if they had taught you that, at the Kinnamon School. To be demonstrative.

TH: No, they teach you everything is strictly, "He's out." When you get in the minor leagues, they tell you that you can start adding a little bit of your flair and flavor to it.

BN: How about vocally? Do you always make sure that the batter and catcher can hear you?

TH: Yeah, I always yell it out.

That still doesn't result in him being recognized an hour after a game. After all, he's wearing his mask behind the plate. Recall Chris Guccione saying in his many years in the game, he'd been recognized maybe once or twice after a game. My quip was that it was because he was wearing his gear. Going to dinner with your face mask on is always going to be something of a tipoff.

Here's a joke told by a contemporary umpire:

"Every so often, somebody's going to recognize you out of uniform in some place you don't expect. In a restaurant, a city you're not from. There's always these umpire fans who'll say, 'I know you.'

"So there's three umpires at the airport. Say John Hirschbeck, Bill Welke, and Jim Wolf. They're running through the airport, say Detroit, trying to make their flight, and a fan stops them. 'Excuse me, I don't want to bother you, sir, but aren't you John Hirschbeck? You're umpire #17. You just had the World Series. Fantastic job. I know that you live in Ohio. I'm a big fan of the umpires.'

"The umpires are shocked by that, but now they're going to stop and listen to this guy. He says, 'I'm just a big fan and I want to say thank you for all you do for the great game of baseball.' He looks at Bill Welke and he goes, 'Bill Welke. I know you very well. Your brother's a major league umpire. I saw you were crew chief here today. You're #52. You live in Michigan. Thank you. Boy, this is going to make my day. I want to get your picture and get your autographs.'

"Jim Wolf's standing there, and Wolf steps forward and wonders, 'Is this guy going to recognize me?' The guy doesn't say anything and he says, 'I'm sorry, Sir, I don't recognize you.' So Wolf takes his Bose noise-canceling headphones – you know, they're going through the airport and they've got their music on – and he puts his headphones back on. And when the fan sees him with the headphones on, he goes, 'I recognize you! You're the guy on TV with all those instant replays.'"

There is the occasional interaction with fans. Rob Drake makes a point of occasionally interacting just a bit with fans. "They just think you're robots out there. That's why a lot of times when I'm on the field, if the stands are close, I'll wander back and talk to people in the crowd. They're always like…they can't believe you're talking to them. So many times I've gotten, 'Hey, we really appreciate you talking to us. That's cool. Thank you.'"

That sort of humanizes things a little. Maybe three or four people realize that umpires aren't so bad after all. Tripp Gibson says, "Jokingly, I say this to people when I speak in large groups – Rotary Clubs or other organizations – I'll say, 'You know, guys, umpires have mothers, too.'"

Keeping some distance can be advisable, though. As we have heard, umpires stay at different hotels from the teams. They do sometimes happen to meet figures from the game away from the field. Sometimes that precedes their career; Kerwin Danley, for instance, was teammates of both Bud Black and Tony Gwynn for two years at San Diego State.

Hunter Wendelstedt grew up in awe of the Dodgers' Steve Garvey. It's no secret. In the *Umpires Media Guide,* it says his first memory of baseball was meeting Steve Garvey when he was 5 years old.

HW: One of my heroes. I had his poster on my wall. I have a letter that he wrote me for my birthday. I had a little issue. Anybody who saw me on television knew that I was not the smallest of people, but at the time I had an issue eating my dinner, eating my vegetables, and Steve – back then, baseball was that accessible that I got a letter from Steve Garvey. And it was awesome. It's the way the media is these days. Back then, some things came out about him which that's his personal life. I would never make a judgment, but I'll tell you right now, as far as being a first-class human being, and being accessible to his fans, accessible to anyone, and a hell of a ballplayer, Steve Garvey, he's my number one.

I went with Dad a lot. Back then, things were different. Baseball was different. I think his first World Series was 1973. I was there. I was only 2 years old. I didn't know what was going on. They had a commercial with Pete Rose and Steve Garvey and my dad was the umpire. It was some Vitalis commercial that they did. Steve Garvey still talks about that. I've seen Pete a couple of times and he's brought that up, too. That's how baseball used to be. It was a big…it was so incredibly family-oriented, to a fault. Baseball always erred on the side of family, and that's what was incredible about it.

Garvey played from 1969-87. Hunter's first game as a big-league umpire was in 1998.

Before a game in Boston, Sam Holbrook and D. J. Reyburn graciously consented to meet at the ballpark with students from Jeff Gerson's Introduction to Politics and Sports course for University of Massachusetts Lowell. One of the students asked, "Either former or present, who's been the most animated coach when there's a disagreement or bad call you've had to deal with?"

Sam Holbrook: Animated, I'd have to say Lou Piniella. Lou is a character. You know what? He was always good to us off the field. Him and Bobby Cox had the most ejections but if you had a flat tire at the parking lot, Bobby Cox would be the first one to help you, even after the game you ejected him from. It's just a job.

I'll tell you a couple quick stories. When Lou was managing the Mariners, I absolutely kicked a play on Joey Cora on first base, called him out when he was safe by about a step, and Joey threw his hat, his helmet down so I ejected him. Lou comes out and throws his hat down, I eject him and we're standing there arguing and he goes to try and kick dirt on me. Well he misses the dirt and kicks me in the leg and I said, "Lou, you just kicked me in the leg, it's time to go." He said, "I did not," and I say, "Lou…" He goes, "Alright, you're right" and leaves. So, he comes in the locker room the next day and goes "Sammy, I just want to apologize to you, I'm sorry for kicking you in the leg," he said. "I only meant to kick dirt on you." I was kind of like, "I'd rather you kicked me in the leg than get dirt on me." That was kind of funny. You know, it's a manager's job to show his players that he's going to stick up for them, and it's a way to fire the team up at times, and unfortunately it's our job to help facilitate that.

There was the occasional player who sought a degree of respite from the limelight by seeking the solace of the umpire's room. Larry Vanover offered a couple of memories.

Larry Vanover: There were only a few people who got to go to spring training right out of school. Luckily, I got to be one of them. They sent me to Boston's camp at Winter Haven. This was the early 80s. I'm 22 years old. I'm told that the dressing room's basically where the grounds crew keeps their tractors and stuff. We're in there with the tractors and the DiamondDry and all the other junk. There's a pipe coming out of the wall that's the shower. But we're in there, working through the month, every day, and about the middle of the month, there's a knock on the door. I don't know who these people are. A guy comes in and it's Ted Williams. I know who *he* is!

He walks in and he closes the door and says, "Can I come in here and hang out?" "Sure." So he pulls out a six-pack of Coke and a bagful of sandwiches. Of course, we're not making any money and they're not feeding us, and here we go. He sits down over in the corner. It's kind of his place to get away from everybody. He's coming in every day and sitting down with sandwiches and Cokes. He's sitting there with the door closed. Nobody knew he was he's doing this. He just wanted to talk to you about baseball.

I'm just a kid in A ball. And he did it every day. Come in there and talk with you about different aspects. What your responsibility is. Your impact on the game itself. After about four or five days of this, he sits down with me and he says, "Listen, I want to talk to you about something specific." "Okay." So we're sitting there and he says, "Listen, I was a big hitter." I said, "I know who you are." He says, "Every time a batter steps into that box, it's a separate game, between him and that pitcher. Who's going to win? If I get on base, I won. If I'm out, he won. It's a separate game, and every hitter takes that really personal."

BN: And he got on base 48.2% of the time.

LV: He said, "You know, you have a whole impact on that." He kind of walked me through a pitch sequence with different counts. "If the count gets this way, he's got to go this way. The hitter's got to..." it was a really unique thing to listen to – to sit with that man and talk about that stuff.

BN: He was taking an interest in you, too. He was often like a teacher.

LV: Right, and it was his time to get away from everybody, put his feet up and have a sandwich, and he liked to talk.

Years later, I'm on the verge of going to the National League and I'm at the Dodgers camp. We're on the back forty, we called it, where the B game's going on. Nobody's there but there's some media people there. And Koufax was the pitching coach. I knew who he was, but I don't *know* him. Anyhow, he's there and something happened when a guy wanted to come on the field with a TV camera during the game. I kind of run the guy off and say, "We're trying to work here. You need to get away." Koufax just happened to like that. After the game he finds us and says, "I was so glad to see that in younger people. Not just to bow down and let them do anything they want. We *are* trying to work here. I really liked your answer." So he sits down in the dressing room and we start to talking and lo and behold he starts talking about the game, and he tells me the same story that Williams told me, about that little game – every time a guy walks in the box, it's a separate game.

I thought that was really unique, that years later, I'm hearing the same type story from the other side. One guy was Ted Williams and the other guy was Sandy Koufax.

BN: That's what bugs me about people who say there isn't enough action in baseball. You don't have whole teams in motion all at the same time. It comes down to that one point, when it's a one-on-one matchup, and if you can focus on that, you can get a lot more out of watching the game.

LV: People don't realize that when nothing's going on, everything's going on. That's the difference. You're setting everything up when nothing's going on.

BN: Anyhow, I gotta get out of your way here. You've got a game in 40 minutes. Let me ask you one thing. Ted Williams played from 1939 to 1960. Do you know how many times he got ejected from a game?

LV: If I had to guess, I'd say zero.

His guess was correct. If Williams had a gripe with an umpire, he'd quietly look at the ground and say, "You can do better than that." Or, "That was one inch outside." He never showed up an umpire and so he never got run. He knew they had a job to do and understood they were trying to do a good job. Joe Paparella told Larry Gerlach about Ted Williams: "He very rarely looked back at an umpire at the plate. And he would help you even to the point of getting players off your back. If you finished the season with Boston, he'd come to the dressing room, shake your hand, wish you and your family a happy winter, and thank you for being associated with the game. He was the only one to ever do that."[12]

Working in Replay, of course, is about the closest thing to anonymity that an umpire can get. Early in most broadcasts, the umpires in the field will be identified. Look up a game while it's online and you can find who's umpiring the game. Check out the boxscore after a game and you can learn who worked which base. Even during the World Series, it's not much different.

As Tim Timmons put it, "Nobody notices you until they notice you." Then it can be bad news. Usually, it's just unfortunate. Some bench jockeying. Catcalls from the crowd. A broadcaster says something about the guy calling balls and strikes. If the call was truly incorrect, it can lead to worse.

For Jerry Meals, the worst thing that happened to him in baseball was the aftermath of a call in Atlanta on July 26, 2011 – in the bottom of the 19th inning. On a close call at home plate, Meals ruled that Julio Lugo had scored – and the Braves therefore won the game. The call stood, but being able to see the play later, Meals agreed that he had missed the call and Lugo should have been out. "No one feels worse than him," said MLB VP Joe Torre.

The Meals family lived in Pittsburgh and his daughter told of threats that were made, ESPN reported that MLB security was "investigating apparent threats made against the family" that included "calls made to the family and people showing up at the Meals' home."[13]

Meals himself minimized it some five years later.

JM: Well, they made statements, this and that. It was more just Internet stuff. It was that kind of stuff.

BN: And this was in July! It's not as though it was in the playoffs.

JM: Yeah, it was one of those things. Today, it wouldn't even be thought about.

BN: Right, you'd have Replay today. It can take you off the hook. It's got an upside.

JM: Oh yeah. Absolutely.

After making a controversial interference call on a bunt in Game Three of the 1975 World Series, Larry Barnett – fearful as well for the safety of his wife and 2-year-old – had to call for F.B.I. protection in the wake of death threats he received.[14] Don Denkinger got hate mail, profane phone calls, and multiple death threats as well after his safe call in the ninth inning of Game Six of the 1985 World Series gave the Royals a runner on first base, a runner who scored the tying run. The Royals won the game, and the Series.[15]

Barnett's call is deemed correct. Denkinger's call would almost certainly be overturned in today's game. Jim Joyce also made a call, which he himself declared incorrect immediately after the game, when seeing the play on television. He called a runner safe at first base; the admittedly wrong call cost Tigers pitcher Armando Galarraga a perfect game. "I just cost that kid a perfect game," Joyce said. "I thought he beat the throw. I was convinced he beat the throw, until I saw the replay."[16]

Hence, in time, the implementation of "instant replay." The trouble was, Jim Joyce didn't see the replay until after the game. Had the system brought in during the 2008 been in effect, Joyce would have been spared all sorts of anguish, knowing his error had cost a young pitcher his shot at baseball immortality.

And for Joyce, there was no such notoriety coming out of the other 3,267 regular season games he worked in the majors. He's remembered for one call on one day.

The Joyce/Galarraga story has an inspirational ending. We won't call it a happy one; it was a tragic story. Ten years later, the two collaborated with writer Daniel Paisner on the book *Nobody's Perfect*, each telling their stories in a book that leaves the reader feeling good – even inspired – about both key participants.[17]

Rob Drake was involved in starting the group Calling for Christ, a Christian group among umpires. He once said, "Umpiring and living a Christian life have a lot of similarities." Asked to amplify, he said, "I think the biggest thing is you are just always trying to be perfect. You're always trying to never fail, to never make mistakes. It's impossible, both in the job and at life. That was the reason that was said.

"That's what I meant. Always trying to be perfect. Only one person ever was."

8

Instant Replay

Umpires are rated on every call they make – even balls and strikes. Automation is not used in the game itself, but is used to evaluate umpires. Major league umpires never would have made the big leagues if they weren't right 98% of the time. But everyone makes mistakes, be it one of positioning (Jim Joyce allowed that he had been a bit further back from the play, his call might well have been different), or simply being "off." We can't say that the system grading them is perfection itself; balls and strikes are tough to call.

For plays on the field, however, it's now a familiar sight, maybe a couple of times during a game, for the umpires to huddle with headphones on and have their call reviewed on the spot. There might also be the occasional crew chief review, where the field umpires come together to discuss a call one of them made. Perhaps one of the other umpires had a different view of the play. Sometimes there is no need to place a call to the Replay Operations Center in New York.

On August 30, 2016, the Rays were leading the Red Sox in Boston and batting in the top of the ninth. With two outs, first base umpire Gary Cederstrom called out the baserunner, Luke Maile. Tampa Bay manager Kevin Cash asked him to look at the call and Cederstrom – the crew chief – agreed to do so. Upon review, his call was overturned and Maile was safe. I asked about it the next day.

BN: Last night, you initiated a crew chief review in the ninth inning there on a call you yourself made. Was there a signal that prompted you to do that, or did you just have a sense you wanted to be sure you had made the correct call?

GC: Kevin Cash asked that we look at it. They looked at it and asked if we would be able to look at it.

BN: But it was your call. It was officially a crew chief review.

GC: Yes.

BN: Have you ever done that? I mean, obviously you are trained to make a definitive call, but there might be a time that comes up when you thought, you know, I really do want to check that one.

GC: I've done that on a home run where…wow, where did that actually hit? Instead of waiting for people to look, I've just said, "Let's just go look at it now, because I'm not real sure where it hit." It was my call.

When the umpires get on the headsets, many fans understandably wonder what's actually said on the headsets.

GC: You get on the headset and you tell them who you are, where you are, what call they're challenging, what the call is, who is doing the challenge – and they take it from there.

BN: And they go silent.

GC: Yes.

Entrance to Replay Operations Center.
(Photograph courtesy of Major League Baseball.)

BN: You can't hear them?

GC: No, the mike has an on/off switch.

BN: On their end.

GC: Yes.

BN: And of course, you've worked down there, too.

GC: They might come back and might have a question for us. That's why we stay on the headsets, but other than that, they'll come back and say, "Yes/no – confirmed, overturned, or stands." That's the gist of being on the headsets. People believe we're standing over there talking…I might be talking to my partner, but we're not talking to New York.

BN: I wondered myself, a few weeks ago on a call that seemed very obvious it was correct. I didn't think there was going to be much time at all. It turned out to be 43 seconds. It wasn't much time. I wondered if someone was saying, "Let's give it another 20 seconds so it looks more respectful of the challenge."

GC: No. The object is to get the correct call, and get it as quickly as possible.

BN: You wouldn't even kill 20 seconds to make it look good.

GC: No. No. I've been over there, in replay, and as soon as they pick up the phones you already know whether you're overturning it or confirming it. I get over there and I say, "Tell me what you've got," and then I say, "Confirmed" or "Overturned" – just like that. They have enough shots there, to get it right.

BN: Are you pretty happy with the way it's worked? I don't mean the implementation of it, but as a system?

GC: My job is to umpire. I do what I'm told to do.

BN: Yes, but at the end of the day, you know the call is "more right" than it otherwise would have been.

GC: Yes, yes. That is true.

BN: I say "more right" because…

GC: It's still subject to people's opinion.

Getting it right is the goal. Umpires will sometimes make the call on their own, not waiting for either a crew chief review or for one of the managers to request replay. In the years before replay, plate umpire Mark Ripperger initiated a huddle himself at Safeco Field in Seattle. Trying to score from third base on a sacrifice fly, Red Sox center fielder Jacoby Ellsbury collided with Mariners catcher Josh Bard at home plate. Ripperger at first seemed to call Ellsbury safe. Asked about it, he still recalled it years later. "I couldn't find the ball. I couldn't see the ball. I was waiting for what felt like forever, and I can't call you out if I don't see you getting tagged by the ball. I called him safe and then after that he [Bard] rolled over and I saw that the ball was in his hand, against his chest. He had control of it, so at that point I got everyone together and said, "I messed this up. I think we should change it and he should be out." The safe call was reversed. Sox manager Terry Francona became Ripperger's first ejection, but the point is that the umpire wanted to get the call right, asked for help, and the correct call was made.

The last thing an umpire wants to do is make a wrong call. Brian Knight was working as a fill-in Triple-A umpire, still three years away from being hired full-time. He was the plate umpire on May 19, 2008. "My first game at Fenway Park," he remembered, "and it can be an intimidating place if you'd never been here and you're not used to it." It was a date fixed in his memory because Boston's Jon Lester threw a no-hitter that night.

BN: You wouldn't be rooting for one team or the other, but you might be rooting for the event, for it to happen.

BK: You know, the crazy thing is I'm rooting for myself to get through it without making any mistakes that would cost me. He was so good that night that I was very aware that he had not given up a hit. My number one thing that I think about is just don't screw up on my end. I really don't have any time to think about any of the other stuff. I'm just so focused on – and I'm sure we all are – one pitch at a time. So I don't make mistakes. That's what it boils down to. I don't really have time to…of course, it's going to be cool, but you don't really think about how neat it would be to be a part of that, until it's over.

BN: And, of course, you can't be part of a no-hitter until the last out is in the books.

BK: I remember walking in here, into this room, after the game, and I didn't know what to do. Like my knees were shaking. It took me 10 minutes sitting in that chair over there, just to kind of take a few deep

Monitoring games in progress, Replay Operations Center. (Photograph courtesy of Major League Baseball.)

breaths and just relax. The adrenaline was pumping through my veins. It was an incredible experience.

What about call-up umpires? They are normally called up from Triple A to fill in for an umpire who is on vacation, out for an injury, or perhaps tending to a family event. Sometimes they will fill in for a day or two, maybe working one of the games of a day/night doubleheader, and sometimes they will be with a crew for an extended period of time. When I spoke with Jansen Visconti in August 2019, he'd been working for a month with Joe West's crew. "This is the fourth consecutive week I've been with them," he said. "They go to Replay from here. I'm going to join with Ron Kulpa and Bill Welke and Gabe Morales."

That raised a question.

BN: Do fill-in umpires ever work Replay – from time to time, to get a sense of what the work's like?

Jansen Visconti: From time to time. I would say it's not very often, but from time to time they'll get us in there.

BN: It would be good to experience it.

JV: Yeah, absolutely.

BN: I guess there could be times when they need somebody quick - injuries or whatever. Family issues.

JV: Absolutely. Family issues. Sometimes they have to pull guys out of Replay to go out on the field and sometimes they'll slot us right in there.

9

Favorite Games to Work and Favorite Positions

Brian Knight's comments about adrenaline help introduce the questions: what do umpires find to be the most exciting games to work? What kind of games do they prefer to work?

Naturally, everyone likes to work a no-hitter or other notable game. Through 2018, Tom Hallion has worked seven no-hitters. He's hoping for number eight, just so he can place first among current working umpires. It's clear that working a no-hitter – or a perfect game – ranks high, particularly if you're the umpire working the plate.

Maybe it's perhaps a little surprising that every umpire seems to remember their first major league ejection, but it's not the least bit surprising that they recall any no-hitter or perfect game.

Jerry Meals worked the plate during one no-hitter and also called Kerry Wood's 20-strikeout game. In fact, both Jerry and Ron Kulpa worked a Justin Verlander no-hitter. I learned they were both on the same crew during a 2016 conversation. Jerry remembered the May 7, 2011 no-hitter. "He walked one guy. That was a 13-pitch at-bat. That was in the eighth inning. He could have had a perfect game if he'd have got him."

BN: That has to be…when did you realize it was a no-hitter? Something like the sixth inning, maybe?

JM: I think it was the sixth or seventh inning.

BN: Did you pick up something, or just happen to see the scoreboard and the zero?

JM: It was just one of those things. The Kerry Wood game, I had no idea he had 20 strikeouts. Zero idea. Chicago, back then, they didn't have anything electronic in the outfield. They just had a scoreboard.

BN: You had to pick up something from the crowd.

JM: I knew he had a lot of strikeouts but I had no idea – zero – until after the game.

Ron Kulpa recalled the Verlander no-hitter he had worked, and how he'd almost been a part of something even more special. He'd picked up on the excitement from the crowd. He knew he was seeing a potential no-hitter unfold. It was June 12, 2007, but fresh in mind was the previous game he's worked the plate, five days earlier.

Ron Kulpa: It's exciting, you know. My plate job before, I was in Oakland and I had Red Sox and A's. And Schilling was one out away from a no-hitter in that one. He gave up a hit with two outs [in the bottom of the ninth]. I called my father after that one and I said, "I'll probably never get that close again." Sure enough, my very next plate job, Verlander threw a no-hitter! I would have had back-to-backs.

One never knows what might occur. Rob Drake has worked five no-hitters, working the plate on one perfect game and one no-hitter. "I've been lucky," he said. It is special to be a part of an historic game. There was an even rarer occasion, in 2009, when he worked second base during an August 23 game at Citi Field. The Phillies were leading the Mets, 9-6, going into the bottom of the ninth. One run scored on back-to-back errors. A single put runners on first and second. Still nobody out, and the potential winning run at bat in the person of Jeff Francoeur.

Rob Drake: "Runners on first and second. There was no reason for them to be stealing. I don't understand it. He just hit a line drive with both of them stealing, he just tagged them both. I remember us standing there and like, 'Oh, the game's over. We're done. OK, let's go.' It's only happened twice in the history of baseball."

BN: You called a game-ending triple play.

RD: Runners on first and second…no reason for them to be stealing…a line drive with both of them stealing, and he [Eric Bruntlett] just tagged them both.[18]

Working the World Series is also a thrill – and, more importantly, an honor. Ted Barrett's crew, though, had an interesting point to make about working in the postseason.

During a conversation on April 14, 2017, I'd started off asking about two very different games that had just been played at Fenway. On Friday night April 14, Tampa Bay had an 8-0 lead over the Red Sox at midgame. The next day, the Saturday afternoon game ended 2-1, with no more than a one-run difference the entire game. Was one kind of game more enjoyable to work, or easier to work, than the other kind?

Ted Barrett allowed, "For me, speaking for myself, years ago the eight-run game would be easier. They wouldn't have as many plays – they wouldn't throw over as much, they wouldn't steal. If you had a close play, they wouldn't get as excited. Now there's the same intensity [for us] whether it's 2-1 or 16-0 because you run the risk of missing a call and getting the replay on it.

"We don't want to miss! So there's not one pitch you can take off during the course of the season. Before, with the older guys, things were a lot more relaxed."

Not only are the umpires graded, but the baseball players themselves are stats-driven. The importance of individual statistics comes out at contract time. A cynical person could suggest that a player might at times be more concerned with their batting averages than they are winning or losing. This can cut both ways. In a blowout game, said player might take a 3-2 pitch for a base on balls because he wants to build up his on-base percentage rather than just fold and go home. This affects replay as well. In a game his team was losing 9-1, the manager might call for replay on a close call at first base, not because he hopes to somehow turn the game around, but because the player might get angry at him for not trying to help him get credit for a base hit.

Angel Hernandez and Lance Barksdale were part of the conversation, too. Was working a World Series game about the tensest game one could imagine? There was general agreement that the first game of the World Series was the most relaxed game of the whole postseason. Both teams knew they had made the World Series. And there were at least four games to be played. If you lose the first one, there's still plenty of time to come back. The tensest games are the Wild Card game, and any other game in which a team's season is over should they lose.

Tom Hallion had a one-word response to the question: What's your favorite kind of game, if you have one?

TH: Quick.

BN: And warm maybe – reasonably warm, maybe. Not hot.

TH: Exactly.

BN: An 8-0 nothing or a 2-1 game, does that matter?

TH: No, they're all the same. You've got to go from pitch one to the last pitch of the game, doing what you do. We really don't get all caught up in the game.

Jeff Nelson's response: "One where the pitchers are throwing strikes, the batters are swinging, the pace of the game is moving. Players are making the plays. They are the best players in the world and they are capable to doing that every day. It's not something we have any control over. But obviously some days are more like that than others.

BN: A quick game is good because it gets over faster, but I think a faster pace in the game helps defense.

JN: I think it's better for everybody, but I also realize that people are playing for statistics, too. That's a factor.

Gerry Davis said, "I like to work the plate. It's more strenuous. It's more demanding – physically and mentally. Obviously, you can't do it every day, but that's how you get to the big leagues. Nobody comes to the big leagues because they're a good third-base umpire."

Favorite Positions

If not a favorite game, is there one position that umpires prefer to work? As one might expect, there were different responses.

Tom Hallion said, "Each position's got its own little pros and cons. If you want an exciting game, you want the plate. If you're tired and you just want to go to a position that…uh…third base. First and second, they're about the same."

Bill Miller: I think we make our money behind the plate. You can't work the plate every day. You just have a lot more control of the game. At the same time, it's nice to go to third base, too.

BN: Then you've got the plate work behind you.

BM: It's just a nice change. If you had to work the plate every day, with the pressure and the stress…Back in the day. Bill Klem, he was working two-man, not only working every other day, but then after a time I think the other guy just didn't want to work the plate.

Doug Eddings concurred: Home plate. Just because you're in charge of the game. You're into every pitch, every play. You don't want to work it every day. Physically, it's very draining, but I think most umpires would say the plate.

Doug then said about Bill Miller, joking: "Billy said right field, probably."

BN: Well, then you're in the playoffs!

BM: Yeah, there you go!

On April 23, 2019, the Red Sox played two games due to a rainout the night before. They played a 1:10 afternoon game and a 7:00 PM evening game. David Rackley worked the plate in the first game and Dan Bellino worked the plate in the second game. Recognizing that working the plate is the most taxing position to work, the policy is that whichever umpire works the plate in such a situation are only asked to work one game that day, with a Triple-A umpire called up to work both games. Jansen Visconti got the call on April 23. The crews for the two games were:

HP - David Rackley, 1B - Jansen Visconti, 2B - Alfonso Marquez, 3B - Larry Vanover.

HP - Dan Bellino, 1B - Alfonso Marquez, 2B - Larry Vanover, 3B - Jansen Visconti.

After the first game had concluded, I met David Rackley as he was leaving and asked him if he had a favorite position to work.

David Rackley: Working the plate is the most challenging. It has the most action. When you have a good game, it's the most rewarding. When you have a not-so-good game, it's the most disappointing.

BN: Brian O'Nora told me, "I think they're all good. After you're done working the plate, it's good to have a mental break. You've got to be constantly in the game…not that you're not at third base, but…"

DR: Yeah.

BN: We just saw a play two or three games ago where the Red Sox picked a guy off first base for the final play of the game. [On April 20, 2019, at

Tampa Bay, the Red Sox were winning 6-5 in the bottom of the ninth but the Rays had runners on first and second with two outs. Red Sox catcher Christian Vazquez caught the pitch and fired to first base, picking off Tommy Pham and thus ending the game]. If the umpire wasn't ready to make that call…

DR: Being ready is…even if you're working third base, you have to be ready for anything that could happen, just like you have to be at home plate.

BN: And Scott Barry said he liked second base because you move around a whole lot more.

DR: Yeah. I could see that. You've got to be prepared for every single play – whether you're at third, second, or first. You're a split-second away from an inning-ending, game-ending, check swing that's very controversial, or a 100 mile an hour ball that lands two feet…

The next day, Dan Bellino had no hesitation: "The plate." Because there's more action at home plate.

Alfonso Marquez agreed: "Yes. You're moving around. Especially on a cold night. And it was cold last night. Really, really cold."

And Ron Kulpa said he liked working the plate the best. "I like working the plate. It's where all the action is. That's where you can make your…for the playoffs that season. I always say that's where you make the playoff money."

Scott Barry had indeed talked about second base. On working the plate, he said, "I think everybody likes that challenge." But then he had added: "I think I like working second as much as any other place, though. I like the freedom. You're able to move all around the bag and take plays from all kinds of different positions."

BN: That's interesting. Working first or third, you're set in the same position where you need to be before the pitch.

SB: Right.

BN: But working second base, you've got to adjust your position to left-handers, right-handers, shifts, what baserunners are on what bases.

SB: Yeah, and just the way plays develop. I think it challenges you more to get into position to see everything. Yeah. I enjoy being able to move. I like the freedom. It's weird.

BN: It makes total sense to me. There are possible steal attempts.

SB: There just always seems to be something to do when the ball's hit.

BN: With the increasing number of defensive shifts, do you get into much dialogue with the players, who might ask, "Could you move a little this way?" Or do you just pretty much see where they're setting up and respond to that?

SB: I do. I just go off what they do and move from there.

BN: Every once in a while someone might ask you to move a bit?

SB: That happens more when you're inside, on the infield grass, and you're trying to get into position. For steal plays, you want to stay out of the way of the second baseman. Whatever side…however he adjusts, that when I'll…I mean, that's when they'll ask you more. I try to be cognizant of it and ask them, "Hey, are you OK? Can you see?" That type of thing. And move before it ever gets to that kind of situation.

BN: I thought Brian gave me a good answer when I asked him what his favorite position was. He pretty much said it was third base – he didn't say it that way, he said "the day after working the plate."

SB: (laughs) Absolutely. That is true.

BN: You've got to work hard behind the plate. You're in more danger. And you've got to call every pitch.

SB: Absolutely.

BN: It's not like when you're working third base you can just wander around and look in the stands to see who's there or anything like that.

SB: Yeah, the day after the plate is always a good day.

Other than wearing protective gear, working the plate isn't necessarily something that umpires need to psych themselves up for. Of course, by the time they've made the majors, they've worked a thousand or more games behind the plate, doing so more often with two-man and three-man crews.

"It's a different animal," Quinn Wolcott allowed, but said, "I don't, like, differently prepare for it, mentally."

BN: [Pointing to notebook on the table, with a table of numbers on it.] I didn't know if that was a secret code for mental preparation.

QW: No, that's a card scoresheet. [A tally for the crew's pre-game card game.]

Paul Emmel: It requires more focus, of course, throughout the game.

BN: And you can get hit more. Not that you could do much about it.

QW: You can't do anything about it. It just happens.

Jeff Nelson concurred about third base perhaps offering a bit of a respite. "Third base, as opposed to the plate, you don't have two or three hundred decisions to make. And you're not going to put yourself at risk for injury. You're not as physically and mentally exhausted. You've got to work them all, but yeah, third base."

Tripp Gibson definitely did not disagree, but entered a note of caution: "Third base has the fewest number of calls, but you could go seven or eight innings and not have anything happen – and then you could have a check swing that could really change a lot of things. So you've got to be on your toes.

"It's easier on the other two bases because you're a lot busier. As far as staying locked in with the blinders on – pardon my horse-racing reference – locked in there. Third base is the most difficult to stay 100% locked-in."

Behind the plate, though, came across as his pick "Behind the plate is the most enjoyable – and also the most difficult – place to be. You're the busiest there…You're in the middle of everything. Every time anything happens on the field, there has to be a pitch thrown first. You have a decision to make before anything else can really happen.

BN: You have to make more than a couple of hundred calls, while at first and third base, or second base…

TG: Yes. And not only that. There's so many calls on the field that don't actually even have a call – the batter's just running up the first-base line to first base and I'm watching to see if he's inside or outside of the lane.

That's a part of calling a "perfect game" – the calls that are not made, because there has been no infraction. Without an umpire keeping a watchful eye, though, one wonders what corners players might be tempted to try to cut.

Tony Randazzo also liked the plate: "You know, I'm going to be honest. I like working the plate. I know it's stressful but you're in the game…not that I'm begging for it, but…"

BN: I had an answer I came up with – down the left-field or right-field line, because that means you're working a playoff game.

Tony Randazzo: (laughs) That's a good one.

Jeff Nelson: If you're working the playoffs, right field's the way to go. We always joke that right field is where you want to watch the game from.

BN: Well, once in a while, just this last year in the 2018 ALCS, Joe West made that call of interference. You've got to be there and ready to make a call.

JN: Absolutely. That's the challenge of working those bases. You don't get calls all the time but when you get them, they're important.

BN: When players these days go into these extreme shifts that they do, does that make things any more difficult for you or do you just simply have to adjust?

JN: I wouldn't say it was more difficult, but different. We have to adjust our coverage. We make sure we communicate who's going to have what responsibilities.

I asked Joe West what was his favorite position to work. He said (of working the plate) that he didn't like people throwing balls at him. He said that third base was the toughest position to work for him because of the wear and tear on the knees.

Joe West: Yeah, because you stand for so long and that, all of a sudden, you've got to run to second base or run to the outfield. There's a lot of starting and stopping without being really loose. That's hardest on your knees.

You also can get all your angles backwards from all your other places. At first base, everything comes over your right shoulder. Everything at third base comes over your left shoulder.

BN: And you've got to be ready to look at check swings on every single pitch.

JW: You do it on both third and first.

BN: You've got to be ready. You can't be looking into the stands and then snapping into focus if you hear the crack of the bat. Second base, there's a lot more movement back and forth, but not the quick burst kind of action that you have at third.

Joe West posing with baseball fan Shawn Gibbons prior to the Red Sox/Braves game on April 28, 2016.

JW: Right.

BN: At first base, you're kind of anchored more to the base because that's the first base every batter runner will come to.

JW: At third base, you can usually walk on some of your calls.

[As it happens, during the game that followed the interview, a mid-game foul line drive in the top of the fifth inning off the bat of Richie Martin struck Joe just above the knee. He shook it off and worked the rest of the game, but did not work the next day's Sunday afternoon game. Brennan Miller was called up to take his place. It was the only game Joe missed. Fortunately, beginning on Monday, he had a respite from field work since he was scheduled to work Replay in New York.]

Call-up umpire Nick Mahrley enjoyed working second base, too.
NM: I do like working the plate. They're all different. There's no night off. But I really like working second base, because there's so many different things you can do. You move around a lot. You really have to umpire. You take different angles on so many plays, because the ball can be coming from so many different places. It really challenges you. I like second base a lot. I do enjoy working the plate on day games, afternoon games. It's a good feel.

"I've got my mind on the plate today," Marty Foster said as he arrived at the umpires' room. But he said he didn't have a preference among positions. "They're all the same. They're all work. Everything is predicated on concentration and focus. You've got to have that at every position. It's just that at the plate you have more decisions than you do at third. Every game at this base, you're going to have a play – whether it be a check swing, a steal play. Ron [Kulpa] had one last night. He didn't have anything in the game and all of a sudden he's got a guy on his knees throwing to third base on a force out. You've got to be ready."

10

Spring Training

Life in spring training is very different for umpires. It's something I had not reflected on until I visited the Phoenix area in March 2019 for the NINE Baseball Conference, the SABR Analytics Conference, and a SABR board meeting. The NINE group went to a couple of spring training games and I went to the Tempe Diablo Stadium a couple of hours before everyone else on March 9, so I could meet the crew working that day. Naturally, I knew that it was good for umpires to get back in working form, too, attuned to the game so they could be at their best when the regular season began. I just hadn't thought about how life was so very different for them during spring training. It's just one of those things most of us don't think about. Mike Winters was the first of the crew to arrive that afternoon.

BN: Is this the crew now that you will have throughout the season?

MW: Oh no. During the season, it's totally different. Some guys are in Florida. Some guys are out here.

BN: Are you just working the Cactus League, or do you go back and forth?

MW: We just work one side. The four of us working today just work the Cactus League. For most of us, it's because of where you live. I live in San Diego, so it's very easy to travel.

BN: Do you get to stay in one area? Most of the parks are relatively nearby each other.

MW: I'm all over the Valley. I've been out in Glendale a couple of times.

BN: But it's certainly not like going from Chicago to Seattle.

MW: No. It's much easier. Half an hour drive.

BN: No air travel once you get here, then. So spring training is very different. The traveling is much lighter. Do you get a place and pretty much just stay in one place?

MW: Oh yeah. It's really nice. My wife's here. She's with me the whole time. The family was out the first weekend. It's much more relaxing. It's all in one spot. The games are mostly day games. You can make plans to go out for dinner.

BN: You can actually have dinner with your family, go to a movie or whatever you might want.

MW: Yeah, it more of a normal lifestyle.

BN: But then comes Opening Day…

MW: Opening Day, things change. Your lifestyle changes. You're up late – and up early for flights.

Spartan accommodations, spring training, Tempe Diablo Stadium, March 2019.

The word "normal" came up more than once, talking with umpires about spring training. Chris Guccione, from Colorado, also worked in the Cactus League. He and his wife and their young daughter come down to Arizona. They're able to spend the month together, while he works games.

CG: It's awesome, yeah. I love it. We're starting to get where she's going to be starting school, so it's going to be a little different. But yeah, I work a full schedule. You can either work 21 games or 15. You can choose. I choose a full schedule.

BN: It's a different experience, spring training. Instead of every three or four days, you're packing up and going to a different city...most of the games are during the day, so you can go out to dinner or a movie if you want.

CG: Right. It's like normal life!

Alfonso Marquez doesn't even have to leave home and rent a place. He lives at Power Ranch, a "masterplanned community in the southeast valley of metropolitan Phoenix." He stays in his own home and simply commutes to every game. Basically, he gets an extra month at home.

Call-up umpire Nick Mahrley also lives in Phoenix. "I live in Arizona. I live in Phoenix, so it's nice when I can stay home and work spring there. I did work spring training in Florida in 2017. My first full big-league spring training was there. It was a great experience, but you can't beat being home."

David Rackley, from Charlotte, works the Grapefruit League. "Spring training is nice," he says. "It's nice to get back out there and get the dust off. Work day games. My family came down for spring break."

Bill Miller says, "I work in Arizona. Being from California, it's easier for my family. I actually do drive. That way my wife has a car when we're down there. That way I've got a car, she's got a car... I'm from Northern California. It's about a 10-hour, 12-hour drive.

It is nice. I'm down there for full spring. For me, it's about 3 ½, four weeks. I think I had one night game this year. Two night games? One o'clock start so you're done by 4. You can go see some people, meet some friends...It's really a lot of fun. Spring training is...we kind of stay right in the Scottsdale area. Man, it's like a glorified spring break for 40- or 50-year-olds."

Spring training – like the Fall League – provides opportunities for aspiring Triple-A umpires, a chance to work alongside major league umpires and improve their opportunities of being assigned a number and employed as a call-up. Seniority accords the well-established big league umpire some options in terms of scheduling. One might, for instance, decide to work two weeks' worth of games to get into form, rather than the full four. "I take two weeks," said Marty Foster. "What do I need four weeks of work for, before the season starts? Two years ago, we started the season in March. I was tired. More so than ever. Some of those games take it out of you. The starters are in for two innings. You're working Double-A baseball. I cut back this year and I started the season feeling better."

Talking about working in Florida, in the Grapefruit League, Hunter Wendelstedt notes that some of the venues are more geographically dispersed than in Arizona, but even in the Cactus League, not all the parks are clustered in Phoenix. "A lot of the young guys have to travel every

Young boy from the Diamondbacks dugout brings out new baseballs to plate umpire Ted Barrett during a Cactus League game on March 7, 2020 at Salt River Field, Talking Stick, Arizona.

couple of days. They do the whole state, just like in Arizona. Seniority has its privileges."

Tom Hallion hails from Louisville, so he elects to work the Grapefruit League.

TH: I could go to either league. I have enough seniority that if I wanted to go to the Cactus League, I could go there.

BN: Do you bring your family down at all?

TH: You try to. You stay for the month. It's the best time of the year. You can go out for dinner.

BN: Civilization, or something like that.

TH: It's very nice. It's like being a normal person.

11

Ejections

We don't want to make too much of ejections. They happen. They offer a little drama. It's almost always obvious why the ejection occurred. The extreme case occurred on October 12, 1984 in Atlanta when umpire Steve Rippley ejected 17 players from the one game.[19] One of the players tossed was Joe Torre.

Since 2011, Joe Torre has served as Chief Baseball Officer of Major League Baseball. He oversees all baseball operations and is the direct contact from the Commissioner to all the GMs, field managers, and major league umpires.

Gerry Davis threw out Joe Torre twice. He ejected his future boss once in 1991 and once in 1992. Rippley and Davis are not the only ones to have ejected the man who became a Hall of Famer…and their boss. Joe West threw him out three times – in 1977 and 1978 with the Mets, and 1992 with the Cardinals.

Umps almost always remember their first ejection. Doug Eddings was asked if he recalled who was the first person he threw out of a game. "Yeah. My boss. [Joe Torre, on August 6, 1999] I've got a signed ball from him. I told him to put the date on it. It was a call at first base, in Seattle." Working five years earlier, in Dominican ball, Eddings once threw out Tito Bell in four consecutive games, but that's another story.

Torre became a convert to the cause of the umpires. Gerry Davis explained: "[He's] talked about that a lot in recent years. From his playing and managerial days, he says he used to believe that the umpires would just make the call and they didn't really care what the fans thought or the teams thought, or whatever. But then in his supervisory and managerial role on behalf of us, he saw how we were when we came in the locker room after we missed a play. How much it affected us, and how much we want to be right. So he has consequently said, 'I'll run through the wall for you guys.' Because he knows how we feel about it. I think that's the biggest thing. We want to get everything right. And when we don't, it eats at us more than it does you."

Sam Holbrook mentioned Lou Piniella and Bobby Cox as managers who earned themselves a lot of ejections. Bill Welke recalled Piniella. "Lou was my first ejection in the major leagues, on national TV. Once you stood up to Lou, he treated you completely different. He treated you like a professional that you could talk to."

That brought to mind Dave Anderson writing about Hall of Fame umpire Bill Klem. "He faced challenges establishing himself, as witness the 25 ejections in his first year in the league. In fact, he averaged more than 19 ejections over the course of his first seven seasons. In all, Klem ejected 279 persons during the course of his career, but after the 1915 season he only reached double digits once, in 1920."[20]

Bobby Cox came up in conversation with Tom Hallion.

BN: You've had 88 ejections before this year, but 12 of them came all in 1989 and five of those were in one game. Houston and Montreal.

Ton Hallion: That was a big brawl. That's really different than other types of ejections. You've got to do what you have to do, but at that point…that was a throwing incident that got out of control.

BN: I saw there was a time that you ejected Bobby Cox because he bumped another umpire. I guess you had to step in.

TH: Yeah. Yeah. Bobby was a classic. (laughs)

BN: Do you remember your first ejection at all?

TH: Sure. Ron Oester. Up in Cincinnati. I called him out on strikes and he said, "Why don't you go back to the minor leagues?" I said, "I'll see ya."

Asked if he remembers his first, Dan Bellino said, "Of course." And he remembered it in detail. "My first ejection was in Tampa Bay. It was Dioner Navarro, on a called pitch to Adam Lind, that I called a ball, low. Navarro argued. I walked out and he kept arguing. I warned him, and then threw him out. It was me, Winters, Layne was the crew chief, and it was Hunter Wendelstedt."

Mike DiMuro was a little surprised at something that came up in conversation:

BN: Mike, there's one question I forgot to ask you. Are you good friends with Bruce Bochy? You know why I ask? Over the course of your career, you ejected 60 people.

MD: Sixty?

BN: Sixty. And five of them were him.

MD: You're kidding me!

BN: I can show you.

MD: I'm sure it's on Retrosheet. I didn't realize that.

BN: It is. I was wondering, 'Gee, do you guys have a thing together.' Two of them were on back-to-back days, and three of them all in one month.

MD: No. I'm sure they were just plays. I've known him since minor leagues, coming up through the minors.

BN: I was just kidding. You haven't thrown anybody out for three years now, though.

John Tumpane or Mark Wegner (from around the corner, not sure who): "You shouldn't have said that! Now it's going to happen."

Vic Carapazza had been an M.P. in the Air Force. Without a doubt that gave him plenty of experience in letting people blow off steam. His first ejection was Miguel Cabrera. It was prompted by what Vic called "a borderline high pitch." Cabrera was waving his arms all around as he was arguing and manager Jim Leyland came out to try to defuse matters. "Leyland came out and was very good. Very calm. He just said, 'Hey, Vic, just let him have his say a little bit more.' You take stuff from guys like that who have been around, and you weigh it. There's days when you just have to handle it yourself. But he's been doing it for 30 years [Leyland]. He wants to keep the guy in the game." Vic probably spoke for most umpires when he said, "I don't like throwing anybody out of any game, but I'll do it if I have to do it. You warn him a couple of times and then, you know, you leave it in *their* hands. Let them decide what they want to do."

Sam Holbrook explained his thinking explained in more detail: "Sometimes a guy will draw a line like where he thinks the pitch is. He knows that's automatic. There's other kinds of stuff that's a little more gray area, but if the guy kicks a bag or something you're going to get run for that. Or throwing the hat, that kind of stuff. But as far as arguing the call, if there's any kind of language we pretty much let go that kind of stuff. My thing is, and I always tell guys, I always try to let the initial emotion of a play go – like especially now – mostly balls and strikes. So if I call a guy out on strike 3 and he gives me a shout or says something, like that F'ing pitch was off the plate or something like that and now he walks back to the dugout, no problem. Once he gets back to the dugout he needs to let it go. Now because he has time to process it and calm down, if he goes in there and slams his helmet he's going to get my attention and then if he wants to pop off again he's probably going to get ejected because I gave him his say, put a warning in, and alright, that's it, let's go. If he goes back to the dugout and he wants to continue, now I'm trying to go back to work and get the next pitch right, and I've got him screaming at us from the dugout."

A manager will, of course, want to stand up for one of their players, sometimes taking the fall to keep a player off the hook, or just wanting his team to know he had their backs. In days long gone, Dave Anderson wrote, "McGraw was one of the toughest on umpires averaging several ejections a season. McGraw claimed that, "...'artful kicking' to keep umpires aware of his presence gained his club as many as fifty extra runs a season."[21]

But as we have seen, there were players such as Ted Williams, who had something of a fiery personality, but never got himself ejected from a single game.

The advent of television no doubt made a big difference, and certainly the implementation of Replay has made a difference.

During his time in the minors, Jeff Nelson had even done some officiating in both basketball and football. He talked about the change in ejections after Replay came in.

BN: When I first heard Replay was being implemented, my first thought was that it was going to take a lot of drama out of the game. The Earl Weavers of the world wouldn't have as much to kick about. Some of those massive arguments were exciting from the fans' point of view. But maybe you just hated them.

Jeff Nelson: Well, you know what, there's an emphasis now on us being calmer during discussions, so the notion of someone coming out and berating you and you have to just zip your lips and fold your arms and just take it and be a whipping post isn't exactly appealing. That part I don't exactly miss. The first year after replay was instituted, there were more ejections than there were the previous year. It just shifted where ejections happen. Now it's shifted more towards ejections on balls and strikes. There's still drama there; it's just different drama and you don't get as many arguments on the basepaths.

BN: A manager will still come out to make a show on behalf of his players?

JN: Yes. That's still an element of the game. When people think that an ejection happened and there was some great wrong that was perpetrated there, a large percentage of the time the manager knew what he was doing. It was calculated behavior and he had a purpose in mind. It's not a surprise to anybody on the playing surface that the ejection occurred. I know it's a strange concept sometimes for the fan because he thinks the ejection was some kind of surprise but that's not the way it works.

BN: You read in Ron Luciano's books that a manager might come out and say, "You know, you're going to have to throw me out of this game. You're going to have to make it look really good."

JN: Most of those were made-up stories, but occasionally that's happened. Most of the time, it's what they're doing. They just don't state it. They come out there with a serious face and they say their whole thing and that's what happens, without their saying it overtly.

BN: Do you remember your first ejection?

JN: Well, we had some chargings of the mound when I was still going up and down. I don't remember those really well. The first ejection I had after I got hired fulltime was Bobby Cox on a checked swing in San Diego. I do remember that one.

As stated, we don't want to dwell on ejections. Those wishing to explore the subject more would do well to read Gil Imber's article on the history of ejections in baseball.[22]

Just as an aside, Jeff agreed with what Angel Hernandez had said – that umpires always remember their first major league game. It was in 1997 and Nelson worked third base. "I had a call in the first inning at third base and that kind of broke the ice. That was a good feeling because it's kind of an out-of-body experience your first time out there. Even though you've worked a thousand minor-league games, it's just a really big deal to be down there and actually be doing it for the first time."

12

Injuries

Injuries are not something we want to dwell on, but they do come with the territory. Umpires get injured from time to time and, as they age, sometimes all the field work begins to take a toll. Concussions and other mishaps occur and Major League Baseball takes them very seriously. There is a medical staff devoted to the umpires, though naturally the first professionals to diagnose and treat an injury on the field will be the medical staff of the home team. Likewise, each team has a designated dentist and, if necessary, umpires will consult the home team's dentist. Overseeing all this is Mark Letendre who serves as Director, Umpire Medical Services, and has worked for the main office since 1999. Dr. Steven M. Erickson is a medical consultant. Dr. Laurence M. Westreich serves as a consultant on behavioral health and addiction. In the conversation with Chris Guccione, he mentions Mackey Shilstone as "our guru nutritionist" who runs a program for umpires urging healthier diets. An interview with Mark Letendre is included in *The SABR Book of Umpires and Umpiring.*

In the 2019 American League Championship Series, home plate umpire (and crew chief) Jeff Nelson was struck twice in the face mask by foul balls, once in the third inning and then again in the fourth inning. After the second one, it was deemed prudent to make a change. Kerwin Danley took over plate duties, the game continued without an umpire on the left-field line, and Nelson was replaced for the remainder of the ALCS by Mike Everitt.

Rob Edelman's biography of Art Passarella in the SABR book details season-ending injuries that the veteran umpire suffered in June 1954 and again in July 1956, as well as a number of minor injuries that seemed to dog him throughout his career.

Ernie Quigley missed most of the 1937 and 1938 seasons due to a severe ankle injury. He'd suffered a number of earlier injuries; in 1934, a foul tip to the jaw left him unable to speak for some days.[23]

After 24 years in the field, bad knees finally forced Larry Young to leave field work. He now works as an umpire supervisor for Major League Baseball and made the trip to England at the end of June 2019 for the London Series there.

Kerwin Danley suffered serious head or face mask injuries due to broken bats or foul tips in 2008, 2009, 2013, and 2015.

As we have seen, after six or seven concussions, Ed Hickox began wearing a different sort of facemask, more or less modified hockey helmet.

Through the start of the 2016 season, David Vincent compiled an historical listing of on-field injuries that were serious enough the affected umpire needed to leave the game. In just the first three months of that season, there had already been 11 such injuries.[24]

At the time I spoke with Gerry Davis, he ranked fourth all-time in terms of the number of games worked – 4,714 major league games through the 2018 season. "I'll pass 4,800 games this year," he said. "That's 120 games a year for 40 years. When you start breaking that down, that means a third of every year. I've been on the road for 40 years."

In 2019, it appeared there might have been an unusual amount of injuries or physical problems that prevented umpires from working the field. It's not a secret when an umpire is out for an injury, but confidentiality and simple respect for privacy leads us to omit the names of umpires so afflicted. When I spoke with Gerry Davis in July 2019, two members of his crew were out, both due to serious long-term problems. "[Name omitted] has a bulging disc that is leaking, which is terrible, and [name omitted] has some real issues with his knee. They're going to try to do some stuff, but if not, he may have to have a knee replacement. Not small things."

BN: Do you have any thoughts about how long you're going to keep going?

GD: I'm still healthy for the most part. I enjoy it. I haven't had any major surgeries. No problems with knees, back, or neck, like a lot of us have had. I'm still healthy. I still enjoy it. This is a contract year for us. We'll see where the numbers go. I'm fortunate that it will be my decision.

Interestingly, it was an injury that led him to become an umpire in the first place. Growing up in the St. Louis area, he played baseball and was a pitcher and first baseman. He wanted to be the next Stan Musial. Around the age of 20 or thereabouts, "I had hurt my arm and couldn't pitch. My manager said, 'Well, since you can't play, you're going to be the umpire.' Whenever we would travel, we would take one umpire and the home team would provide one. So he could save the eight or ten dollars or whatever he was paying the guys, he said, 'You're going to be one of the umpires.' I did it, and he said, "You know, you're pretty decent. You should think about going to umpire school.' I didn't know there was such a thing. The manager sent away for the application to umpire school for me, and had it sent to my house. At the time, I had this new crazy job as a computer operator. I worked in the Federal Reserve Bank in St. Louis, but I worked the third shift. I hated the job. So when the application came for umpire school, I thought, 'You know, I want to stay involved in sports somehow if I can.' So I went to umpire school, not knowing if that's what I wanted to do. but I fell in love with it while I was there. And here we are."

Not all are as fortunate in terms of health and injury.

Tony Randazzo missed the entire 2008 season. He said why. "I've got a plate in my neck. Spring training game. Randy Johnson was pitching. Todd Helton batting. Straight to the jaw. I went down. My whole arm... About three days later, I still couldn't sleep. I had to put my shoulder into the couch. Finally, there was a game and I looked up like that and I got a stinger down my back. Gooch goes, 'You need to get to a doctor.' I went to the doctor and they told me I had a crack in my vertebrae."

[During a game in 2016, Tony took four foul tips off his mask in one game and had to leave with concussion symptoms. The next year, during the May 13, 2017 game in San Francisco, he took a fastball to the mask in the fifth inning and stuck with it but eventually had to leave after the 13th inning.]

Tony was able to return after his 2008 season and put in full seasons the next five years.

Some umpires suffer injuries on the field that prove to be career-ending. In 1996, John McSherry, only 51 years old, collapsed on the field and died during the first inning of the Opening Day game in Cincinnati. The game was called off and played the following day. McSherry was seriously overweight. When the two leagues were merged into Major League Baseball in 1999, Mark Letendre instituted a health and wellness program for the umpiring staff. MLB was the first of the major professional sports to institute such a program.

It is possible that Cal Drummond died due to an on-field injury. After he was struck by a foul ball in 1969, he was unconscious for some days and had surgery to remove a blood clot from his brain. Less than a year later, he suffered a fatal stroke involving that area of his brain.[25]

Above, we saw Tim Welke express his appreciation for the program and Mark's dedication: "The health and welfare of the umpires has just turned into something outstanding. It's a demanding job. The guys are healthier today. [Mark] oversees that. He's done a terrific job maintaining people. It's improved tenfold."

They baseline all umpires and then monitor them. As Letendre explained, "We do baseline pysch. We do baseline vestibular balance. We do baseline vision."

Increasingly, umpires have come to select hotels which offer swimming pools and good gym or exercise facilities.

There are the occasional games where something unexpected happens that makes for a very different game. One such game occurred on August 26, 2009. Three different umpires worked the plate (not all at the same time!) A hard-hit foul off the bat of Aaron Hill struck plate umpire Jerry Crawford in the mask; he shook it off but had to leave the game after the second inning. Tom Hallion moved from second base to work the plate. In the bottom of the sixth, a Scott Kazmir fastball eluded catcher Gregg Zaun entirely and struck Hallion in the chest. He was knocked to the ground and there was a 21-minute delay while he was seen to by medical personnel. Brian O'Nora worked the plate for the rest of the game.

Brian O'Nora: I worked that game with Scott [Barry]. He was the call-up guy. Scott and I worked a two-man.

BN: They both had to leave the game?

BO: Yes, sir.

BN: I thought Tom got hit by a ball in the chest, but then moved to third base.

BO: No, they wouldn't let him back in the game.

BN: You're saying you had two umpires ended up working a major league game? You and Scott worked a two-man crew?

BO: Yeah.

BN: I would have come out and helped. I guess that kind of took you back to the old days, working in the minor leagues as a two-man or three-man.

BO: Yeah.

BN: You just kept cycling people through home plate.

BO: Yeah, that was…actually, the game was headed for extra innings when Rod Barajas hit a two-run homer in the bottom of the ninth to win it. [Toronto 3, Tampa Bay 2]

BN: We had a game here the other night that went for 19 innings.

BO: The other night, yeah.

BN: I stayed for the whole game…as did every one of the umpires!

BO: (laughs)

One indicator of a possible injury can come from the number of games a major league umpire works in a given year.

Rob Drake only worked 66 games in 2018, well below the 155 games a year he worked on average as a call-up umpire in 2007-9, or the 120 games that is the more-or-less typical workload of a major league umpire.

Rob Drake: Yeah. I had knee surgery in July last year.

BN: There's a lot of guys who have been out recently this year.

RD: Yeah, the game's changing. It's just a lot more intense. There's a lot more wear and tear on your body.

13

Evaluation and Selection for Postseason Play

When Tony Randazzo was named to work the World Series in 2016, he got the phone call inviting him and became very emotional. Tony's father, George Randazzo, founded the National Italian American Sports Hall of Fame in Chicago. George told an ABC News reporter, "Tony called me up. He was crying. He had me crying and said, 'Dad, I made the World Series.'"[26] He'd been in the majors for 17 years and it was his first World Series.

It was an honor that every umpire aspires to.

Gerry Davis has worked a "special event" in 24 consecutive seasons. "The All-Star Game is one. The Division Series in one. Those kind of things. The thing that I am most proud of with that is that those are selected on merit now. Years ago, before my streak began, it was on a rotational basis. Now it's chosen by merit. I'm humbled by those numbers. It means that I've been good enough to be chosen and I've been able to do it for a long time."

To be selected to work the World Series is the highest honor of all.

As noted, to become a major league umpire in the first place, one is subject to constant oversight and evaluation for more or less 10 years. Even after reaching the final rung on the ladder and being promoted to the majors, evaluation never stops. When you work the plate, every call you make – ball or strike – is rated as correct or incorrect by an internal monitoring system to which the public is not privy. But umpire supervisors are well aware of the ratings. It is public information how often a given umpire's play calls are overturned on Replay. These sorts

Umpires arrive outside umpires room, dressed up ahead of Game Two of the 2018 ALCS, Fenway Park, October 6, 2018. L to R: Dan Bellino, D. J. Reyburn, Fieldin Culbreth, Mike Winters, Cory Blaser.

of figures are taken into account when making postseason assignments and selecting umpires for what are deemed "Special Events."

Of course, umpires earn additional pay for working special events.

Evaluations have, of course, changed over time. Jeff Nelson worked his first major league games in 1997.

Jeff Nelson: Back then, they didn't have as much formal supervision but the crew chiefs at the time – in the National League – were very close to the office and gave a lot of informal feedback. There was no shortage of feedback, even back then, despite the fact that there weren't as many formal supervisors.

BN: Were the games video'd then, or did that only come in later?

JN: Games were taped on a VCR in the umpires room. Obviously, the production quality of the games in 1997 wasn't what it is today. The older umpires then came from a different era when the production quality just wasn't that great. And the game was played differently. When they first started, there was a lot of expectations from everybody in the game that you called things from the way they looked. Maybe not necessarily the way they were. I'm not saying they were wrong. If the tag beat the runner and it was a good tag, and it was down, there might be a huge cloud of dust or dirt and everything gets obscured, but it looked like he was going to be out…the guys were very talented but maybe the expectation of the umpiring wasn't as precise as it is now with the high-definition, slo-mo video.

When I was coming up, it was just changing and the effects of television were just starting to be felt where the supervisors were emphasizing that you had to call exactly what television showed – what the people could see on TV. Now they can slow things down and see more – not nearly as much as we can see today, but more.

Some of the old-timers resisted some of the video back then, but through my time video has become second nature and a part of our jobs.

What is the evaluation process like? Sam Holbrook said, "We get graded on every single pitch and play that we have on a field. We have an electronic strike zone that we get a score on for every game and Major League Baseball obviously gets those numbers, too. We get graded on every single play, and we have a website we go to where we can find out exactly what our numbers are. They're not compared to other umpires but you know, Major League Baseball has all the numbers and that's one aspect of their evaluations of us. When you look at the numbers we're all pretty close; we're all working around a 98% success rate so that 2% is what we place for."

Call-up umpire Nick Mahrley was preparing to work the plate on July 27, 2019. I asked him, "When you work the plate tonight, you'll get a report like an hour or two after the game? You can look up a rating of how you did?"

NM: Usually, it's the next day. You can log onto our strike zone grading website and it'll tell you how many callable pitches you had, how many you got right, how many you got wrong, and how many of them were maybe...

BN: Borderline?

NM: Yeah, borderline maybe. Pitches that you can't pick up. Sometimes they could go either way. Then they give you a grade – what you got – a percentage grade. And it just goes in your file. Every night you just try to get every single pitch right that you can, and do your best.

Umpires on the major league staff – those who have made it – are still evaluated, after every game they work. For those who have worked the plate, there is feedback within a number of hours. At the end of each series, each umpire receives an individual evaluation.

Will Little: We have a website, through the league. We log on and view all the plays and pitches, etc.

BN: Do they edit it for you? You don't have to watch the whole game?

WL: It's edited. It's cut down to where it's just the pitches and just the plays. We're not watching the six-hour video from last night's game. [The game from the night before lasted 5:54, a 15-inning game. Joe West worked the plate.]

BN: They give you a score, too, a numerical score?

WL: Sure, there's a numerical score that goes along, on the total number of pitches that we actually call.

BN: You don't need to call a foul ball.

WL: Correct. Or a pitch that's swung at. Yeah, pitches that we have to call. Based on my own games, I would say there's probably 175-200 pitches a game.

BN: You get evaluations after each series.

WL: As soon as they get done with them, they'll send them on and we review them. The league takes this whole job seriously, and they certainly take our jobs seriously.

We're held accountable for every call we make, every decision we make on the field – good or bad – and all of it's taken into our reports, put into our reports, and they reflect on how they want to drive forward to make a positive business for MLB. We're all one family at the end of the day. We all want the game to be successful and profitable while maintaining its integrity on the field that we as umpires take full responsibility for.

They hold us very accountable, but we hold ourselves more accountable than anybody.

On the very last day of the 2019 regular season, I asked James Hoye about working in the postseason. He and Brian O'Nora were the two umpires on the crew that had been notified, the previous Saturday, that they would be working in the first round of postseason play. James would be working the ALDS.

BN: How do you find out the postseason assignments?

James Hoye: We get a phone call.

BN: One of the supervisors.

JH: Yes. They'll say, "Hey, we want you to work the LCS" or whatever it is.

BN: And you could say, "Naah, no thanks."

JH: You can, but I'm not sure that's a good idea. They don't tell you who else is on the crew, because they have to call all the guys on the crew – the guys that you're working with in the LCS or whatever.

BN: After they reach everyone, then they post the list on the website.

JH: Correct. I'm going to Houston on Friday.

BN: You've worked several Special Events now. The first WBC but also the Division Series in 2011 and 2015. A Wild Card game. And last year you worked the first couple of games on the ALCS here at Fenway Park. And then you went on to work Replay? Is that what happened?

JH: Yeah.

BN: Was that the same kind of feeling? What I was wondering was about you working the games here and then working Replay? You don't have 38,000 people screaming and yelling, and you're not on TV.

JH: Replay is the same.

BN: But the intensity…

JH: The intensity…it's a big game, right? Any call is a big deal. There's a lot of people in that room, and a lot of people are moving…there's a lot of moving parts in that room. When there's a challenge in the playoffs, it's kind of an end-all-end kind of thing.

BN: Everybody's a little hyped up.

JH: Yeah. Doing Replay in April is not like doing Replay in the postseason. Absolutely.

Working the plate in Game Seven of a World Series is as special as it gets. There have been 39 times, through 2018, that a series has ended in a seventh game. I asked Jeff Nelson about it:

BN: There's one more game I wanted to ask you about. I suspect it's one of the games you might have been most happy to work. That was Game Seven of the 2014 World Series at Kansas City. There you are – Game Seven of the World Series. Home plate.

Jeff Nelson: Did I work that? [pause, then a chuckle]

I'm kidding. I'm kidding. Now that it's done, it was an interesting experience. It's the biggest game that you can work. There's a lot of pressure. Very intense atmosphere. It's not an experience that I feel I would have missed had I not worked it – because of the pressure. But I worked it. It went well. So now it's a good officiating memory. But it was very intense and very pressure-packed and I'm thankful everything went all right.

BN: 2016 had to be intense as well. Two teams battling each other, neither one of which had won a World Series in ages and ages. Then you had the Indians coming from behind. Then it goes into extra innings – and then there's a rain delay! Talk about a dramatic conclusion.

JN: Yeah, Sam [Holbrook] did a fantastic job, under the toughest conditions you can imagine. That's pressure. That's serious pressure. He answered the bell on that one.

BN: That was really a highlight of his career.

JN: Especially in the rear-view mirror. An hour before you walk out there? I don't care who you are, if you don't feel anxious about the experience, you're lying. There's a lot of pressure and you want to do a good job. You're feeling it. It's like waiting for a race to start. Once the race starts, you're kind of in your element but the build-up prior to the race, it's like 'Come on, let's go. Let's get this thing started. Let's do this now.' You don't want to make a mistake that costs a team their chance. Everything comes down to every decision you make during that game.

It's a big experience. There haven't been that many guys who have gotten the chance to do it, so looking back, yeah, that's a memory they can't take away from you. It's a pretty cool thing.

14

Keeping a Clear Mind to Work That Perfect Game

For someone who is a fan of baseball but who has never trained as an umpire, it may be astonishing to hear from Jerry Meals that he could work home plate during the May 6, 1998 game when Kerry Wood struck out 20 batters and not realize that Wood was on his way to tying (or maybe setting) the major league record.

We have seen umpires explain how they have to keep their mind clear as a way to avoid problematic calls. Focus is essential. Anticipation might be tempting, but is not something an umpire can afford. Batters need to anticipate, and try to wait for their pitch. Umpires have to take each pitch as it comes. They have to know the count, of course, to be able to signal a walk, perhaps call a strikeout on the exceptionally rare two-strike bunt, and maybe show some extra flair on a third-strike call. But they have no need to be counting strikeouts.

We've also seen that umpires often couldn't tell you the final score of a game they just worked once it's an hour or so after a game.

When they do get a break, will umpires watch a ballgame on TV, or take as complete a break as they can?

Jeff Nelson said: "No. When I get a haircut, I get asked that all the time and I ask them, 'When you go home at the end of the day, do you watch the Haircut Channel?' You know what, I'm lucky because I've been able to umpire thousands of games but at the end of the day I like a break just like everybody else. I think most of us are like that. Having balance in life is good. Life exists outside the baseball bubble.

BN: I just wondered if you did find yourself watching a game, since you wouldn't have a rooting interest in one of the teams, if you would end up watching the umpires – their positioning and so forth.

JN: If there's ever a sporting event that I go to, I'm watching the officials more than anything, for sure.

BN: Regardless of the sport.

JN: Yeah. I go to NBA games a lot. I'm not that knowledgeable about the intricacies of NBA officiating, but I like watching them work and I like seeing how they carry themselves. I like seeing how they interact with people. How they do their jobs, and to me there's a lot of carryover and similarities in what they do and I'm a student of officials. I enjoy the basketball, but I watch the officials a lot.

Angel Hernandez: The only time I watch baseball when I'm off the field is when I'm in Replay, because I get paid to watch. Otherwise, no. I don't watch football, basketball, hockey. I'm not into sports. Sports has been in my whole life. I had five brothers growing up, but I could care less about any other sport. I've had enough of sports. This is a job. That's the way I look at it. I'm not into sports. I'm not a fan of the game. This is a job. That's my approach.

Jordan Baker: That's all I do, is watch the officials.

Ron Kulpa, a diehard St. Louis Blues fan (who had attended Game One of the 2019 Stanley Cup finals the evening before our May 2019 talk) said, "I watch Blues games as much as I can. If there's a hockey game on, I'll turn it on. Even when I go to a hockey game, I find myself watching the officials."

Gerry Davis is a little atypical, even among crew chiefs. I asked him, "When you're not working – maybe in the offseason or when you get a week off, do you ever watch sports?" His response: "All the time. All the time. I'm always checking my crew. We get four weeks' vacation throughout the year. Two of them are individually. When I'm at home, I'm always watching the crew to make sure things are going well. Like a mother hen."

BN: Do you send them a note?

GD: We talk. We talk.

Hunter Wendelstedt emphasized the sacrifices that umpires make, the time away from home and family. "Hey, any day you can get home to be with your family is a big day. Whoever umpires, no matter what field it is, no matter what level, the umpire is sacrificing.

"From the umpire's side, what we teach at school is no matter if it's Little League or a big-league game, you've got to go out there and work hard – because that game really matters to somebody. There might be a grandfather who flies in and is only going to see his grandson play T-ball one time…It's a T-ball game.

"Some people will say Boston/Yankees is more important. No. That day, that T-ball game is the most important thing in that grandfather's life. That's how you put everything in perspective."

Angel Hernandez followed up what Hunter said: "We are an essential part of the game. When it's time for the game, that's when we need to be there. Everyone thinks the job is easy – whether it's at the Little League level or the high school level or college. And it's not.

"You every played golf? It's a really hard game. The analogy I use is a professional golfer. Why are they so good at what they do? They've hit thousands and thousands – hundreds of thousands – of balls. Everything's repetition. When we're watching, it can look like it's really easy because they've done it thousands of times. It's the same for our profession. The game is really hard. The profession is really hard. Just the basics are hard, unless you attend an umpire school. Where to stand. The mechanics to use. That's just the beginning. At this level, you need serious years of repetition. The years we spend working in the minor leagues are vital."

"If you decide to do this work, you're not doing it to draw people to you, to like you. You're doing it because of something you feel in your heart. How many people are able to do for a living what they really have in their heart?"

One needs to keep a clear mind, and one way he keeps his mind clear is by not following sports when he's not at work.

Jansen Visconti, working as a call-up umpire, sees the benefit – at least during the baseball season – of a similar approach. "For me, I think – we don't really get the same vacation as these guys (umpires on the major league staff), so I think any time you can get away for a day and take your mind off it, I think it's healthy. We wake up every day and that's all we think about is baseball and what we have to go through that day to get prepared to come here. For me, at least, I find that it's kind of healthy to just get away – don't think about it, don't watch it."

Jansen has a degree in finance from Penn State and might well have done into financial consulting had he not chosen to pursue umpiring. He has been umpiring since he was 9 or 10 years old, and for pay since he was around 15.

At the same time, during the offseason he follows sports.

Jansen Visconti: I'm a big hockey fan. Big football fan.

BN: When you do, do you tend to watch the officials?

JV: I do. I do. One nice part of at least getting some exposure up here is that I've found that a lot of the NHL guys are in communication with the baseball guys, so I've gotten to meet a lot of NHL guys. And some NBA guys. Scott Twardoski in the NBA. Shandor Alphonso and Garrett Rank in the NHL. [As it happens, both Twardoski and Alphonso wear #52 – the same number Jansen was assigned.] Gord Dwyer, who worked the Stanley Cup this year. It's been a lot of fun. Just getting to go out with them, have some dinner, a little bit to eat. It's refreshing to talk to somebody who goes through what you go through.

As we sat talking on a grounds crew vehicle under the stands at Fenway Park, Tripp Gibson was asked about the professional pride in being a major league umpire.

Tripp Gibson: Being a major league umpire means being as professional a person as possible. You understand the fact that everyone has a job to do out there. The home team and the visiting team, they have their own job to do. They're out there to win the game. And we have a job to do, keeping the game fair, keeping things consistent. We have to understand that there are emotions that go with being very competitive athletes. They're the best athletes in the world, right? Our job is to maintain the consistency and to do the best we can.

We're as competitive as they are. I don't want to miss anything. I don't want to miss a single call. And when I do – when I miss a call – it hurts. It hurts a lot.

With video, we've been able to analyze our plays, to analyze our work with a lot more scrutiny so we can improve, but it still doesn't feel good at all. I don't sleep very good at all, when I miss a call. We take enough pride in our job that I don't want to make a mistake out there. Replay has allowed those mistakes to be fixed, but it hurts just as bad. You don't want to make that mistake in the first place.

Marty Foster said, "They say, 'Oh, you get to travel!' I'm sick of travel. I want to be home with my wife. But this game deserves my full attention, concentration, and focus every night. That's probably something people don't fully understand.

"We're our biggest critics – each and every one of us. Nobody thinks more than the calling umpire about how he could be better."

The need for feedback never stops. Gerry Davis said, "One of the things that you have to do all the time as an umpire – you have to self-evaluate all the time. When you miss a call, did you miss it because you were out of position? Did you use your judgment at the wrong time? Or did you really just miss it because you're human and you're going to miss it? Those are all parts of the lure of baseball.

"I think Replay's helped us a lot in that regard. Number one, the vast majority of the time we're right. Before that was available – even before it became part of our decision-making process, before it was first available for the fans to see after the play…before we had that, we were just automatically wrong if it went against their team. Kill the bum! But then when they saw over and over that we were right the majority of the time, the fan – which is short for fanatic – their mindset changed so that. 'Well, you know, they *are* usually right…' Fans have a very different perspective about our profession now than they did even just a few years ago."

Gerry's wife Linda had a different perspective on Replay, one shared by a number of fans who follow the game. As Gerry expressed it, "Years ago the runner would slide in and we'd call him out and he'd get up and slam down his helmet and get in our face. The manager's there. My wife always says that from an entertainment standpoint, that would be one of the most exciting parts of the game.

"People would stand up or get on the edge of their seat, she said, because they were anticipating what was going to happen. Now when the same play happens, the guy doesn't get up. He just cups his hand over his ears – go to Replay – and she says people get up and go to the bathroom then.

"And the other thing I know that happens – because as a crew chief I go to the headset – they'll be showing it on the [electronic message board] and I'll be looking in the stands and half the people are going 'safe' and half the people are going 'out' – and they're looking at it in slow motion!"

Will Little said: "I was a former college player. I've taught at umpire school. One of the toughest habits to break in umpire school – you bring in former players and one of the hardest habits they have to break is: when the ball is hit, they follow the ball. As an umpire, that's one of the worst mistakes you can make. You have to learn that when the ball is hit, you have some other part of the field that you need to be looking at, that's going to help guide you to put you in the right position to make a call that's about to happen.

You start following the ball – especially at this level, with the game happening so fast – by the time you turn away from it, you're already way behind.

BN: You have to be aware where the ball is headed – say, to right-center field – and calculate the possible things that might happen, perhaps with a runner on base.

WL: Correct, but there's a lot of other aspects of the game that you need to be watching, that's going to put you in the right position for that call that is potentially about to develop.

I'd talked with Alfonso Marquez about this earlier.

BN: In the little game between the batter and the pitcher, the batter's thinking one thing and the pitcher's thinking another. The batter's trying to psych out the pitcher and the pitcher's trying to psych out the batter. When you're working the plate, do you kind of anticipate what kind of pitch it might be or do you just try to keep your mind as blank as you can on that?

AM: In my opinion, any time an umpire tries to anticipate anything, that's when you get in trouble.

BN: You do that a little on the bases, though, depending on who's on what base.

AM: You anticipate as far as the angle of the plays [that are possible] but if you tell yourself where this guy's going to be, that's when you start to get in trouble. Behind the plate, especially, if you say, "Is this guy going to throw a curveball" – and all of a sudden he's coming the other way with it…if you're expecting one thing and he throws something else…You just want to react on whatever happens.

Will Little wrapped up with some thoughts about the work:

Will Little: We enjoy it. Everybody who does this has a love for the game. Most people have at least played the sport at some time in their lives, so they have some understanding of what a player goes through. A lot of people coach the sport in some way, shape, or form. They might have coached a youth league – or just being a parent in general, they have an understanding of governing the play of your kid with each other's kids. But very few people have ever umpired a game. At any level. Or in any sport, for that matter. So to have an understanding of what we really go through – not only on the field but behind the scenes, especially at this level of major league baseball – there are no words that can describe it.

"Really, at the end of the day – we as a staff and as individual umpires, we just want to be right. We're very, very over-competitive people. And competitive within our job. Every call I have tonight, I want to be correct."

I asked Marty Foster, "What do you think that people who are not umpires don't appreciate – don't understand or appreciate – about the work you do?"

Marty Foster: "Probably the amount of care we give in upholding the integrity of the game. We're doing this for future generations. We don't just go out there and run around. We actually care about it as a game – the game we're working and the game overall. We want to do the best job we can every night."

One final note: No one is ever going to be perfect, but over the five years in working on this book and talking with umpires, it continued to impress me how much the umpires who have made it to the major league level truly care about approaching that goal.

15

After Umpiring

Prior to the 2020 season, there were four retirements -- Gary Cederstrom, Dana DeMuth, Mike Everitt, and Jeff Kellogg. Both Everitt and Kellogg will become Major League Supervisors. Four new crew chiefs were named: Kerwin Danley (who becomes the first African-American crew chief), Alfonso Marquez (who becomes the first Mexican-born crew chief), Dan Iassogna, and Jim Reynolds. Because of the retirements and the tragic death of Eric Cooper late in the 2019 season, there are five new additions to the major-league umpiring staff: Nic Lentz, Ryan Blakney, Ramon De Jesus, Chris Segal, and Jansen Visconti.

As a way to wrap up this book, it struck me that it might be worth asking just a couple of former major league umpires what life had been like in the first few years after retirement. Did they miss the game? What was life like? I asked Tim Welke and John Hischbeck. Life, it seems, was pretty good.

Interview with Tim Welke on November 8, 2019

Recuperating from left shoulder surgery for a torn labrum, he said his 13-year-old grandson asked him, "Shouldn't it have been your right shoulder, since that's where you called all the strikes and the outs?" He said, "Braden, I guess I made too many safe calls."

BN: I wondered if you had done anything like umpired Little League since the time you retired.

TW: No, I haven't. I do have five grandkids and the two oldest are boys. They're at that Little League stage – 11 and 13. I'm just a fan there.

BN: You retired after the 2015 season.

TW: In 2016, I was on disability. I had two total knee replacements. I had one done in January and one done in July. They're a lot better. And those were from being an umpire. That was the issue there. My official retirement date was in January 2017.

BN: You were approaching 60 and you'd worked 33 years on major league fields. 4,216 games. So what have you done since then?

TW: Kept busy. We live in Kalamazoo, but we have a vacation place up in northern Michigan where my mom lives. It's called Beaver Island. I spend about half the time there in the summers and falls. My mom lives there seven or eight months a year.

I come from a large family so we do a lot of family stuff.

BN: You told me at one point that one of your goals was to go back and finish college.

TW: Yeah. That never happened. Instead, I've done a lot more things. We've got a little farm up there that…I didn't realize when my dad was alive that he did so much work. I put in like nine rye fields for the deer. Feed the deer. Watch the deer. Next week we'll all go up hunting. I have four brothers and we'll all be up there, with some kids and grandkids.

I've become a farmer. I spend a lot of time in the summer on a tractor, mowing up there and doing things. We just do it basically for fun. Me and two of my brothers own 270 acres up there. There's a lot of mowing to do. A lot of painting of fences. Fixing things and stuff. Planting the rye and the clover for the deer. It keeps me busy.

We hunt. We harvest. One of my most favorite meals is venison, and my wife can make it pretty well. That's one of her specialties. We feed them, we harvest them, and we enjoy eating them.

BN: You get a pension from Major League Baseball?

TW: Yes, I do. Once you've reached 20 years you're kind of maxed out. Your pension is fully maxed out when you're age 62 and I turned 62 in August so I will officially start to take the pension on January 1 of next year. I wanted to wait because I've been on disability. It was better for me to do it that way. It's going to be comfortable and that's fine. I don't have a luxurious lifestyle anyway.

BN: Have there been times when you…miss it?

TW: I miss the guys. And I miss the locker room. The before and after the game. I definitely miss the guys but, you know, I did it for so long. I don't miss the travel. I don't miss the hotels. I don't miss the restaurants. The early morning flights. All that kind of stuff. Trying to make a flight to get to the next town. You're in the 13th inning on a Sunday and you're going from Baltimore to Kansas City and you know you're probably going to have to spend the night in Baltimore and get up very early in the morning and go to Kansas City. I don't miss that stuff, no. I did it long enough.

The thing that sticks with me is, boy, it went by fast! It seemed like it went by really fast, the 30-plus years.

BN: You keep in touch with your brother Bill and with Jeff [Kellogg], I'm sure. Do you keep in touch with some of the other umpires at all?

TW: I keep in touch with a few. Mike Everitt. Gary Cederstrom. And then there's some retired guys like John Hirschbeck and Tim McClelland and Joe Brinkman. Not a whole lot of the guys. They have busy lives, too. Obviously, the active guys are busy during the season and in the offseason they decompress and they're enjoying their families.

BN: I wondered if there might be a golf tournament that you go to once a year or something like that.

TW: I was, until my shoulder got bad. They have a big tournament in Arizona every year in conjunction with the active umpires who are out there to go to meetings. I haven't made that yet. In January, leaving Michigan it is a chore.

BN: Do you watch much sports – of any kind – on TV? Will you occasionally go to a game in Detroit?

TW: I haven't been to any games. I do turn on...we obviously get the Tigers here every day and I'll turn on the TV and see who's working the game. My brother sends me the schedule so I can kind of know where the umpires are at. I'll check in and see who's working. And I will watch some of the postseason.

The year after I retired, my brother Bill invited me – he had spring training where I always had spring training, in the Sarasota/Bradenton area, and I did go down there. My wife and I went down for a week. He had a two-bedroom condo. And that was fun. The last three years he invited me down but we haven't gone. I went to Florida for 30-plus years. Sometimes in March, the weather's nice around here. I've got things to do outside, like rake up leaves and that kind of stuff.

I keep busy. A couple of years ago I helped one of my sons coach one of the Little League teams. I was an assistant coach. That was fun.

But I remember when my dad retired. He said the best thing about retirement is you look at your calendar and it's snow white. When you're a working man there's something written every day on your calendar – what you've got to do, where you've got to go. So I thought, "Gee, I'd have all this time on my hands." But I don't. There's something to do every day. Once you get one thing done, there's something else.

BN: So it's all good, then. You've just got to get through these physical problems.

TW: Yes, but I'm still a young man. I just turned 62. It's just the wear and tear of being an umpire, I guess.

Interview with John Hirschbeck on November 22, 2019

JH: All my family still lives in Connecticut but we live in Ohio now. Youngstown area. I was 62. Thirty-four years in the big leagues, and 41 years overall. I had just done something long enough.

BN: 3,589 games was enough for you?

JH: Is that what it was? I did not know that.

BN: So what have you done since then?

JH: We live in Florida half the year. I always loved to hunt. I've been hunting, fishing...Now that I've got more time, I play a lot more golf. I fish. Work around the house. I'm always busy. I'm just having the greatest time of my life. I wake up every day and literally say, "Thank you, God, for another day of retirement."

BN: You retired after the 2016 season. The following spring, 2017, did you find yourself kind of missing it?

JH: Not at all. I have a very, very close friend who asked me that in January and then he purposely called me in March when my wife and I were in Florida. He said, "OK, tell me now if you miss it." He knows I am very truthful with him. I said, "No, I really don't."

I see the guys in the Sarasota area. I see my friends. They come for dinner. We play golf. We fish when they have off-days. I'm very glad to see them but I don't need to go to the ballpark anymore, that's for sure.

BN: You don't miss those 6 AM flights, the morning after a night game?

JH: No. Now I get up at 6 AM to take the dogs out. It's wonderful.

I still talk to a lot of guys. We have guys come to for lunch when they have an off-day in Pittsburgh or Cleveland. Some of them will come for dinner and spend the night and then go on to Pittsburgh or Cleveland the next day. I still see some of the guys.

BN: Have you gone to a game, as a spectator?

JH: No, I have not yet. Nothing against the game. It's just that I don't have time, or I guess I haven't wanted to make time. The game of baseball has changed immensely.

BN: Do you follow on TV at all?

JH: I'll watch the MLB Channel once in a while, just to keep up on the news. Just to know what's going on in the game. I know that the Winter Meetings are coming up and I know who the new managers are that have been hired. Just to keep up on the news. I don't disassociate myself from it, but I don't have time to sit and watch a four-hour marathon.

I did watch the playoffs quite a bit. I did sit and watch quite a bit. Not the whole time, but I did watch my friends work. There are certain guys that I want to say, "Hey, congratulations. Great job" – and I don't want to say that just to say that. I want to see them work. I watched quite a few playoff games, actually.

BN: You were able to retire when you were still young enough to be very active.

JH: Right. You just thank God for your health and to be able to enjoy it now, as long as I can.

—end

Appendix

Umpires interviewed for this book:

Lance Barksdale – April 18, 2016
Lance Barrett – September 4, 2015
Ted Barrett – April 30, 2015, July 11, 2015, & April 18, 2016
Scott Barry – September 10, 2017
Dan Bellino – June 23, 2017
Cory Blaser – July 3 & 5, 2015
C. B. Bucknor – September 4, 2015
Vic Carapazza – September 17, 2016
Mark Carlson – October 1, 2016
Gary Cederstrom – August 30 & 31, 2016
Chris Conroy – July 3 & 5, 2015, and June 5, 2016
Fieldin Culbreth – September 9, 2015
Phil Cuzzi – August 4 & 11, 2018
Bob Davidson – July 22, 2016
Kerwin Danley – May 13, 2016
Gerry Davis – July 13, 2019
Dana DeMuth – January 13, 2017
Laz Diaz – July 3 & 5, 2015
Mike DiMuro – June 5, 2018
Rob Drake – July 31, 2019
Doug Eddings – July 28, 2018
Paul Emmel – July 22, 2016
Mike Estabrook – June 20, 2016
Chad Fairchild – September 26, 2015 & April 20, 2016
Andy Fletcher – May 13, 2016
Marty Foster – August 17, 2015 & May 29, 2019
Greg Gibson – September 26, 2015
Tripp Gibson – August 6, 2019
Manny Gonzalez – April 27, 2017

Brian Gorman – October 1, 2016
Chris Guccione – July 3 & 5, 2015, May 9, 2016, & October 1, 2016
Tom Hallion – August 15, 2017
Adam Hamari – June 23, 2017
Angel Hernandez – July 11, 2015, April 18, 2016, & June 11, 2019
Ed Hickox – June 23, 2016
John Hirschbeck – September 22, 2015 & November 22, 2019
Pat Hoberg – July 11, 2015 (promoted to major league staff on February 21, 2017)
Sam Holbrook – May 2, 2017 (plus U Mass Lowell class that day)
James Hoye – September 22, 2015 & September 29, 2019
Marvin Hudson – May 20, 2016
Dan Iassogna – September 4, 2015
Jim Joyce – September 26, 2015
Jeff Kellogg – September 21, 2016 & June 9, 2018
Brian Knight – August 9, 2016
Ron Kulpa – June 5, 2016 & May 29, 2019
Will Little – April 18, 2016 & September 18, 2019
Alfonso Marquez – May 9, 2016
Jerry Meals – June 5, 2016
Bill Miller – August 9, 2016
Gabe Morales – June 26, 2018 & May 29, 2019
Mike Muchlinski – August 17, 2015
Paul Nauert – April 6, 2017
Jeff Nelson – May 18, 2017 & May 10, 2019
Brian O'Nora – August 15, 2015 & September 10, 2017
David Rackley – May 9, 2016
Tony Randazzo – August 9, 2016 & May 10, 2019
Mark Ripperger – July 4, 2016
D. J. Reyburn – September 15, 2016 & September 12, 2018 (plus the U Mass Lowell class on May 2, 2017)
Jim Reynolds – September 9, 2015
Stu Scheurwater – April 13, 2018
Paul Schreiber – September 9, 2015
Dale Scott – September 4, 2015
Todd Tichenor – August 9, 2016
Tim Timmons – October 26, 2018

Carlos Torres – September 26, 2015 (when a call-up umpire) & April 6, 2017
John Tumpane – September 22, 2015 & July 1, 2016 (the day he was promoted to the major league staff)
Larry Vanover – May 9, 2016
Mark Wegner – August 17, 2015 & May 16, 2018
Bill Welke – September 22, 2015
Tim Welke – July 30, 2015 & November 8, 2019
Hunter Wendelstedt – November 29, 2016 & June 11, 2019
Joe West – May 13, 2016 & August 17, 2019
Mike Winters – August 17, 2015
Quinn Wolcott – October 1, 2016
Jim Wolf – August 27, 2016 & September 12, 2018

Supervisors:
Randy Marsh – July 11, 2013
Steve Palermo – August 20 & 21, 2014; January 15, 2015
Rich Rieker – November 22, 2016
Larry Young – February 10, 2015

Call-up umpires:
Ryan Additon – August 1, 2017
Sean Barber – June 5, 2016
Toby Basner – August 8, 2016 & August 1, 2017
Clint Fagan – July 3 & 5, 2015
Nic Lentz – May 17, 2018 (promoted to the major league staff before the 2020 season)
Shane Livensparger – July 22, 2017 & May 6, 2018
Nick Mahrley – July 27, 2019
Ben May – May 16, 2018
Brennan Miller – July 13, 2019
Roberto Ortiz – July 22, 2017
Jeremie Rehak – August 1, 2017
Jansen Visconti – August 17, 2019 (promoted to the major league staff before the 2020 season)
Chad Whitson – July 31, 2018

Triple A umpires:
Adam Beck – August 1, 2017
Ryan Clark – July 22, 2017
Scott Costello – July 22, 2017 & May 22, 2018
Rich Grassa – May 6, 2018
Skylar Shown – May 6, 2018
Alex Tosi – May 22, 2018
Ryan Wills – May 22, 2018

My appreciation to all who took the time to help me gain a better understanding of the work and lives of today's umpires. There were only a handful who declined to be interviewed. Some were minor-league or call-up umpires who quite reasonably could worry that something that they said might have been misinterpreted by someone, and hinder their hopes for promotion. There were only seven major league umpires who declined – as was their complete and total right – less than 10% of the total.

In particular, I want to express my profound thanks and appreciation to Larry Gerlach. This book grew out of the book he and I co-edited for the Society for American Baseball Research, *The SABR Book of Umpires and Umpiring*. I found I couldn't stop, and just had to keep going, and this book is the result. As I conducted the interviews along the way, I ran them by Larry for his comments and asked for suggestions for questions to put in future interviews. He was both a mentor and a superb sounding board as the book progressed – and then graciously agreed to write the foreword. It's hard to believe it's been nearly 40 years since his pioneering *The Men In Blue: Conversations with Umpires* was published. It is still available from Bison Books, and highly recommended.

End Notes

1. Minor-league compensation in 2019:
Class AAA: $2,900–$3,900 per month
Class AA: $2,500–$3,100 per month
Class A – Full Season: $2,100–$2,600 per month
Class A – Short Season & Rookie: $2,000–$2,300 per month
Per diems:
AAA: $58–$66 daily
AA: $50–$58 daily
A: $44.50–$52.50 daily
Source: http://www.stevetheump.com/minor_league_umpires.htm

2. Larry Mayer, "Umpiring Is No Minor Calling," *Chicago Tribune*, June 23, 1992.

3. Author interview with Tony Randazzo, August 9, 2016.

4. A strategy employed in 1999 labor negotiations between the Major League Umpires Association and the American and National Leagues resulted in a mass resignation of umpires. Some were rehired, and some were not. The individual status of the various umpires is listed here.

Umpire	Employer in 1999	Status
Drew Coble	AL	Retired with back pay; never returned to major league umpiring
Gary Darling	NL	Rehired in 2002; retired in 2014
Bill Hohn	NL	Rehired in 2002; worked through end of 2010 season before retiring for health reasons
Greg Kosc	AL	Retired with back pay; never returned to major league umpiring
Larry Poncino	NL	Rehired in 2002; retired in 2007 after injury
Larry Vanover	NL	Rehired in 2002
Joe West	NL	Rehired in 2002
Frank Pulli	NL	Retired with back pay; never returned to major league umpiring; died 2013
Terry Tata	NL	Retired with back pay; never returned to major league umpiring
Eric Gregg	NL	Retired; never returned to major league umpiring, and died in 2006
Paul Nauert	NL	Rehired in 2002 with no back pay
Bruce Dreckman	NL	Rehired in 2002 with no back pay
Sam Holbrook	NL	Rehired in 2002 with no back pay
Rich Garcia	AL	Never returned as an umpire but worked as MLB umpire supervisor until he was fired in 2010
Bob Davidson	NL	Rehired in 2007
Tom Hallion	NL	Rehired in 2005
Jim Evans	AL	Retired with severance
Dale Ford	AL	Retired with severance
Ed Hickox	AL	Rehired in 2005
Mark Johnson	AL	Retired with severance; never returned to major league umpiring, and died in 2016
Ken Kaiser	AL	Retired with severance; never returned to major league umpiring, and died in 2017
Larry McCoy	AL	Retired with severance; never returned to major league umpiring

5. As is evident in some of the interviews that I conducted, some of the current staff rescinded their resignations or otherwise reapplied to be rehired. In every case that I encountered, this was done after talking with those who elected not to return. During the interviews, we also hear appreciation for umpires such as Frank Pulli. Those who have died in

recent years, such as Mark Johnson and Ken Kaiser, have been honored with a memorial patch worn on the sleeve by today's umpires.

6. Email from Paul Emmel, September 11, 2019.

7. Tom Gorman and Jerome Holtzman, *Three and Two* (New York: Scribner's, 1979), 18.

8. Ira Berkow, "Tom Gorman's Final Call," *New York Times* August 17, 1986.

9. Alan Cohen, "Tom Haller," SABR BioProject, https://sabr.org/bioproj/person/399c055e.

10. Bill Nowlin, "U. S. Secret Service Agent Puts His Life on the Line Posing as a Major league Umpire," in Larry Gerlach and Bill Nowlin, eds., *The SABR Book of Umpires and Umpiring* (Phoenix: SABR, 2017).

11. Bill Nowlin, "Chris Guccione," in *The SABR Book of Umpires and Umpiring*.

12. Jim Prime and Bill Nowlin, *Ted Williams: The Pursuit of Perfection* (New York: Sports Publishing, 2002), 111. The Paparella quotation comes from Larry R. Gerlach, *The Men in Blue* (Lincoln: University of Nebraska Press, 1980), 139.

13. Aaron Gleeman, "MLB Investigating Threats Made Against Jerry Meals' Family," NBCSports.com, July 27, 2011. See https://mlb.nbcsports.com/2011/07/27/mlb-investigating-threats-made-against-jerry-meals-family/.

14. See, for instance, Murray Chass, "Umpire Gets Death Threat," *New York Times*, October 22, 1975.

15. Dan Greene, "After the Call," *Sports Illustrated*, at https://www.si.com/longform/2015/1985/world-series-cardinals-royals/index.html.

16. Larry Lage, Associated Press, "Blown Call Costs Galarraga Perfect Game in 9th," *Boston.com*, June 2, 2010. http://archive.boston.com/sports/baseball/articles/2010/06/02/galarraga_loses_perfect_game_with_2_outs_in_9th/.

17. Armando Galarraga and Jim Joyce, with Daniel Paisner, *Nobody's Perfect – Two Men, One Call, and A Game for Baseball History* (New York: Atlantic Monthly Press, 2011).

18. The triple play can be seen on YouTube: https://video.search.yahoo.com/search/video?fr=yfp-t-s&p=eric+bruntlett+triple+play#id=1&vid=16b05f28d6fe9a14cedd039689672272&action=view.

The only other time an unassisted triple play closed a game was on May 31, 1927, the feat executed by the Tigers' Johnny Neun.

19   Bill Nowlin, "Throwing Out 17 Players in One Game," in *The SABR Book of Umpires and Umpiring*.

20   Dave Anderson, "Bill Klem," in *The SABR Book of Umpires and Umpiring*.

21   Anderson, in his article on Deadball Era umpiring which appeared in *The SABR Book of Umpires and Umpiring*, cited Robert F. Burk, *Never Just a Game: Players, Owners and American Baseball to 1920* (Chapel Hill, North Carolina, University of North Carolina Press, 1994), 134.

22   Gil Imber, "You're Out of Here – A History of Umpire Ejections," in *The SABR Book of Umpires and Umpiring*.

23   Larry Gerlach, "Ernie Quigley," in *The SABR Book of Umpires and Umpiring*.

24   https://www.retrosheet.org/Research/VincentD/umpgmchg.htm.

25   See Larry Gerlach, "Death on the Diamond – The Cal Drummond Story," in *The SABR Book of Umpires and Umpiring*. For further detailed information on umpire health concerns and care, see Etic Frost, "Umpires and Health" in the same volume.

26   Michelle Gallardo, "Roselle umpire Tony Randazzo to call his 1st World Series," ABC7chicagocom. https://abc7chicago.com/sports/roselle-umpire-tony-randazzo-to-call-his-1st-world-series/1572486/.

www.ingramcontent.com/pod-product-compliance
Lightning Source LLC
Chambersburg PA
CBHW030305080526
44584CB00012B/452